Josh Dowse, Ian Woods
ESG Unlocked

Josh Dowse, Ian Woods

ESG Unlocked

How successful companies and investors build our natural, social, human and financial capital

DE GRUYTER

ISBN 978-3-11-142837-6
e-ISBN (PDF) 978-3-11-142894-9
e-ISBN (EPUB) 978-3-11-142917-5

Library of Congress Control Number: 2025943776

Bibliographic information published by the Deutsche Nationalbibliothek
The Deutsche Nationalbibliothek lists this publication in the Deutsche Nationalbibliografie;
detailed bibliographic data are available on the internet at http://dnb.dnb.de.

© 2025 Walter de Gruyter GmbH, Berlin/Boston, Genthiner Straße 13, 10785 Berlin
Coverdesign: Dörte Nielandt, Berlin
Typesetting: Integra Software Services Pvt. Ltd.

www.degruyterbrill.com
Questions about General Product Safety Regulation:
productsafety@degruyterbrill.com

On *Unlocking ESG*

This book is an essential read for anyone seeking to understand the evolution, impact, and future of ESG. It offers a comprehensive, clear, and balanced overview from multiple perspectives—investors, businesses, policymakers, and citizens—making it a valuable resource for both seasoned professionals and those new to the field. At a time when ESG is at a crossroads and under more scrutiny than ever, Dowse and Woods provide a rigorous, insightful, and pragmatic guide to why ESG matters, how it has shaped markets and investment decisions, and where it goes from here. A timely and necessary contribution to the ESG conversation—I encourage everyone to read it.

Fiona Reynolds, *former CEO of the UN PRI*

Many have struggled to articulate why ESG matters to our corporate and investment decisions. That's part of the reason some seek to dismiss it. Dowse and Woods have made sure you won't. It is a coherent, practical and enlightening coverage of the topic, whether you're new to the topic or deep into it.

Martijn Wilder AM, *Founder & CEO, Pollination*

Working out how capitalism can operate sustainably on this planet is one of the greatest challenges of our time. We cannot just keep pushing the answers down the road for future generations. Dowse and Woods have offered an incisive account of why that's important, and what to do about it.

Keith Tuffley, *Ocean and Polar Explorer*
and past Chairman of Energy Transition & Sustainability at Citi

ESG Unlocked is an insightful guide to ESG and its importance in shaping the future of business, investments, and personal decision-making. Dowse and Woods have grounded the ESG story with a fascinating dive into the historical business context, drawing parallels to the evolution of financial reporting. Their conversational style, and use of high profile case studies, creates an engaging and practical resource for anyone looking to harness ESG principles to create value and drive positive impact.

Merren McArthur
retired airline CEO (Tiger Air, Lynx Air and Virgin Regional Airlines)

The idea of ESG is thriving. But so is the lip-service paid to it and so are the ranks of its soothsaying protagonists. There is also, inevitably, political and commercial pushback to ESG's noble aims. The antidote offered by Dowse and Woods is therefore especially welcome. Not only for their insightful analyses of the inherent value of genuinely committing to ESG principles but also for their practical suggestions of how to do so in ways that really can benefit people, planet, and profit. It really is a mighty fine read.

Professor David Kinley
Chair of Human Rights Law, The University of Sydney and
Academic Expert Member, Doughty Street Chambers, London

https://doi.org/10.1515/9783111428949-202

Contents

Authors

Josh Dowse has been an independent consultant, facilitator, writer and editor for the past 20 years, becoming one of Australia's most trusted thought partners on ESG, sustainability, energy, climate change, and related communications. He has prepared or reviewed dozens of ESG or sustainability strategies, numerous public policies and articles, and facilitated and/or ghosted significant public documents such as AEMO's *Integrated Systems Plan* (Australia's national energy plan) and CSIRO's *Australian National Outlook*.

After a brief stint as a lawyer and authoring *Australian Corporations Practice*, he has focused on helping specialists to develop and articulate their ideas, as a publisher with Allen & Unwin, a communication consultant with McKinsey & Company and SenateSHJ, and editor of the *McKinsey Quarterly*.

Josh has an Honors degree in History, an LLB, and a Master of Environmental Law and Economics, and learned as much as a father of four, a director of a disability NGO, and a long-time coach and president of a junior rugby club.

Dr Ian Woods is Principal of Ian Woods Advisors, advising asset owners, asset managers, and investment industry associations on responsible investment strategies. He is a global leader in responsible investment strategies, having been Head of Responsible Investment at AMP Capital for 19 years, and cofounder of the Investor Group on Climate Change (IGCC) and its Deputy Chair for 10 years. He is currently a member of Chronos Sustainability's expert network and serves on a number of company and fund manager ESG advisory committees.

Before entering the finance sector, Ian was a manager at a leading environmental consulting firm, assisting companies with the assessment and management of environmental issues, and spent three years at an environmental and safety risk consulting firm in London.

Ian has a PhD in Chemical Engineering, a Master of Environmental Law, an Executive Master of Business Administration, and is a Graduate of the Australian Institute of Company Directors.

https://doi.org/10.1515/9783111428949-204

Introduction

The world is awash with money. Yet people often overlook what creates it.

It all comes from natural capital, the natural resources of this planet. People then add their thinking and effort (their human capital), attract other people to do things with them (their social capital), and through their labor and machines create the products and services that can be sold for money (the financial capital). So, the more we look after the natural, human, and social capital, the more financial capital we can have.

Many companies and investors know this. They keep one eye on their money, and another on the natural, human, and social capital on which it is based. By keeping an eye on these nonfinancial factors, they do themselves and their communities a power of good.

In investment circles, these nonfinancial factors are known as 'ESG' – the environmental, social, and governance competencies that generally lead, as we will map out, to better financial performance.

But ESG can also be a double-edged sword for company executives. It can force them to choose between competing interests, and take them down for acts or oversights that may have been legal but represented only short-term thinking (to be kind).

As a result, ESG is viewed with skepticism in some quarters. Some criticize it as being 'woke', and wish it would go away.

It won't.

This book helps you understand what ESG is, why it is here to stay, and how you can use it to add value to your business, your investments, and your family decisions.
It will help anyone facing these decisions. If you are already a specialist in these decisions, this book might be something to hand a colleague to start a conversation.

We offer a clear and actionable way of thinking about ESG, in four parts:

- **Part A: ESG and why it's here to stay.** The basic concepts and how they fit into the history and future of capitalism. We introduce what ESG is, how it came to be here, why it makes sense on many levels, and why it won't be going away. It underpins the other three parts.
- **Part B: Creating organizational value with ESG.** The principles of ESG apply to any corporate, public, or nonprofit organization. Those that improve their ESG performance and engage stakeholders on its journey will get access to more capital: financial, human, social, and natural. This part will help them do so, or help you understand what they are trying to do.
- **Part C: Investing other people's money with ESG.** Institutional investors have to be very clear on how they integrate ESG into their investment philosophy, and how they communicate that to those whose money they manage, and to the com-

https://doi.org/10.1515/9783111428949-001

panies or assets in which they invest. This part will help them do so, or help you understand what they are trying to do.

– **Part D: Making your personal choices with ESG**. Because most companies now publish their ESG information, you have much clearer information with which to decide how you might participate in our economy – as consumers, shareholders, employees, and as voting citizens. More than anything, we aim to show how people can be true to themselves and their values in each of these domains. And to show that if we are, we will nudge our economy in a healthier direction.

Our book captures the heart of conversations found in companies, in investment firms, and, we hope, in families. It also riffs on some of the great themes of capitalism and its sometimes uneasy coexistence with the planet and the people who dwell on it.

We are capitalists, and suspect almost everyone who reads this book is too. We have both worked in support of capitalism throughout our careers. Capitalism is the great engine of our economy, building the potential and means to fulfill our needs and desires. Markets are indispensable to what people need.

However, we fear that in the wealthiest nations on earth, the market capitalism of the early 21st century is no longer meeting the reasonable needs of most of the people, most of the time. Unless it responds, two things are likely to happen. In the long term, we are reducing the ability of future generations to meet their own needs. In the short term, people who feel they are missing out will feel the pressure to reach for more and more radical political solutions.

We believe that drawing on ESG to nurture our natural, human, and social capital can ensure people are not missing out in such numbers, can ease those pressures, and can help our market economies get back to delivering what people want and need.

Part A: **ESG and why it's here to stay**

Create the world you would like to see

Sustainable or responsible investing grew slowly but steadily as the 20th century ticked over to the 21st. These forms of investing seem worthy and interesting beasts, allowing money to flow to the most deserving companies and causes. Yet even though major investment firms had those options, they were almost an underground movement. Few people knew they existed, let alone what they meant, and few invested in them.

Perhaps it was what they were called. Did they suggest mainstream investing was unsustainable, or irresponsible, or even unethical? In any case, they are vague and loaded terms. The term 'sustainability' was business's answer to a late 20th century global policy push toward 'sustainable development' — leaving future generations with the same or better opportunities as past ones. But the term morphed into 'corporate sustainability', was abused to mean 'sustainability of the corporate', then petered out into a morass of acronyms like CSR and a general suspicion of do-gooders wanting to take the oomph out of capitalism.

From about 2006, the financial community focused more pointedly on what lay underneath responsible or sustainable investing — the environmental, social, and governance or 'nonfinancial' factors behind a firm's financial performance; investing that took these 'ESG' factors into account became, simply, ESG investing. And those nice, safe, and neutral initials opened all sorts of doors.

At first, the people who studied ESG factors were tolerated by their harder core investment colleagues. They could do some neat things – identify the risks of a large pollution event, or poor people management practices, or a board that was too close to a CEO–owner – but this was a sideshow compared to analyzing the financial results.

Very gradually, the hard men of the markets (and yes, most of them were men – 'diversity' meant different colored ties) came to grasp how ESG factors could affect financial performance. The evidence kept piling up. As a whole, funds that considered ESG factors did better than those that did not.

In 2021, $649 billion poured into ESG-focused funds worldwide, up from $542 billion in 2020 and $285 billion in 2019. In the same year, the MSCI World ESG Leaders' Index rose 22%, compared with the MSCI World Index's 15%. ESG funds now account for 10% of worldwide fund assets.[1]

More importantly, though, funds that are not labeled ESG are almost certainly incorporating ESG factors into their analysis. In other words, in just 15 short years, integrating ESG into investing became totally orthodox.

That has had a telling effect on the companies being assessed. While 'corporate social responsibility' and 'corporate sustainability' have been nice-to-haves, ESG has become essential. Any company, public or private, that does not respond to investor expectations on ESG performance is at risk of losing its investor support, access to financial and other forms of capital, and ultimately value.

https://doi.org/10.1515/9783111428949-002

If that's the case – that ESG is now mainstream – why care about it? If every investor and company is doing it, wouldn't the advantage just cancel out and everyone is back on an even playing field? Well, every investor looks at (or should look at) financials, management quality, and industry dynamics as well; but that doesn't mean they're all doing it with the same success.

In one sense, ESG is just like anything else – what counts isn't whether you do it or not, but *how* you do it. If you do it well, as a company, a fund manager, or a private investor, it will pay off. If you do not, it will just be a time-consuming distraction. Perhaps those who oppose ESG have experienced it in this way, as a distraction, and not seen it executed well.

But in another sense, ESG is not just like other investment factors; as an investor, **ESG helps you to use your money to create the world you would like to see.** If we didn't care how our money was invested, then we wouldn't care whether we invested in a company that pays children $2 an hour to make poker machines that are installed in local milk bars or a company that pays graduates $25 an hour to fix computers in local businesses. If both make you the same amount of money, who cares?

Instead, **ESG helps you decide what is important not only to you, but to a healthy economy and society, and to invest in those things.** That investment, big or small, makes a difference. Little by little it is changing the world, for the better. Small investors like us choose where to put their pensions or superannuation funds or any savings that they have. Those funds accumulate, layer upon layer, to build an immense pool of opportunity.

These pools of money, owned by us and invested by conservative professionals for our benefit, can change capitalism for the better. By including ESG in their thinking, they can do a lot to protect the natural, human, and social capital on which our financial futures depend (not to mention our environmental and social futures). When these investors act together, it matters. And when a business or sector finds it difficult to raise capital, you can expect it will fight back, using everything it has.

This first part of our book introduces what ESG is all about. There's a bit of history and a bit of hope, but in the end there's just logic. You can't expect the world to be a decent place to live in, if all its financial resources are dragging it down.

In this part, we look at:
- What ESG is, and how it is used
- How it came to be here
- Why it makes sense in granting access to all types of capital, and
- Why ESG isn't going away any time soon.

A few interesting strands of investment theory, corporate governance, and industrial history come together with sometimes surprising results.

Chapter 1
What ESG is, and how it is used

'The stone age didn't end because they ran out of stone.
Don Huberts, Shell (often quoted by Amory Lovins)

What is ESG? As you'll find many times in this book, there is a short and a long answer.

'ESG' literally stands for the <u>e</u>nvironmental, <u>s</u>ocial, and <u>g</u>overnance factors that may affect a company's performance, whether or not they are disclosed. They are the 'nonfinancial' factors that an investor might assess, alongside the company's financial performance factors.

More completely, ESG analysis considers how a company interacts with the world around it. It considers the choices the company makes about risks and opportunities in that world, the way it engages with others on them, and the way those choices affect the community, the environment, and the company's own health.

This chapter gets to the crux of the issue first – answering 'what is ESG?' – while the following short chapters trace its origins, its current significance, and why it will remain part of corporate and investment life, indefinitely.

The 'hard and soft': financial and ESG metrics and standards

A company's financial performance has been expressed in hard numbers since Egyptian times. A company's accounts were set out in their current form by the 15th century Venetians, typically appearing as the profit and loss, balance sheet, and cash flow statement. These were tested and refined for centuries, leading to accounting standards developed in the 1920s. They continue to be refined to meet the needs of the owners and investors. The International Accounting Standards Board is as busy as ever trying to meet those needs.

The numbers in these statements measure financial performance over and at the end of a single period, e.g. performance over the last financial year. The P&L and cash flow statement reflect what a company has endured or achieved financially over the last year. The balance sheet measures the 'book value' of the financial and physical assets the company has available to create more 'value' in future years.

While these financial concepts have been around for a long time, the nonfinancial ESG factors and their meaning are less familiar. To distinguish them from the 'hard' financial numbers, many call them 'soft' or nonfinancial. Yet, as we will see, calling them 'soft' is inaccurate and rather misses the point, as they also focus on 'capital' and 'value'.

https://doi.org/10.1515/9783111428949-003

Only in March 2022 has the International Sustainability Standards Board published a set of standards for disclosing general sustainability and climate-related data. This global effort is significant, as several previously independent attempts at setting a standard have now converged for the first time. So, to be fair, the effort is a hundred years behind 'hard' financial accounting. Let's give it a few years to catch up.

While new terminology can get in the way, the concept is simple. A company is more than its numbers. Pretty much anything apart from its ultimate financials can be captured by ESG. ESG ratings agencies – the earliest of which have now become part of the well-known ratings agencies S&P, MSCI, and Morningstar – trace anything up to 1800 individual metrics for a listed company.

That's a numbers game for them, as they push for an illusory competitive edge. Individual companies and investors can work out which few of these metrics are most important to their needs. Table 1 sets out a logically grouped starting list of ESG factors.

ESG and the Sustainability Family

The ESG factors are what they are – the nonfinancial factors of a company. As simple as that sounds, many people have looked at those factors in different ways and called them different things.

It's like being at a museum, with the ESG exhibit in the middle. Instead of people looking at it in open space, they see it through a window from separate rooms – and in each room the labels on the window are different; see Figure 1. Those labels include CSR (corporate social responsibility), corporate sustainability, the triple bottom line, shared value, and stakeholder capitalism.

This family of terms has been bubbling along about 30 years, arguing among itself as to which has the better name and forgetting that they are all basically the same. We believe 'ESG' has trumped all of these labels simply because ESG is a value-free, neutral acronym of the relevant factors, while the others compete against their own histories, people's biases, and the very different meanings they ascribe to the same words.

Here is a handy guide to this family of terms.

– **Corporate Social Responsibility** is likely to mean that companies have a social duty to act responsibly, both toward society and toward the environment, and that there are consequences if they do not. 'Responsibility' flows from long-held debates on corporate ethics: the idea that companies should do more than just comply with the law but should behave ethically. That, of course, begs the question of what is ethical or responsible. For most, it is a negative definition: that is, for companies not to act irresponsibly. Doing so implies that companies consider others and the environment they depend on.

– **Corporate sustainability** came from the language of 'sustainable development', a term coined in the 1987 Brundtland Commission Report on Environment and

Table 1: Common groups of ESG factors.

Environmental	Social	Governance
Use of and impacts on natural capital	Use of and impacts on human and social capital	Use of and impacts on financial capital
– **Management** including policies, governance, and compliance – **Biodiversity** including forestry, native vegetation, GMO, and soil – **Climate change** including emissions, adaptation, energy – **Circular economy** including sustainable sourcing, resource efficiency, packaging, recycling – **Water** including use and impacts – **Waste** including pollutants, hazardous waste	**Workforce** – **Human capital development** including engagement, education, innovation, research and development – **Employee human rights** including labor practices, diversity and inclusion, freedom from slavery, safety and wellbeing, education and development **Local community** – **Basic human rights/ philanthropy** including affordable access to education, health, care, and opportunity – **Community engagement** including use of public lands and assets, community-led transitions, asset closure management – **Avoiding harm** Local operational impacts, local economic impacts, **Value chain** – **Suppliers and industry** Trade practices, supplier diversity and inclusion, supply chain management – **Customers** data privacy, product stewardship, customer safety,	– **Effective governance** including independent directors, diversity, remuneration, accountability, management systems and culture – **Business conduct** including anti-crime, anti-bribery and corruption, marketing practices, trade practices, government influence – **Risk management** including corporate governance, financial stability and systemic risk, cybersecurity, privacy protection, business continuity, crisis management

Figure 1: Different windows onto the same thing.

Source: The authors.

Development, *Our Common Future*.[2] The very reasonable proposition of the Brundtland Report was that each generation should meet its needs 'without compromising the ability of future generations to meet their own needs'. (The word 'sustainability' only came afterward, captured in the Macquarie Dictionary in the late 1990s as a derivation of 'sustainable development'.)

So 'sustainable companies' are those that take their place in a sustainable economy by engaging with the threats to future generations and seeking solutions to them. Companies may even do this strategically, so that in seeking these solutions, they strengthen their reputation, their innovation, and their relationships. A sustainability strategy might ask 'what can we do that we're not doing now that would be good for a particular social and environmental issue, and good for us.'

However, 'sustainable' has another well-established meaning: able to last. And since the special meanings of 'sustainable' and 'responsible' were poorly defined, it is this meaning that really won over in the boardroom. If companies say they want to be sustainable, many mean they want to be here for the long term — it is the company's sustainability they are talking about, not the planet's.

- **Shared value** took the idea that sustainability could be an opportunity as well as a responsibility a little further. In their 2011 *Harvard Business Review* article "Creating Shared Value"[3] Michael Porter and Mark Kramer defined the term as "policies and operating practices that enhance the competitiveness of a company while simultaneously advancing the economic and social conditions in the communities in which it operates." Once that mouthful is digested, you get a clear picture of a win-win for the company and its communities and everyone gets to share in the value. For many, though, the environment doesn't get a mention; while for others the true problems arise when the value is divvied up.

– **The triple bottom line** gets closer to the nub of ESG. It was coined by sustainability leader John Elkington in the 1990s as a call for analysts to measure the emerging concept of sustainability performance. It suggests that a company (or an industry, community, city, state, or nation) should be assessed not just on its financial bottom line but on its impact on broader social, environmental, and economic dimensions. ***People, Profit, Planet*** is the way it is often neatly, and accurately, expressed. The triple bottom line should be able to be measured and reported, just like the financial bottom line, with the 'economic' bottom line extending to both short-term financial and longer-term economic performance, for both the company and the economies of which it is part. It was this triple bottom line that formed the basis for early standards of ESG reporting.

– **Six Capitals** is a relatively new term that takes the triple bottom line further, perhaps twice as far. It opens up the triple bottom line and looks at the six forms of assets that lie underneath: two forms of traditional 'hard' capital (financial capital and assets that can be turned into financial capital), three forms of 'soft' capital (intellectual, social, and human capital) and the asset on which it is all based, natural capital. We will look at these capitals throughout this book. They are particularly well described in Jane Gleeson-White's book of the same name, *Six Capitals*.[4] They are the basis for the international Capitals Coalition, a group of international companies and firms that promote them, and are the basis for international frameworks that ask or require companies to report on their access to and impact on the capitals.

– **Stakeholder Capitalism** is another relatively new term, that focuses less on the specific issues of ESG and more on who is worried about those issues. Many believe that 'corporate sustainability' or ESG is simply about engaging transparently with stakeholders on the things that matter to them. However, the term became controversial when used by Larry Fink in 2021, speaking as the head of BlackRock and the US$13 trillion that firm manages.[5] "Stakeholder capitalism is not about politics. It is not a social or ideological agenda. It is not 'woke'. It is *capitalism*, driven by mutually beneficial relationships between you and the employees, customers, suppliers, and communities your company relies on to prosper. This is the power of capitalism." Fink was not denying the role of shareholders but asserting that broader stakeholder relationships are at the center of the capitalist firm. Under pressure from a range of political participants and investment commentators, BlackRock has since softened its public rhetoric on ESG and stakeholder capitalism, although ESG is still integral to its investment philosophy.

– **Purpose** is often wrapped up in ESG conversations but is more like a cousin to the ESG family. All the above terms in the ESG family are about *how* an organization interacts with the natural environment and its various stakeholders. 'Purpose', on the other hand, can be about *what* an organization does, or *why* it does.

Having a positive purpose does not necessarily correlate with a strong ESG approach and performance. A company or nonprofit organization may declare its purpose to provide affordable housing in a community, or even to provide shelter for every one of its residents. In that noble social quest, it may not show any interest in the environment, or governance, or other aspects of human rights – let alone disclosing its performance on those factors.

Individuals and their organizations will find the term that suits them best. None are perfect. For now, the point is that most of these terms have to date been used by organizations and their stakeholders – other than their investors. The investors have instead used the term ESG. The organizations are now adopting that term as well – after all, their investors usually have the final say in most things.

Before going deeper into what ESG is and how it is used, it's worth taking a short detour backward in time to see how it got here in the first place.

Chapter 1 summary
- 'ESG' is short for the environment, social, and governance factors of a company's performance. Investors want to know about those nonfinancial factors, alongside the financial factors they've always been interested in, because they give clues about the company's future financial performance.
- There are hundreds of these ESG factors, but some are more important than others, and most are not relevant to most companies.
- ESG is the investor world's simple term for what companies have called many things, including 'corporate sustainability' and 'the triple bottom line'. These terms do have slightly different meanings – debated at length in academic and consulting circles. But really they're all trying to do the same thing, so choose one you like and move on.

Chapter 2
How ESG came to be here

Ever since the Cognitive Revolution, Sapiens have been living a dual reality. On the one hand, the objective reality of rivers, trees and lions; and on the other hand the imagined reality of gods, nations and corporations.

Yuval Noah Harari, *Sapiens*, 2011

To understand how ESG got here, sit back with us and watch an imaginary doco on corporate history – as in, the history of the corporation – viewed at 9 million times normal speed.

As you know, companies don't really exist; they are a figment of our imagination. But, as Yuval Harari tells us in *Sapiens*,[6] it is this ability to imagine what cannot be seen that sets us we *Homo sapiens* apart from all other creatures on this fine earth. And the corporation is one of our most productive imaginings.

The first companies were created by royal charter, giving their promoters exclusive rights to trade or to minerals, and so to build a mercantile empire. The Brits kicked things off in the 16th century with the Muscovy, Spanish, Turkey, Venice, Barbary, and Levant Companies, culminating with the East India Company in 1600. Other countries soon followed – for example, the Dutch East India Company in 1602 and the New Netherland (read Australia) Company in 1614. As both East India companies were to show, this was colonialism in brutal mercantile form, backed to the hilt by the British and Dutch navies. ESG was not an issue at all.

These companies not only had exclusive territorial rights, but had the special privilege of being able to raise money from the public, without having to repay it if things went pear-shaped. This went well for the companies, but not so well for the public. The South Sea Company was established in 1711 to trade with European colonies in South America. Promising untold wealth to investors, its share price blew up in a speculative frenzy. The happy speculators cashed up and exited, bursting the bubble and bankrupting half of the UK government. Not in a mood to finesse the regulation, the government passed the Bubble Act 1720, *banning* new companies for 104 years. Long before the ES mattered, the G did – if these companies couldn't be governed properly, then they could not exist at all.

The prohibition of UK companies finally ended in 1824, as the Industrial Revolution gathered steam and needed more capital fuel. After a bit of legal to-and-fro, the Joint Stock Companies Act 1844 enabled business promoters to create companies by registration. The Limited Liability Act 1855 then went further and protected *investors* as well as promoters from losing more than the money they invested, no matter how much damage their companies did elsewhere. So the G was again tightened to protect investors, but the ES remained outside their care. That was the agreed price of adding the capital to capitalism.

https://doi.org/10.1515/9783111428949-004

The next 100 years of corporate history makes a roller coaster look steady. Free from any duties except to their shareholder owners, company managers sought profits when and where they could find them. They rose and fell with the economic tides, through the peaks of the 1860s, 1890s, and 1920s, and horrendous lows of the 1870s, 1900s, and, of course, the 1930s. As companies crashed and burned, so too did the people they employed, the communities they serviced, the businesses with whom they traded, the investors who believed in them, the fields they harvested, and the skies their owners breathed. Sure, all their stakeholders benefited when things were good, yet somehow it seemed that the benefits weren't so well shared in the good times as the pain was in the bad times. Trade unionism grew through these ups and downs, to help temper the impact of market volatility and capitalist enthusiasm on workers and others, and to have at least some say in how companies operated. They and others, including the political mainstream, suggested the E and S were worth a look at, too.

By the time the West had endured the Great Depression and World War II, many had had enough. People argued for and secured global institutions to buttress national governments against the harm that unbridled capitalism could render unto their people. The United Nations was declared open on March 1, 1945, even before the end of World War II. It immediately commenced work on the Universal Declaration of Human Rights, adopted in 1948. In that Declaration are all the core principles of the S in ESG. Only the E remained.

With war out of the way, for the time being, Western economies switched their focus from the war effort to consumer needs – meeting the long-held ones and inventing more than could be imagined. It took only 20 years of accelerated progress for the E to have its day. Rachel Carson woke one morning to realize that the birds she grew up with were no longer singing. Not only those, but birds and other noisy creatures throughout the United States had seemingly vanished. Her 1966 cry for the lost, *Silent Spring*,[7] became part of the late 1960s counterculture movement across the USA and Europe as much as any Bob Dylan song. Carson's book and other clear examples of how environmental degradation harmed people led governments to think about limiting the corporate freedom to pollute, and so the field of environmental law was launched. However, it was soon recognized that the law, while necessary, was never going to be enough.

Silent Spring set the wheels of science and the United Nations in motion along new environmental tracks. An entire new branch of the law was spawned – environmental law – complete with its cross-border cases. Other research titles gave rise to new phrases: *"The Tragedy of the Commons"* and *"Limits to Growth"*. Finally and poetically, in 1987, the UN World Commission on Environment and Development coined the phrase 'sustainable development' – development that meets the needs of the present without compromising the ability of future generations to meet their own needs. Climate change was the Commission's primary issue as early as its 1992 Conference. (There, the UN Framework Convention on Climate Change was adopted, the very same one being debated at Glasgow in 2022.) The E was all locked in.

The three strands of the ESG family were pulled together in the 1990s. Its early advocates were perhaps responding to the Gordon Gekko 'greed is good' mantra of the 1980s, the Chicago School insistence on the primacy of the shareholder, and the weakening ability of governments around the world to solve social and environmental problems. Gordon Gekko was Michael Douglas' character in the film-of-the-times *Wall Street*, which depicted the brutal market life that the University of Chicago School of Economics theorized in pseudo-mathematical abstractions. Or perhaps the response was an expression of Maslow's hierarchy of needs – people just wanted their work to mean more than money.

Every now and again, the ESG family gets a burst of energy. An event so appalling in its greed-driven harm that it manages to nudge thinking. In the USA – the governance debacles of Enron and WorldCom, and the destruction of environments and livelihoods by BP's Deepwater Horizon. A Global Financial Crisis triggered by layers of banks, investors, and ratings agency who turned a blind eye to the simple fact that housing loans were being written that could never be repaid. In Asia, the single explosion of Bhopal, and the everyday social erosion of modern slavery. In Australia, a succession of blind eyes – James Hardie to asbestos, Rio Tinto to the cultural value of the Juukan Gorge. In the UK – the Murdoch's abuse of the Fourth Estate at *News of the World*. And everywhere, climate change, the COVID-19 pandemic, and war.

Every now and again, too, there was a statement of support from an authoritative source. When some argued that considering ESG issues was contrary to a company director's duty to consider only the company's shareholders, the legal firm Freshfields confirmed[8] that directors must also consider future shareholders, and so cannot trash the company's reputation for quick cash today. When strategy consulting firms suggested that corporate sustainability was a distraction, Michael Porter wrote a powerful article[9] in the Harvard Business Review saying it must be embedded in strategic thinking.

One recent marker was Larry Fink's 2022 Letter to CEOs.[10] Mr Fink sits on top of BlackRock's $13 trillion pile of investments. His letter was a flag jammed at the top of that pile, saying it would only be used with ESG in mind. Larry's letter was not a game changer, but rather announced that the world has changed. Referring to views that expected employees to be subservient, seen but not heard, he declared: 'That world is gone.'

That declaration is now being tested, as a backlash against ESG rides the same cultural waves that flow through social media and a resurgent political right. The question is now whether 'that world' is making a comeback, or is in its last gasps before history washes it away.

The UN Principles of Responsible Investment

Perhaps the most durable of all sources of ESG influence has been the UN Principles for Responsible Investment (PRI). The PRI was launched in April 2006 to little fanfare, an initiative of 67 institutional investors in partnership with UNEP Finance Initiative and the UN Global Compact. On 31 December 2022, there were 3,900 signatories, in charge of US$121 trillion; see Figure 2. A year later, there were 5,372 signatories, of whom 740 were pension funds and other institutions holding assets on behalf of members like us.[11]

The PRI has just six simple principles. By the first three, the signatories commit to incorporate ESG issues into investment analysis, ownership, and disclosure:

1. We will incorporate ESG issues into investment analysis and decision-making processes.
2. We will be active owners and incorporate ESG issues into our ownership policies and practices.
3. We will seek appropriate disclosure on ESG issues by the entities in which we invest.

These principles were clear enough, but the second set of three have arguably had more to say on the history of ESG investment:

4. We will promote acceptance and implementation of the Principles within the investment industry.
5. We will work together to enhance our effectiveness in implementing the Principles.
6. We will each report on our activities and progress toward implementing the Principles.

The PRI has now been joined by the Principles for Responsible Banking and the Principles for Sustainable Insurance. Together, they have made ESG the orthodox reality it is today.

Chapter 2 Summary
- Companies and company accounting, in the modern formal sense, have been evolving for over 400 years. Their rules and realities will continue to evolve.
- For most of that time, investing in companies has been a high-risk affair – both for investors and for the economies, societies, and environments in which they operate. In fact, they were so risky that they were banned in the UK for over a hundred years, from 1720 to 1824.
- More recently, companies and investors have seen the negative impacts on company values and on society when companies do not manage their ESG issues effectively.
- Conscious of those risks, global investors moved in 2006 to formalize notions of 'responsible investment'. Members of the UN Principles of Responsible Investing began to incorporate ESG issues into investment analysis, ownership, and disclosure, and to collaborate on doing so. They now represent over $160 trillion of our collective money.

Figure 2: The rise and rise of the PRI.

Assets under management

USD trillions   — Number of signatories

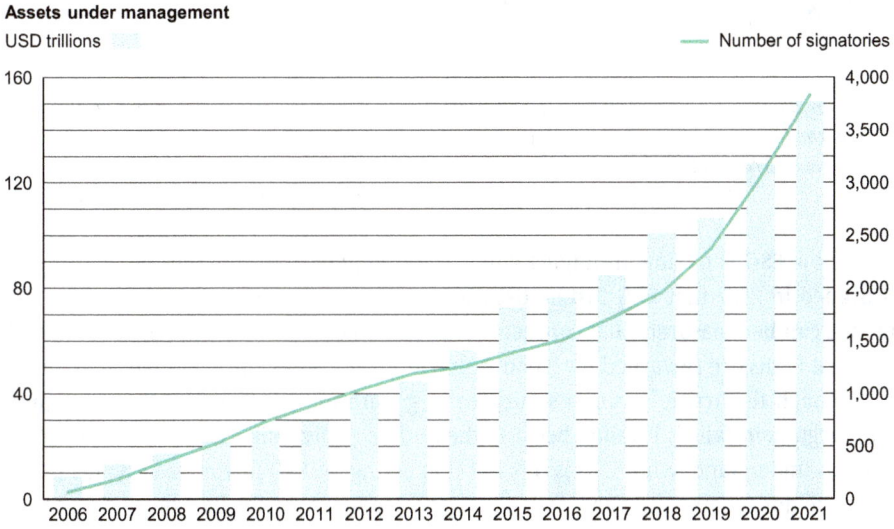

Source: Principles of Responsible Investment (PRI): https://www.unpri.org/about-us/about-the-pri.

Chapter 3
ESG gives access to all forms of Capital

If anyone had told me as a child that I couldn't fulfil my various childhood ambitions to be an astronaut, or pilot or James Bond due to my gender or ethnicity, I would have dismissed their views as irrational.

Shemara Wikramasingh, CEO, Macquarie Group, 2020

You know ESG is having an impact when *The Economist* calls for it to be abolished.[12] It argued in 2022 that ESG fosters delusion, claiming that its users suggest that ESG factors can be measured, that conflicts between ESG objectives can be easily resolved, and that firms are rewarded for 'good' behavior. Best just focus on climate change.

Though the article served its purpose in generating reaction, the esteemed journal's argument failed; it failed because the author really didn't understand, or didn't want to understand, what ESG is. It's not that acting on ESG factors is easy; it's that it has to be done. Companies can no longer expect to make profits by externalizing their costs to society. The delusion is that companies can ignore ESG factors, focus solely on financial ones, and expect to be around in a generation.

The journal isn't alone in this confusion. ESG has been called everything from 'scrambled eggs' to, famously, 'the Devil Incarnate' by Elon Musk. Is it what a company does, or how it is rated, or what an investor considers, or a special type of investment fund? Is it new, or has it been around for a while? When you read the press, nobody seems really sure, which makes it hard for companies and investors to focus on what they really should be doing about it. Since unfamiliarity breeds fear and possibly contempt, there is a risk that the great value of ESG may be lost to many markets.

This section puts forward a new model for thinking about ESG, one that builds on quite familiar and valuable concepts and puts them together in a recognizable way. It helps understand what ESG is, how it is used, and who uses it. In Part B, we use that model to help guide an organization's approach to ESG.

The model we suggest is simple. Consider first a financial performance-and-engagement cycle: a company that can generate financial capital will be more likely to engage with investors and get access to more.

ESG is best understood as a similar performance-and-access cycle. However, it embraces *all* the types of capital that an organization relies on – financial, yes, but also human, social, and natural – and engages with *all* the stakeholders that have or control access to that human, social, and natural capital.

Seen this way, ESG is at worst an innocuous representation of reality. At best it becomes a powerful, holistic way for organizations to improve their performance and get access to the capital they need.

https://doi.org/10.1515/9783111428949-005

Using four or six capitals to understand intangible value

Any organization, indeed our economy as a whole, relies not just on financial capital, but a range of different tangible and intangible capitals. Together, those capitals tell a simple story.

Let's say we started with just the Earth's natural capital. To that we added our human capital (the whole gamut of productive imagination, labor, and leadership). As individuals and organizations we then add social capital – all that it takes for *others* to join us in what we're doing, or just consent to it: trust, relationships, reputation, brand, and social license all rolled into one.

With that natural, human, and social capital, over millennia, we produced everything there is in the world (beyond of course the natural capital). Some of those are material, manufactured things; some of them are ideas and services (more human capital). Many of them can be sold, in turn, for money, which can be reused to restart that cycle.

There are two good models that capture this story. The first is Six Capitals, best described in Jane Gleeson-White's excellent 2015 book, *The Six Capitals: The revolution capitalism has to have.*[13] These six have been merged into four in the other model, adopted by the Capitals Coalition, an international association of companies, organizations, and advisory firms; see Figure 3. Either works, so choose the one that helps you most.

Figure 3: The Capital Coalition's four capitals with which to build a world.

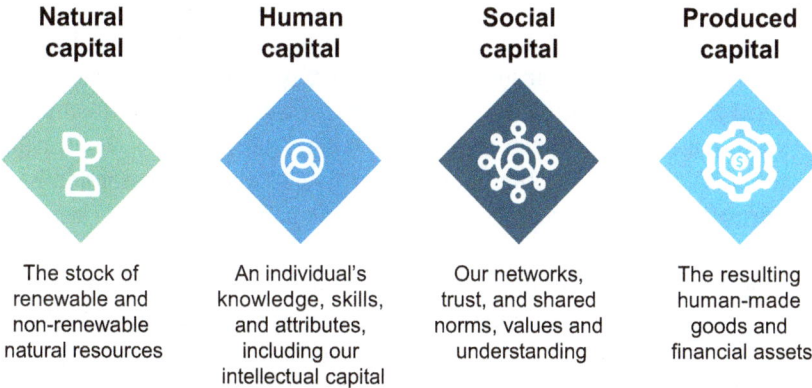

Natural capital	Human capital	Social capital	Produced capital
The stock of renewable and non-renewable natural resources	An individual's knowledge, skills, and attributes, including our intellectual capital	Our networks, trust, and shared norms, values and understanding	The resulting human-made goods and financial assets

Source: Capitals Coalition 2024 (text simplified).

Now let's look at these models from an organization's perspective, as shown by the four oval or ellipse shapes in Figure 4. The inner shape is the firm's financial and manufactured (or produced) capital. Up to and including the 20th century, that's the book value for which companies were valued: their financial and material capital, and the earnings they made from those two things – i.e., cash or the things that could be readily sold for it.

Figure 4: An ESG perspective of the six capitals.

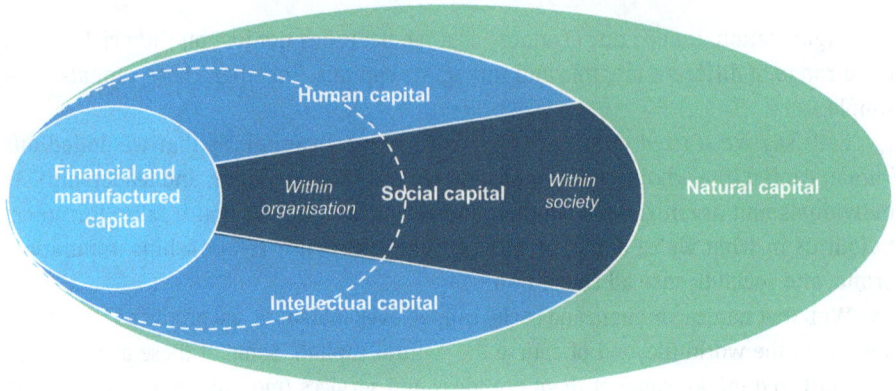

Natural capital	All the planet provides
Human capital	The productive power of safe, healthy, educated people
Social capital	The relationships, trust and regulation between people
Intellectual capital	The ideas used by people to create physical and intangible things of value
Manufactured capital	Physical things of value
Financial capital	Transferable money in all its forms

Source: The authors.

The next oval out, shown as a dotted line, represents the firm's intangibles:

- **human and intellectual capital** enable an organization to do things by itself. It includes its people (in all their numbers and diversity, and all their abilities and willingness to use them, including their culture), as well as its intellectual property (which the organization can draw on no matter who its people are). For the company Meta, this includes the information it knows about its users and how that information can be used and sold to enable companies to undertake targeted advertising.
- **social capital** enables an organization to do things with others. It is its brand, trust, relationships, networks, and social license all wrapped into one. Again, in the case of Meta, it is the trust its users place in how the company is going to use personal information or moderate the content on Facebook and Instagram.

We have used Meta as an example of a trend that has accelerated since the dot-com boom at the turn of the millennium. Then and now, companies like Amazon and Alphabet, owner of Google, have been sold for huge multiples of their capital and earnings. What did those multiples represent? The intangibles: the human, intellectual, and social capital that were not easy to value individually, but could together draw in future customers and revenues. For investors, this is the juicy part of the framework – the stronger these intangibles are, the more the company is worth.

The next oval out suggests that the firm's intangibles are just a small share of the world's intangibles. The amount of intellectual, social, and human capital available in the world is, truly, infinite. Every unit of this capital brings the capacity to generate more. The total amount typically grows when there is wealth, security, and education in the world. Firms can draw on that capital, or add to it, so the boundary is always in flux. Not only can a firm or an economy expand its intangibles by securing it from the rest of the world, but it can expand the world's human, social, and human capital. It is not a zero-sum game at all.

Finally, the outer circle is the boundary of the system: **natural capital**. That is a finite circle, and all the other capitals are built from that one, nonexpandable thing. Human activity can erode and restore natural capital, but it cannot expand it. The laws of physics and chemistry are beyond our reach.

Unfortunately, for most of history we have not valued this natural capital nor recognized its limits. Science is littered with evidence of our erosion of natural capital. An estimated 500 species have gone extinct in the last 100 years. Just this century, we have lost 99 million hectares of forest (four times the size of the UK). Much remaining natural habitat is at the mercy of weeds and feral animals. Our water resources must recover from about 80% of all industrial and domestic wastewater being released without any prior treatment.

Global warming is reminding us in no uncertain terms that there are limits. People are facing fires, storms, and floods that they have not experienced before and that they are not prepared for. There are glimmers of hope that, in response, we might now value clean water, our climate, and the contribution of biodiversity. Your reading this book adds to that hope.

The value of intangible capital

These 'intangible' human and social capitals have become more and more significant in how investors value companies. Ocean Tomo, a firm specializing in financial valuations, has measured how much more significant over the last 50 years. It estimates that, back in 1970, about 80% of the aggregate market value of listed companies in the USA represented material assets: cash or physical things that could be turned into cash. Only 20% of that value represented what investors thought of as 'intangible' capital: its people, brand, reputation, intellectual property, and the like; see Figure 5.

Over the last 50 years, Ocean Tomo suggests that the balance between the tangibles and intangibles has been turned on its head. The 20% ascribed to the intangibles has risen steadily to an astonishing 90% today, with all of the balance sheet and physical stock and plant making up just 10%.[14]

Figure 5: Human and social capital are becoming more and more valuable.

Ocean Tomo components of S&P market value
Percent

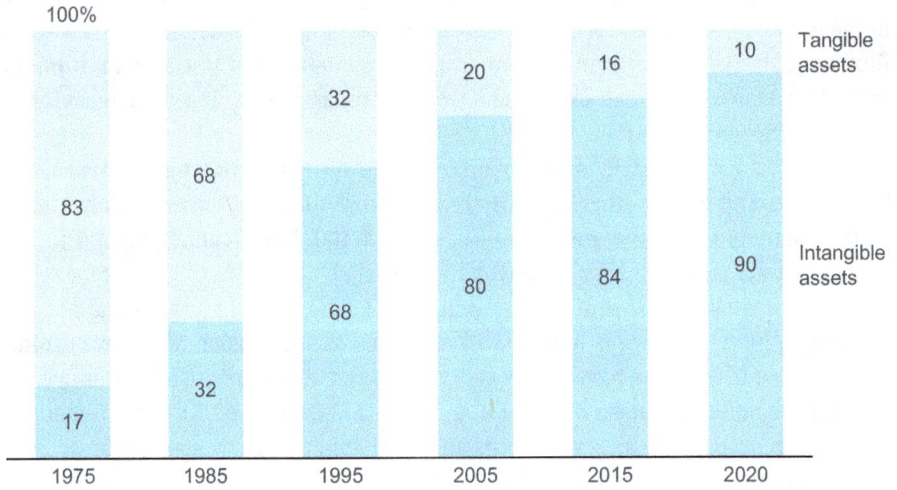

Source: Ocean Tomo: https://oceantomo.com/intangible-asset-market-value-study/.

Other firms have questioned whether the value of intangibles really has risen to 90% of all market value, but all agree in the rise of that share and that they do now account for well over half.

The rise reflects that our economies are now less about physical products, and more about data and services. Investors realized that the tangible capital represented past performance, but the intangible capital represented the potential of future cash flows. There is more profit in the future than the past.

That's why, for instance, Tesla shares in 2021 were valued at more than all other car companies in the world put together. But perception can be a double-edged sword. The desire to own a Tesla depends in part on the shared values or even admiration for the company and its founder. Actions by the company or its founder may lessen that desire. To understand how, we turn to a short- and long-term performance cycle.

The short-term financial performance-and-access cycle

Let's start by suggesting a model for considering how financial performance data is produced and used, shown in Figure 6.

Figure 6: The standard financial performance-and-access cycle.

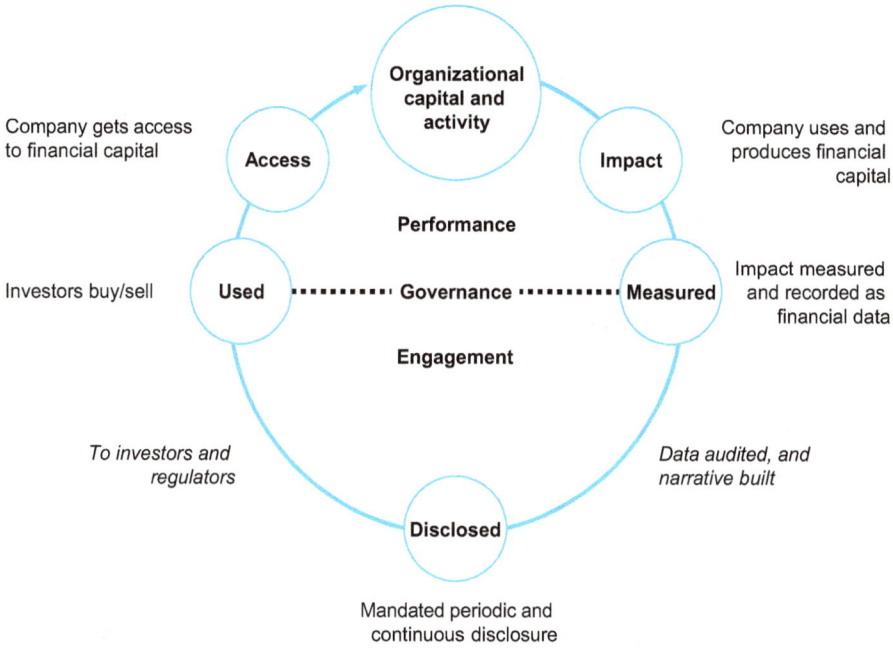

Source: The authors.

As soon as a company acts in any way, it affects its financial capital. A single paid person working for an hour will draw down the hour's wage from the company, immediately affecting a 'live' P&L and balance sheet. Anything the person does, any assets or materials they use, will have a similar effect. With a bit of luck, that person will generate some profit, adding to the company's capital. At the end of any given period, or in real time, all those impacts are measured in dollar terms and reported internally.

Assuming the company needs to report externally at some point, it may need to audit the numbers and it may want to create a narrative around them. There may be regulations and standards involved to ensure that those using the numbers can rely on them. All this financial data is packaged up and shared with markets and regulators, through reports, presentations, and, most importantly, discussions.

Why the need for that engagement? The whole purpose of all this is for investors to know what's happening with their money. If they like what they see, they'll keep it there, or even chip in more. If they don't, they might sell their stake, assuming they can.

In other words, all that effort to measure, report and audit financial impacts and then engage with investors is for one sole purpose – to get access to financial capital. Without that capital, the company – or any organization – will cease to exist.

The company is pedaling on a financial performance-and-engagement cycle that, all going well, will give it access to more capital. At the heart of that cycle is governance – everything the company does to make sure that the cycle is reliable and legal and also that the company's directors won't be liable for either the breach or the loss.

The performance-and-engagement cycle captures the company's impact on the investor's capital. Nothing really new here.

The long-term ESG performance-and-engagement cycle

The Capitals Coalition or Six Capitals models are immensely powerful constructs with which to see the world. As Paul Druckman says, "Without a focus on a range of capitals, providers of financial capital simply do not have the information needed to allocate resources most effectively".[15]

Figure 7: The ESG performance-and-impact cycle.

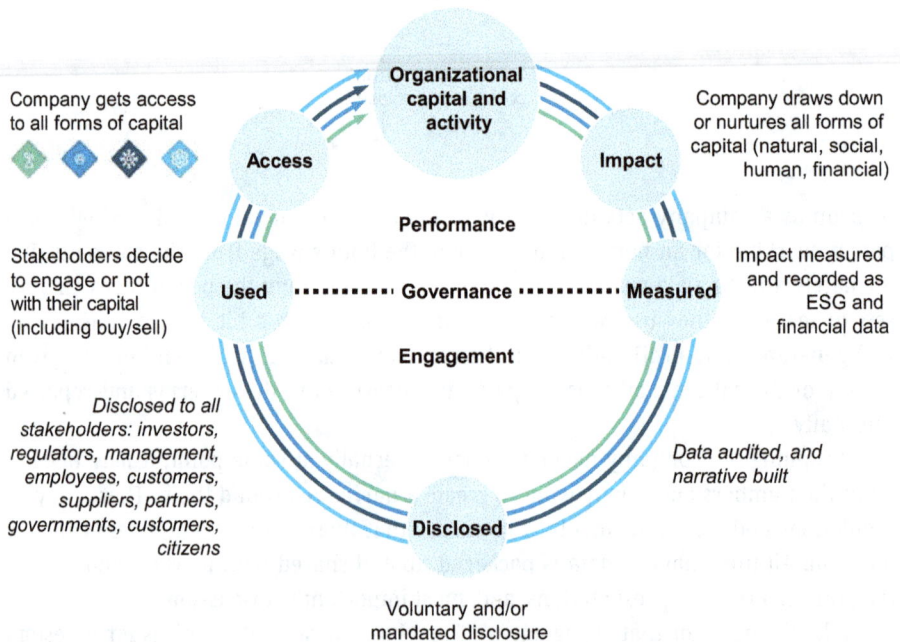

Source: The authors.

If the intangibles, in the form of human and social capital, do account for such a large proportion of an organization's value, it makes sense that investors would want any data they could access to understand what they're buying. Increasingly, they're asking for that information in the form of ESG data. And just because it's hard to turn that information into simple numbers doesn't make it any less valuable.

To understand how ESG data meets that need, we can go back to the simple performance-and-engagement cycle for financial capital and expand it to take into account all forms of capital, as shown in Figure 7.

Each stage of this cycle bears a different meaning of the term 'ESG'. That's why the term can be so confusing.

At the top of the cycle is what a company[16] does, its **ESG performance**. It is the meaning of 'ESG' which is displacing terms like 'Corporate sustainability' or 'Corporate Social Responsibility' or the 'the Triple Bottom Line' – i.e., how a company interacts with the environment, society, and the economy, for better or for worse. Every action affects both the total capital it has and the total capital it can access. Most importantly, each type of capital affects the others, so you only know how much capital the organization has by considering all capitals together.

Next, **ESG measures**. Companies work out how they can measure their ESG performance, i.e., their impact on the four capitals. They can do so in many ways, from fuel efficiency or carbon emissions, to headcounts and employee engagement, to compliance, community actions, and awards. Some of these measures are needed to make ESG disclosures; others are desirable because progress on that metric will help build the four capitals and drive business performance.

Then, **ESG disclosure.** The company then decides how to report on these measures to others, whether there are any standards that apply, whether they need to meet the expectations of ESG ratings agencies or investors and the need for any audit. They then choose, to a greater or lesser extent, to share this information with others. Until recently, that has been voluntarily, but there are an increasing number of mandatory disclosures, in Europe, Asia, and Australasia in particular.

Any disclosure should be part of broader **ESG engagement**. A company uses its reports to support conversations with the stakeholders that matter. Its investors will also be pursuing ESG engagement, so it will in most cases be a mutually beneficial conversation. A new class of stakeholder looking to engage are the agencies that produce **ESG ratings** from disclosed measures and other sources. These ratings are used by investors who want to support, or in place of, their own engagement.

The success or otherwise of the company's ESG engagement is whether the other party offers access to their capital. A government may give a resort operator access to a national park. A farming community may give a mineral explorer access to an opportunity. A university may join a collaborative initiative, giving it access not only to its human capital, but to its reputation or social capital. An up-and-coming manager may give it their personal human capital, by joining the firm. An investor may give the company access to more, or less, financial capital. A new **ESG fund** may be created with the explicit purpose of taking all of the cycle into account in its investment decisions, i.e., the company's ESG performance, measures, disclosures, engagement, and ratings.

In Parts B and C, we'll look at each of those stages and phrases in turn.

Together, these meanings of ESG are making a dramatic impact on how people decide to engage with organizations, either as investors, employees, consumers, or citizens. The impact has been so dramatic that some US states have legislated to outlaw their own investing institutions from taking ESG factors into account. It may seem ironic that the party of the free market seeks to constrain the free market's ability to do things for financial and societal benefit, but courts are having the final say.

Chapter 3 Summary
- The Four Capitals model of our world suggests that everything we have is based on natural capital. People add their thinking and effort (human capital), attract other people to do things with them (social capital), and through their labor and machines create the products and services that can be sold for money (financial capital).
- The Six Capitals model splits our intellectual capital from human capital, and adds manufactured capital as a stepping stone to financial capital. Choose the model that suits you best. In both models, only natural capital is finite. All the others are infinite, so nothing has to be a zero-sum game.
- The intangible capitals (human and social) are the most valuable to a company, and investors value companies largely on their assessment of those intangibles.
- The more that organizations nurture their four capitals, the more they can access more human, social, natural, and financial capital from others. That is the whole point of ESG.

Chapter 4
The evidence is in, and ESG is here to stay

The single biggest problem in communication is the illusion that it has taken place.
George Bernard Shaw, quoted by William Whyte, 1950

So far, we have introduced what ESG is, how it came to be here, and how it supports companies to get access to the capital they need to operate and prosper. We believe that ESG has such an inherently sensible place in modern capitalism that it will stay here for as long as there are capitalists.

The first reason for that belief is the democratization of capital over the past 40 years. More people have an interest in publicly listed companies than ever before and they have a more diverse range of lives and outlooks than earlier stock traders. Importantly, they are represented less by company directors, and more by the institutional investors who manage their pension or superannuation funds. Many of those institutions are insurance companies, whose deep study of risk has convinced them of the need for action – for long-term financial reasons – on emerging social and environmental realities. The more that they and other investment professionals have adopted ESG thinking, the more it has paid dividends. They have also considered the arguments as to why they should not adopt ESG and found reason to dismiss them one by one.

While there will always be cowboys in capital markets, the more that investing in those markets is a profession, the more likely it is that ESG will stand.

The democratization of capital markets

ESG has not been a standalone trend over the past 40 years. It has accompanied other movements that have fundamentally changed the nature of our capital markets and of people's expectations of those markets.

In many respects this has been a democratization of capitalism. More people hold substantial investments than ever before, both directly and indirectly through their retirement funds. These decades have seen the greatest privatization of public assets in human history. In countries where the assets were not just handed over to oligarchs, thousands of 'mom and dad' investors signed up for shares. The rise of personal wealth has also driven questions about the purpose of that wealth and the influence it may wield. Information has become more readily available and social media has amplified its scrutiny.

All these trends support a greater analysis of the nonfinancial performance of our companies, by more people, for more reasons.

https://doi.org/10.1515/9783111428949-006

The rise of share ownership through privatizations and pension funds

The ownership of companies in the USA has changed markedly since the 1970s. Figure 8 tracks that change with the Visual Capitalist's usual vision and insight. Until the early 1970s, just over half (51%) of the market value of all US stocks were held by the 1% of US families (including single individuals) who had the largest personal income. Almost three-quarters (74%) of market value were held by just the richest 10% of families.[17] While the wealth of those families has not decreased, their share of a rising stock market fell to just 24% of market value in 2019. Replacing them have been retirement accounts managed by investment firms, i.e., US pension funds and foreign funds that also typically represent pension or superannuation accounts. These funds represent the retirement savings of over a billion global workers, and they are the same organizations that are signatories to the Principles of Responsible Investment. The stock market has become less a plaything of the wealthy and more a steward of retirement funds, and ESG has become more and more important to that stewardship.

Figure 8: US stock ownership within taxable accounts fell from 80% in 1965 to 24% in 2019.

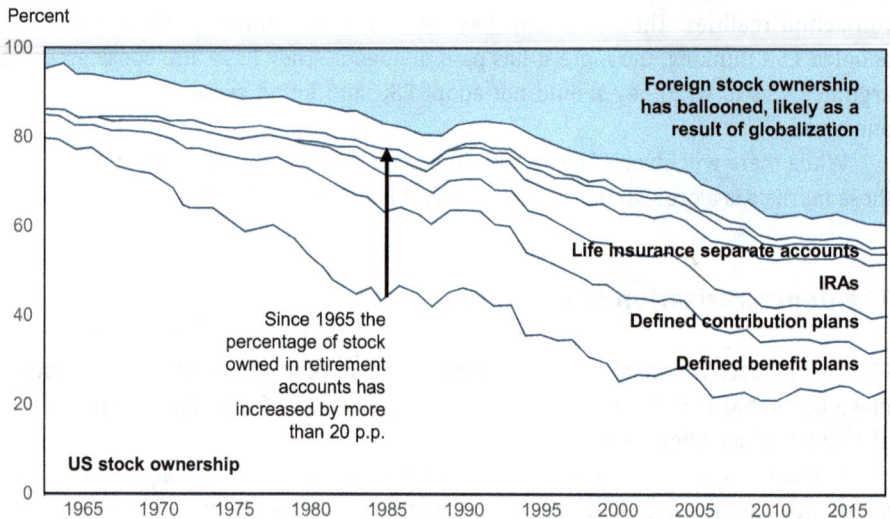

Source: Visual Capitalist.

A similar trend is visible in Australia, with the introduction of compulsory superannuation in 1992 and an opening up of the Australian financial market. The democratization of share ownership was accelerated in the 1990s when the government sold off publicly owned enterprises such as Telecom (now Telstra), the Commonwealth Bank, the Commonwealth Serum Laboratory (now CSL), and QANTAS, and mutual organizations such as AMP and NRMA (now IAG) were listed on the stock exchange. In just a decade, the proportion of Australian adults with a share portfolio quadrupled from 10% to 41%; see Figure 9.[18]

Figure 9: Australian became a 'democracy of shareholders' by deliberate government policy in the 1990s.

Proportion of the Australian adult population with on-exchange investments
Percent

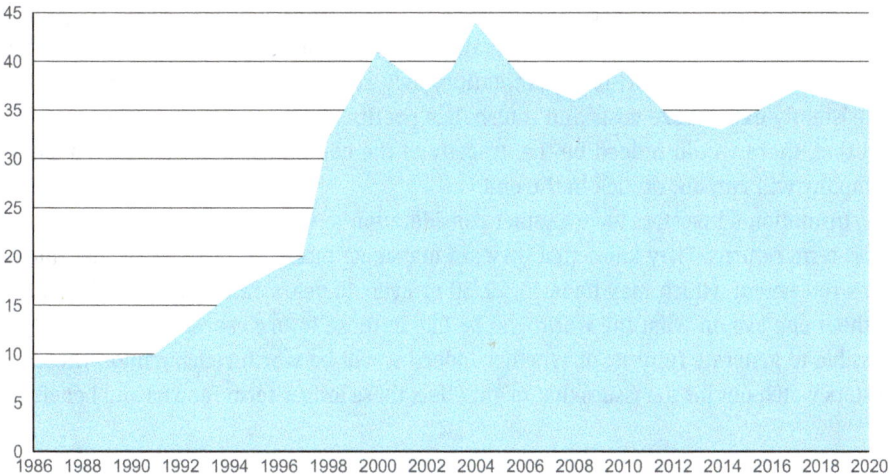

Source: ASX (2023), 'Australian Investor Study 2023', ASX, https://www.asx.com.au/content/dam/asx/blog/asx-australian-investor-study-2023.pdf, accessed 15 December 2024.

Professional scrutiny of company ESG performance

This revolution in share ownership is not just a change of hats, it has brought an equally dramatic change in how companies have been governed and managed. The new directors were not, as before, in close cahoots with the company's own management or indeed one and the same. They did not, as might be thought, represent the vast new class of 'mom and pop' investors, who rarely bothered to vote and if they did give their proxy to the Chair.

Rather, the new directors represented the investment funds who now dominated the share registry. Even if they took the view that they were on the board just to look after the owners' interests, then they are very different owners than before. The new owners were no longer just the extremely wealthy, the top 1% of incomes, with a surprisingly high degree of shared values. The new owners were all working people, with unsurprisingly diverse values. At the same time, the trustees of many large re-tirement funds have had a professional shakeup. Where once they might have been dominated by industry and union representatives, appointed as a reward and with no particular skills in investment, now those trustees are largely appointed for those very skills.

More importantly, the new owners are universal owners. They own shares not just in one company but tens of thousands of companies around the world. As univer-sal owners, they are unlikely to be impressed by a company that makes its profits only at the expense of the social, human or natural capital that *all* companies may draw on. Despite the short-term temptation, they are unimpressed by companies that consistently externalize costs and internalize profits. They know that if all companies did that, there would indeed be the 'tragedy of the commons', and that even a single company will run out of luck in the end.

Institutional investors have another consideration to weigh against the temptation of short-term returns. They know that they are managing money to provide for their mem-ber's retirement, which may be in 10, 20, 30 or even 40 years' time. How can they do so without one eye on what the world will be like in those future years, whether it will be possible to generate returns, or whether indeed it will be worth retiring into? These in-vestors watch out for the issues that might affect those longer-term returns and benefits.

Societal expectations and scrutiny of ESG performance

While companies are now under ever more effective scrutiny from institutional and professional investors, the digital age has extended that scrutiny far and wide.

More people are aware of company decisions, actions, and impacts than ever be-fore. It doesn't take much for that information to be posted to the Internet – by the company or others – and shared through social media. Where once a company may be able to sweep an embarrassing incident under the carpet, now that is extremely unlikely. If an incident occurs, it is impossible for companies to control the narrative in the way they might have done with traditional media. News and views are spread instantaneously, magnifying the power and reach of any initial whistleblower.

This societal scrutiny increases the level of accountability of companies. That can be uncomfortable for some organizations because societal expectations have also risen. Thankfully, there are now many more things a company might be embarrassed about than there were a generation ago. We will explore these in Part B, but they in-clude the familiar advances in human rights – toward diversity and safety and away from modern forms of slavery – as well as essential environmental action. Often, these expectations are stated directly by a company's workforce or customers. Just as often, they are expressed through personal relationships. Many have said in (semi-) jest that the most powerful force toward good corporate behavior are the progressive children of corporate executives.

As well, the privatization of public assets in many countries has meant the private sector provides many of the services that were traditionally the domain of government – roads, hospitals, aged care, childcare, retirement incomes, transportation infrastructure, even data registries. Many of these services rely on government payments. The question arises, if companies are providing a social good, which is subsidized by the government, should not the company also be accountable to the public for the quality of the service and its ESG impacts?

Figure 10: ESG as an outcome of social, economic, and technological progress.

Environmental and social issues	Enabling technologies	Enabling wealth	Stakeholder expectation	Competitive advantage
	• Biotech	• Maslow's hierachy	• Government: ESD	
	• Alternative energy		• Clients/consumers	
	• Whole system design		• Investors: UN PRI	
	• Service-based businesses		• Employees	
	• Stronger economic models		• NGOs	

Source: The authors.

This is just the start of the long-term societal, economic, and technology trends that support the emergence of ESG. Figure 10 suggests how this might have occurred. We have always had social and environmental issues, and always will. Solve one and another two pop up in their place. But we do have the technology to deal with many of them, if we choose to use them. We also have the wealth to deal with them, if we choose to apply it. If we are aware of a problem and have the wealth and technologies to address it, it becomes likely that one or more stakeholders will call for the issue to be addressed. Companies can either wait for that call and be reactive, or seek out a competitive advantage by addressing it appropriately.

Not for nothing has the term 'ESG' risen on the same wave as 'social license'. However, while much of this discussion seems to be phrased in the negative, it is actually a very positive story. Companies, especially the large modern international corporation, seem to be the way our society organizes its resources to get things done. The more that companies do that with strong, genuine ESG performance, the more our communities and environments will benefit. Happily, it also seems that, on the whole, the companies and their investors will benefit more as well. It is simply a better way to do business. As Don Huberts from Shell put it, often quoted by Amory Lovins, 'The stone age didn't end because they ran out of stone'.[19]

Integrating ESG leads to better investment performance

Nowadays, most investors intuitively see value in ESG. They acknowledge, for example, that a diverse group of company directors are more likely to make better decisions, or that companies that abide by the law and preserve their resources (human, financial, social, or environmental) have more options to perform well, with less risk.

This was not always the case. Until quite recently, the idea that nonfinancial factors might be a useful guide to financial outcomes was considered 'novel'. Many investors pointed to long-recognized legal and investment axioms to refute the idea. Indeed, for many years, corporate sustainability practitioners stopped short of asserting that good practices *led to* better performance. They were content with calling out the correlation, and few had the research appetite to even attempt showing causation.

Better performance over time

In the end, comprehensive investment research has identified the correlations between ESG factors and financial performance and identified some elements of causation. We take a first look at the research here and offer more in Chapter 11.

Care is needed here. One can always find a research study to support a pro- or an anti-ESG case. It is more important to look at 'survey' articles: those that survey all of the published research to assess the weight of evidence. Two large and independent studies have found remarkably consistent results.

In 2015, a joint team from Deutsche Asset & Wealth Management and Hamburg University reviewed over 2,000 empirical studies since the 1970s, still the most comprehensive review of academic research on the topic.[20] They found that around 63% of the studies showed a positive relationship between ESG and corporate financial performance, with just 8% suggesting a negative relationship. This was the average finding over a range of asset classes (equities, bonds, and real estate), and after considering the ESG factors either individually or in combination; see Figure 11.

More recently, researchers took a magnifying glass to the MSCI All Country World Index (ACWI), which tracks the performance of 2,933 large- and midcap stocks across 11 industry sectors, representing about 85% of the market capitalization of all listed companies in 23 developed and 24 emerging markets. The researchers compared the relative financial and ESG performance of those companies over 7 years to November 2020. The results are shown in Figure 12. The companies in the top third of ESG ratings outperformed the ACWI by 1.31% annually, while those in the bottom third or ratings lagged their peers by 1.25% in annual returns – with earnings growth a disappointing 9.2% below their peers.[21]

Figure 11: Most studies find that ESG performance correlates with financial performance.

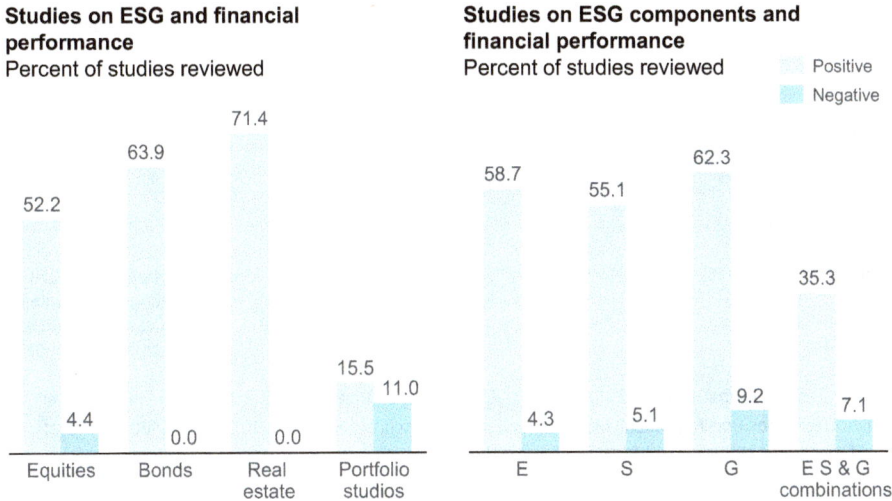

Studies on ESG and financial performance
Percent of studies reviewed

Studies on ESG components and financial performance
Percent of studies reviewed

Positive
Negative

Equities	Bonds	Real estate	Portfolio studios
52.2	63.9	71.4	15.5
4.4	0.0	0.0	11.0

E	S	G	ES & G combinations
58.7	55.1	62.3	35.3
4.3	5.1	9.2	7.1

Source: Friede, G., Busch, T., & Bassen, A. (2015). ESG and financial performance: aggregated evidence from more than 2000 empirical studies. *Journal of Sustainable Finance & Investment,* 5(4), 210–233.

These major research pieces make a strong case for believing that integrating ESG considerations into investment analysis and into corporate strategies do contribute to greater risk-weighted returns for those investors from those companies.

A sampling of the research reviewed by the Hamburg teams, and more conducted since, shows the many investment nooks and crannies that researchers have explored – over time and in distinct markets. They keep getting the same results: stronger ESG performance correlates to stronger financial performance. For example, when Morgan Stanley reviewed US-based mutual funds in 2015,[22] they found that "sustainable equity funds had equal or higher median returns and equal or lower volatility than traditional funds for 64% of the periods examined". This was on both an absolute and a risk-adjusted basis, across asset classes and over time.

Similarly, when Envestnet PMC investigated what lay behind the differences in US equity fund performance, they found that "on average, socially conscious investing does 'no harm' relative to unconstrained, conventional investing", that there was less variance between the best- and worst-performing SRI funds than there was for the respective non-SRI funds, and that SRI funds tend to have less downside performance, especially during bear markets.[23]

Figure 12: Strong ESG performance translates to strong market returns.

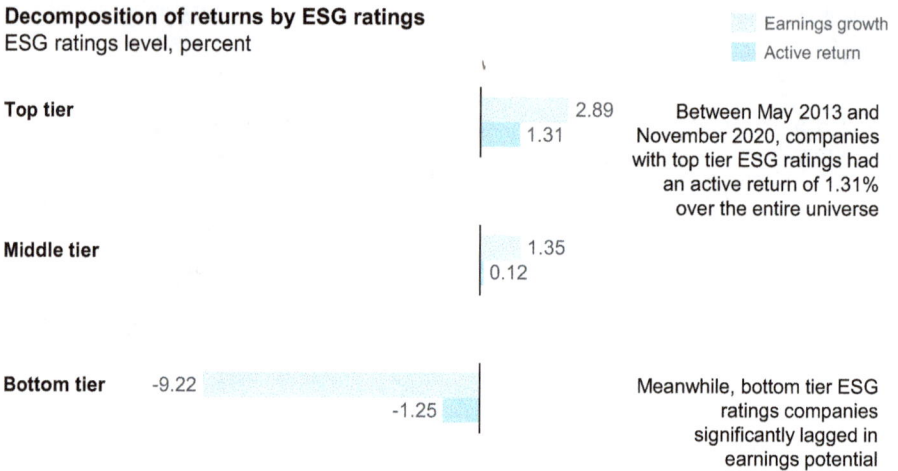

Decomposition of returns by ESG ratings
ESG ratings level, percent

Earnings growth
Active return

Top tier 2.89
1.31

Between May 2013 and November 2020, companies with top tier ESG ratings had an active return of 1.31% over the entire universe

Middle tier 1.35
0.12

Bottom tier -9.22
-1.25

Meanwhile, bottom tier ESG ratings companies significantly lagged in earnings potential

Source: Giese G, Kumar N, Nagy Z, Kouzmenko R, (2021), 'The Drivers of ESG Returns – A Fundamental Return Decomposition Approach', MSCI, https://www.msci.com/documents/10199/f31964d0-c79b-02af-45cc-fada2887d085# accessed 16 December 2024.

Better performance when the markets crash

We mentioned above the surge of ESG interest in 2006. That was the year when the UN Principles of Responsible Investment were launched, and international interest in climate change rose markedly with the launch of the UK *Stern Review*, Al Gore's documentary movie *An Inconvenient Truth*, and the European Emissions Trading Scheme.

The Great Financial Crisis (GFC) of 2007–08 put a stop to all that. All but the deepest green corporates and investors dropped their interest in climate change to focus on meeting the next payroll. As markets settled down, those who still believed in ESG continued to build experience, collaboration, and research; Companies focused on long-term exogenous risks as much as immediate waste and community initiatives. Membership of the PRI continued to grow, but for another decade remained very much under the radar.

The COVID-19 pandemic has given researchers another chance to compare how ESG and mainstream funds fare when times are very tough. ESG researchers were particularly nervous that the pandemic would focus eyes on the immediate at the expense of the longer term. However, the intervening 12 years had brought a lot of maturity to both corporate and investor approaches. Yes, the pandemic was hell but companies did everything they could to keep safe whatever human and social capital they had. Investors could see which strategies were working and which were not. Would interest in ESG and sustainability wane in 2020 as it did in 2007?

Not this time. Analysis by Morgan Stanley revealed that US sustainable equity and bond funds outperformed their peers through the worst of the pandemic of 2019 and

2020; see Figure 13. While the benchmark traditional equity funds averaged a 27.7% re-turn in the upturn of 2019, their peer ESG-related equity funds averaged a 30.5% return.[24] Then, in the downturn of 2020, traditional funds lost an average 8.7% of their value, while the ESG-related funds lost only 4.8% of theirs. Over the two years, the net returns were 19% for the traditional funds and 25.7% for ESG-related funds. Their very success put them in the firing line of ideological commentators. The performance of ESG-related bond funds was even more impressive, according to the same study, out-performing traditional funds by 3.1 percentage points over the two years.

Figure 13: ESG funds outperformed their peers through the COVID-19 pandemic.

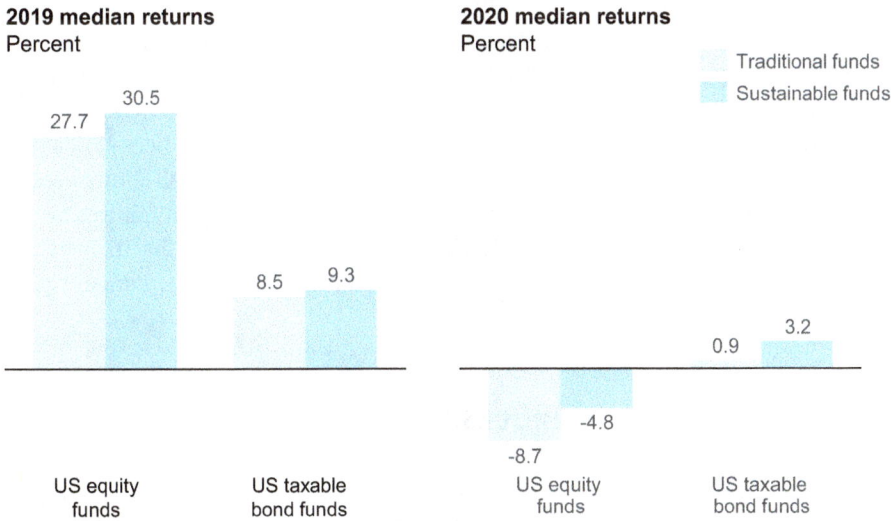

Source: Institute for Sustainable Investing (24 February 2021) 'Sustainable Funds Outperform peers in 2020 Coronavirus' Morgan Stanley, https://www.morganstanley.com/ideas/esg-funds-outperform-peers-coronavirus accessed 16 December 2024.

Given the thousands of academic and investment house studies into correlations be-tween ESG and financial performance, any two pages here are necessarily selective. But we believe not dangerously so. McKinsey also found that just 8% of the 2000 articles it reviewed found a negative correlation, and they were in isolated markets. Those find-ings are inevitable, just as there will be isolated, local, short-term falls in temperature despite the global reality of a warming climate. And in 2023, the consulting firm shared findings that "reveal that while strong ESG scores do not compensate for weak funda-mentals, companies that achieve stronger growth and profitability than their peers while improving sustainability and ESG scores" deliver two percentage points more re-turns to shareholders than companies that excel only on financial metrics.[25]

The big downside risk of overlooking ESG factors

Marginal outperformance over time may not, however, be reason enough to keep an eye on ESG factors in all decision-making. The aim is to sidestep the big, value-destroying crisis that a company may innocently walk into, or more likely bring upon itself. Our colleagues at SenateSHJ researched 312 well-known corporate crises over the past 40 years to determine their immediate financial impact, and how long that impact lasted.[26] The crises spanned the environmental (the Vale tailings dam failure), the cultural (Rio Tinto's destruction of Juukan Gorge and its 40,000-year-old artworks), the ethical (VW's false emissions data), and tragic human loss (Boeing and Ardent theme park crashes).

On average, the studied companies suffered a 35.2% drop in share price, ranging from 2.1% after publication of VW's dishonesty, to 50.4% for BP's Deepwater Horizon explosion and oil spill, to AIG's 97% collapse after its exposure to mortgage-backed securities triggered a government bailout. On average, it took share prices 427 days to recover the lost ground, and some never did.[27] Some were technical failures seemingly remote from ESG considerations. Some were avoidable human failures, as we will see when considering Deepwater Horizon in Part C. In all, 181 of the 312 incidents were a failure of environmental or governance controls, the abuse of human rights, or white-collar crime.

The arguments made against ESG come up short

Despite the evidence, some still argue against considering ESG factors in managing companies or investing in them. Some of their arguments sound good on first hearing. It's axiomatic, isn't it, that if you exclude some companies from the 'universe' of potential investments, your returns will fall? And don't we have a duty as company directors to increase shareholder returns, and as an investment trustee to increase investment returns? And what about the 'sin-stock' index that outperforms the 'do-gooder' index every week of the year?

While some of these arguments have some merit under some circumstances, none of them stand up to detailed scrutiny – or to a longer-term view of what is in the best interests of the company or the investor.

Directors actually do have to look past the current share registry

Many people who have studied law, formally or informally, this century or last might remember that company directors are duty-bound to act in the best interests of their shareholders. That broad duty was interpreted very narrowly, by some, to put the interests of current shareholders ahead of any other stakeholder – the doctrine of shareholder primacy. While the duty has been clarified by recent legislation (see below), the narrow view meant that returns to current shareholders was the be all and end all.

In fact, directors have always used their business judgment to decide how much of a potential profit to pay out to investors, and how much to reinvest in the company. In that decision, they may consider any number of factors and are considering the interests of future shareholders, not just the current ones.

So, like so many other business decisions, the real issue is one of balancing short-term and long-term needs and duties. A company could be 'wasting money on a social cause', or it could be investing in its social and human capital. Who is to say which, other than its management and directors?

This has been clarified by recent law reforms in most countries. For example, the Canada Business Corporations Act was amended in 2019 to expand the factors that directors may consider in exercising their business judgment: shareholders, employees, retirees and pensioners, creditors, consumers, governments, the environment, and the long-term interests of the corporation. It followed two Supreme Court of Canada decisions that suggested directors and officers should take those factors into account in seeking to make a 'better corporation'.[28]

A similar provision is now written into section 172 of the UK Companies Act 2006, confirming that directors must "act in the way he considers, in good faith, would be most likely to promote the success of the company for the benefit of its members as a whole" which includes considering the long-term consequences of actions and the interests of employees, commercial relationships, the community, and the environment. To make sure directors and investor interests align, many countries mandate the disclosure of ESG considerations. That's been required of Europe's listed companies since its 2014 Nonfinancial Reporting Directive, or the EU's Corporate Sustainability Due Diligence Directive, requiring large companies to report regularly on their human rights and environmental due diligence. We will consider more of these disclosure obligations in Part B. For now, it is enough to confirm that directors are not only permitted to consider ESG issues, but that they have a positive obligation to do so.

Even in countries like Australia where legislation is not so clear, the case law, declarations by regulators and business associations, company norms, and investor action combine to make the legislation redundant. Company officers, in meeting their duties to existing and future shareholders, must take broader factors into account. As Andrew Lumsden and Saul Fridman put it

> [I]n a world of open, knowledge-based competition, 'companies do not function in isolation from the society around them'. The success of a corporation depends upon the organisation's ability to most effectively use capital, labour and natural resources to produce goods and services. That, in turn, depends upon 'workers who are educated, safe, healthy, decently housed and motivated' and operate in an environment with less waste, lower pollution levels and free from the outrage of the community about corporate 'misconduct'.[29]

Investment trustees actually do have to look past financial performance

A similar debate has been settled on the duties of investment trustees, the individuals legally responsible for managing the funds entrusted to them, which they may invest in a range of company stock, bonds, physical assets, or other funds. A lead role was played by the 2005 paper "A Legal Framework for the Integration of Environmental, Social and Governance Issues into Institutional Investment", published by the international law firm Freshfields Bruckhaus Deringer at the request of many of those institutions. Widely referred to as the 'Freshfields Report', the landmark paper argued that, "integrating ESG considerations into an investment analysis so as to more reliably predict financial performance is clearly permissible and is arguably required in all jurisdictions".[30] A sequel in 2009 confirmed that taking ESG factors into consideration was in keeping with an investment trustee's fiduciary duties.[31]

Throughout this book, we will see how ignoring ESG factors can risk the value of a portfolio. Equally, an investment trustee who falsely claims they are taking ESG factors into account may face prosecution for 'greenwashing', a subject that we turn to in Part C. Just as many market regulators have imposed ESG obligations on investment trustees, they are quite ready to take action against those who overhype their ESG credentials. In the USA, ESG has become an increasing focus of the Securities and Exchange Commission's Enforcement Division, with staff applying "time-tested principles concerning materiality, accuracy of disclosures, and fiduciary duty, as codified in federal statutes, regulations, and case law" with respect to both public companies and investment products.[32] Among the Division's 760 enforcement actions for 2022 is one charging BNY Mellon Investment Advisers for "materially misleading statements and omissions about its consideration of ESG principles in making investment decisions for certain mutual funds".

All investors shrink their universe

According to investment theory, reducing the universe of investment options also reduces investment returns. So, some argue, since ESG exclusions reduce that universe, investment returns should reduce also.

This argument seems to ignore that all active investors reduce their investable universe. They might focus on a class of assets, or apply certain financial criteria, or seek certain managerial characteristics. Even the choice to invest passively in the S&P 500 is a choice to choose one country's public companies over another. And that style of passive investment may be exposed to known systemic or sector-specific risks, such as poor governance or climate change risk.

The issue is not whether the investable universe has shrunk, but whether the selected subuniverse leads to better investment risk and returns. That test applies equally to ESG funds as it does for other active funds.

Jeremy Grantham tested the impact of excluding different sectors from the investment universe in his seminal piece on investment and climate change, "The Race of Our Lives Revisited".[33] He found that over any long term "you can divest from oil – or anything else – without consequence". As shown in Figure 14, over the long term, it made very little difference which sector was excluded, and you were equally likely to perform better or to perform worse. As Grantham puts it:

> . . . if you were to consider it unethical to own these oil companies (whose scientists wrote . . . about the serious dangers of climate change in the 1970s only to have management later ignore it all and fund deniers and obfuscators), you can believe the cost of your ethics is about +/- 20 basis points!

With most of today's ESG investment representing the retirement funds that are intended to build over a person's working life, typically over 30 years, arguments about excluding even whole sectors become very moot indeed.

Figure 14: Excluding particular sectors makes little difference to overall returns.

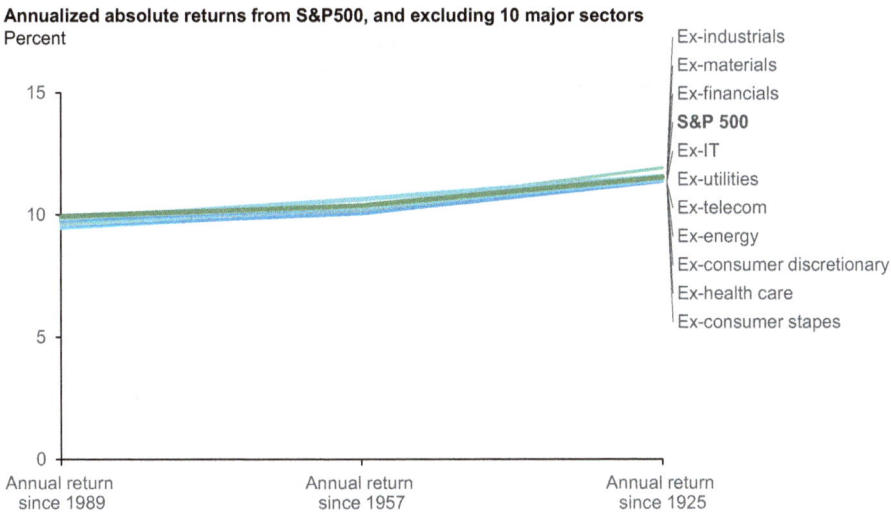

Annualized absolute returns from S&P500, and excluding 10 major sectors
Percent

Ex-industrials
Ex-materials
Ex-financials
S&P 500
Ex-IT
Ex-utilities
Ex-telecom
Ex-energy
Ex-consumer discretionary
Ex-health care
Ex-consumer stapes

Annual return since 1989 — Annual return since 1957 — Annual return since 1925

Source: S&P, GMO (prior to March 1957 the S&P is represented by the S&P 90 index).

All investing is an expression of values

One of the arguments used against investing with a strong ESG emphasis is to question 'Who are you to enforce your values on others?' or 'Whose values should be used?'. These types of arguments seem to suggest that managing or investing in a company was 'values free' before ESG came along, and should remain so. However, values-free investing has never really existed, and wishing it did is really a value in itself. People who make the argument for values-free investing or corporate governance are seeking to impose implicit values such as 'the only things of value are those that can be monetized', or 'compliance with the law is all I need to do'.

The problem is that such a minimalist value can be dangerous, not to mention out of step with societal expectations. That's the lesson of the Banking Royal Commission in Australia, the behavior that led to Deepwater Horizon or the destruction of Juukan Gorge, or indeed the decisions which led to the Global Financial Crisis. Laws are written within the context of those societal expectations and compliance with them is only the start of responsible behavior. Indeed, 'corporate sustainability' has long been considered to be actions taken 'beyond compliance' and ESG performance retains that emphasis. Where companies and investors stick to the letter of a law that falls short of societal expectations, then those laws will be changed.

Capitalists are working out what corporate policies are effective and supported and what policies are not. It is undeniable that corporate policies have been put in place in the name of ESG that do not reflect broad societal values, or that are simply ineffective in what they are trying to achieve. Those policies are typically rejected sooner or later.

The values that ESG seeks to embed in corporate and investor performance are universal values that have been adopted by individuals and by community, national, and international organizations to respect the natural, human, and social capital we depend on. Most capitalists insist on the intrinsic worth of natural, human, and social capital in their family and community lives. The question is 'Why exempt companies and investors from the same values'?

Pushing back on the 'anti-woke' pushback on ESG

Nonetheless, the broad economic and ethical values that are driving ESG's adoption are not universally shared, particularly in the United States. In June 2024, an interim staff report was circulated through the US Federal Judiciary Committee, with the evocative title "Climate Control: Exposing the Decarbonization Collusion in Environmental, Social, and Governance (ESG) Investing."[34] The report alleged that a 'climate cartel' of major financial institutions was colluding with left-wing activists to impose radical environmental, social, and governance goals on American companies.[35] Soon after, the Republican heads of the Judiciary Committee sent letters to over 130 US-based companies, retirement systems, and government pension funds who were members or otherwise associated with the cartel (otherwise known as Climate Action 100+; see Chapter 13). The companies and investors denied any collusion or that ESG goals were radical. Climate change, they stressed, is an investment risk and it is well within their fiduciary duty to consider and, if necessary, act upon that risk.

Similarly, a number of US states have sought to remove their public and retirement funds from banks or fund managers that may 'boycott' fossil fuel companies. A 2021 Texas law requires the State Comptroller to publish a list of the offending fund managers. As of August 2024, the list included 16 of the world's largest fund managers, including BlackRock, BNP Paribas, HSBC and UBS, and 353 specific funds. Yet the Texas action may well have been counterproductive. Five of the state's largest underwriters of municipal bonds closed down their Texas business in response, and the subsequent lack of competition led to higher borrowing costs for Texan municipal governments.

Other states in the USA, typically those with a Democrat majority, have enacted legislation *encouraging* public pension funds to include ESG factors in investment decisions. Needless to say, both positions have been challenged in the courts. No court has yet found that a consideration of ESG issues is inconsistent with either board decisions in a company, or investment decisions in an investment fund. On the contrary, there will be many events and incidents in this book that show exactly why an ESG lens is essential.

* * *

The continuing backlash against ESG in the USA seems to suggest that even considering ESG factors is somehow contrary to traditional business decision-making. That would imply that 'traditional' decisions are made purely for the short-term financial benefit of current shareholders: the narrowest view of shareholder primacy. On the contrary, businesses should be free to consider ESG factors. They may not find all of them relevant or material – and they may ultimately ignore them all and press on for a short-term benefit. But there is strong empirical evidence that companies that integrate ESG factors into their governance, strategies and operations will perform better, financially. In Part B, we turn to how companies should do just that.

Chapter 4 Summary
- We are all capitalists. Through direct shareholdings or indirect pension funds, more of us have a financial stake in companies than ever before. These companies provide more of our public goods and services than ever before.
- We have a common interest to make sure companies are not 'robbing Peter to pay Paul', by harming our shared natural, social, and human capital to make a short-term financial gain. Being (on average) wealthier and more educated, our expectations are (on average) higher. With more and more widely shared information on company conduct than ever, companies that do the wrong thing will lose value. These trends may pause but will not be reversed.
- Professional investors manage our money on our behalf. They too want companies to build their own capital and add to the shared pool, rather than achieving a profit at the expense of the shared natural, social, and human capital that will generate future profits. They've also noticed that companies that add to the shared pool do better financially than those who don't. Or, at least, they don't do any worse.

- Many people don't believe these results are possible. They argue against the possibility on many grounds, but their arguments – and the numbers – fall short.
- Measuring a company's impact on our shared natural, social, and human capital is the whole point of ESG for investors. It will never be a precise science. But investors will continue to seek information on a company's ESG performance, both as a way to identify and manage risks, and a way to identify and pursue opportunities. These trends may pause but will not be reversed.

Part B: **How to gain access to the four capitals using ESG**

The principles introduced in Part A apply to any organization, large or small, public or private. Any organization that improves its ESG performance and engages its stakeholders on that journey will get access to more capital: financial, human, social, and natural. For convenience – mainly it's easier to say 'company' than 'organization' all the time – we'll talk about companies in this Part. It's true also that companies, listed companies in particular, are subject to more social media, investor, and ratings agency scrutiny on their ESG performance.

In this Part B we take a deeper look at the ESG performance-and-access cycle: *how* a company can use an ESG or sustainability lens to secure access to more of the four capitals. This is the core of ESG or sustainability work from the corporate perspective. The people in that company are the ones that have to decide what ESG issues to engage with and for what purpose, and to take the appropriate action and bear the consequences.

For the purposes of this Part, you are one of those people. You may be leading the ESG effort, but are as likely to be someone asked to be part of that effort, and want to know what's going on. You have your own priorities and challenges, and may not want these ESG asks to be added to your pile. This Part should give you confidence that it is worth your while, and can be done. It considers:

- **Chapter 5: Understanding what's at stake: the core dualities of ESG performance.** These dualities must be kept in mind in every corporate decision. The first duality splits the four capitals: the tangibles and intangibles. Next is to consider both the risks and the opportunities of any action (or inaction). There is the risk that actions may erode human, social, natural, or financial capital; there are also opportunities to nurture those capitals. The third is 'double materiality': the materiality of those impacts on the four capitals from the perspective of both the company and its stakeholders. And the fourth is balancing the short-term and long-term consequences of a decision.
- **Chapter 6: Deciding what to do when capitals are at stake.** You might want to consider ESG issues in three types of decisions that create (or erode) capital. Operational decisions are those made every day in the ordinary course of business. Strategic decisions change or confirm the 'what, where, or how' of what the company does. Lastly, companies make specific ESG investments to nurture their four capitals. Each applies the core dualities in different ways.
- **Chapter 7: Getting people involved in ESG decision-making.** If ESG is to matter to your company, then it really has to matter to your people: the leadership, people on the front line, and most importantly and most overlooked, the middle rungs of management. This section suggests what people can do to assist the ESG effort and how you can get them involved.
- **Chapter 8: Reporting and engaging to access more capital on ESG performance.** You are engaging with people with whom you want a lasting relationship, as they have capital that you would like to draw on for a long time. Like any relationship, it helps to be on a shared journey and to be honest through it. You'll

https://doi.org/10.1515/9783111428949-007

need a narrative that appeals to the audience you're targeting: your own people, investors, customers, business partners, ratings agencies, regulators, or the public at large. Ideally, it's the same narrative for all.

At the end of each chapter, we will offer a summary of the key questions and issues. Together, those summaries can form the basis of a sustainability strategy for your organization.

In thinking about such a strategy, companies need first to agree on some basic principles. They can set whether their ambition is to be industry leaders, experimenters, or followers; whether their focus will be on risk or opportunity; whether they will bias internal or shared external efforts; and whether they will focus on social, human, or natural capital. Then they can make their organizational choices: to make sustainability a standalone effort or integrated into all decision-making; to pursue it in operations or at the corporate center; and to be methodical or nimble. Each of these principles is touched on in this part.

While this book focuses on ESG performance, there is obviously a lot more to a company's ability to foster the four capitals. There are the core strategic, leadership, cultural, operational, and organizational aspects to performance as well. We believe ESG performance is part of that mix; you can still perform without it, but it is harder to perform well.

Chapter 5
The core dualities of ESG performance

It's like with anything else in life: hard work, being thorough and breaking challenges down into small pieces.

KAJSA VON GEIJER, SVP HR and Sustainability, Thule

As we saw in Part A, companies have financial, natural, human, and social capital to play with. Decision-makers in those companies have to work out how to make and access more. In doing so, you will need to consider the four core dualities of ESG performance:

- *Tangible* and *intangible capital.* As we saw in Part A, these two essential forms of capital map to the four (or six) capitals. Tangible capital is the measurable, material goods and assets that can be quantified on the balance sheet: raw or manufactured goods, real property, and financial assets. Intangible capital is the human and social capital that we can apply to that tangible capital to create more of it.
- The *risks and opportunities* of action or inaction. ESG factors affect value in two ways: there is a risk that actions may erode the human, social, natural, or financial capital of either the company or its communities; there are also opportunities to nurture those capitals.[36] As we have seen, the value of intangibles in modern corporations far exceeds that of their tangible assets, so it is the risk to and opportunities for intangible assets that are far more important.
- The '*double materiality*' of ESG issues to both the company and its stakeholders. The ESG issues or factors that matter most are those that are material to both the company and its stakeholders (including the environment). For the company, some ESG issues are relatively easy to identify: those relevant to the successful execution of an operational, strategic, or ESG investment decision. Otherwise, we propose a simple test for both the company and its stakeholders. An issue is material if a party *says* it is important to them, *or* whether objectively it may have a material effect on the party's four capitals, or its ability to draw financial, human, social, or natural capital from others.
- *Shorter-term* costs and *longer-term* investments. One of the most difficult things to overcome in the world of ESG is the belief by some that it is a cost to business. The main premise of this book is that any company action on an ESG issue should be considered an investment. On most issues – diversity, governance, safety, community engagement – the company is investing directly in its human and social capital. If it doesn't think the action will pay off in the medium term, it should not be doing it. On environmental issues, the payback may be just as direct (savings from energy efficiency or waste reduction), or the investment may gain indirect returns through access to markets, innovation, or employee engagement.

https://doi.org/10.1515/9783111428949-008

In fact, some believe that ESG is not anything new at all. It is just sound business judgment, applied over a longer timeframe and more factors than the pressures for short-term performance typically allow.

The risks and opportunities to tangible and intangible capital

The value that ESG can add over time is shown in Figure 15. In the short term, sound ESG performance can reduce immediate costs or risks to people, the business, and the environment. Over time, good performance will be recognized by those sharing their capital: companies would be able to borrow for a lower interest rate and hire people for less than otherwise. This is not being cheap, just recognizing that people are more likely to want more money to work for companies that don't really care about the social costs of their business. At the extreme, for example, the International Red Cross could hire someone in the same role for a lot less than, say, British American Tobacco. More likely though, the company will gain better value from the salaries they do pay, as those salaries are typically higher in companies with higher ESG ratings.[37] They might also increase revenues through getting more business. Governments might grant access to markets, large corporates might put the company on their vendor panel, and selective consumers might include their brands in their shopping.

The big value, however, is building up intangible capital – social and human capital – the things that bring more opportunities to take calculated risks and make greater returns in the future. That converts to financial benefits down the track, which is what the investors are really interested in.

The double materiality of ESG issues

Companies need to act and report on the issues that are important or 'material' to their company. They also need to act and report on the issues that are material to their stakeholders. What is material to a company may not be necessarily be material to a stakeholder and vice versa. However, it is important for companies to understand both their material ESG issues and their stakeholders', which introduces the idea of double materiality.

The definition of 'materiality' has been notoriously varied, with no conformity yet on whether regulated reporting should insist on single or double materiality and how either one should be defined.[38,39] A company can make its own choices but does need to consider double materiality no matter how it later reports on it. If an issue is material to both the company and its stakeholders, that will help determine what actions to take, how to effectively report on, and the metrics used to assess performance.

Figure 15: ESG adds value to both tangible and intangible capital.

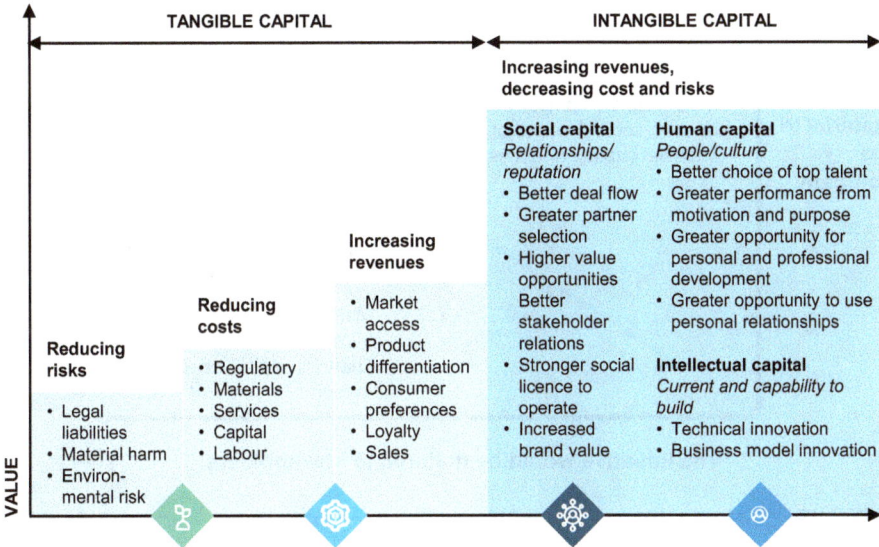

TANGIBLE CAPITAL			INTANGIBLE CAPITAL		

Increasing revenues, decreasing cost and risks

VALUE	Reducing risks	Reducing costs	Increasing revenues	Social capital *Relationships/ reputation*	Human capital *People/culture*
			• Market access	• Better deal flow	• Better choice of top talent
			• Product differentiation	• Greater partner selection	• Greater performance from motivation and purpose
			• Consumer preferences	• Higher value opportunities	• Greater opportunity for personal and professional development
			• Loyalty	Better stakeholder relations	• Greater opportunity to use personal relationships
	• Legal liabilities	• Regulatory	• Sales	• Stronger social licence to operate	
	• Material harm	• Materials		• Increased brand value	Intellectual capital *Current and capability to build*
	• Environ- mental risk	• Services			• Technical innovation
		• Capital			• Business model innovation
		• Labour			

Source: Dowse CSP, based on McKinsey & Company and PwC intangible asset models.

So, materiality for the company can be identified by asking two questions, as shown in Figure 16:
– whether it is relevant to what the company says is important in its corporate, brand, or operational strategies and risk management, and
– whether it would potentially have a material effect on the company's four capitals, or its ability to draw financial, human, social, or natural capital from others.

Issues that are material to stakeholders can be considered on the same two dimensions:
– whether it is relevant to what the stakeholders *say* is important to them, in their published statements or policies, or in research that asks the question, and
– whether it would potentially have a material effect on the stakeholders' four capitals, or its ability to draw financial, human, social, or natural capital from others.

Note that the second dimension is independent of what the parties say: it is an objective test of whether the action would negatively affect that party's assets, whether or not they realize it. It is an extended form of the legal principle of negligence. At law, an entity that negligently harms a person to whom they owe a duty of care will owe that person damages. In ESG, whether or not there is a legal duty of care, the entity's social capital will be penalized if there is harm, let alone harm with knowledge or negligence (an outcome considered below).

Figure 16: Consider what is material to both the company and its stakeholders, including the environment.

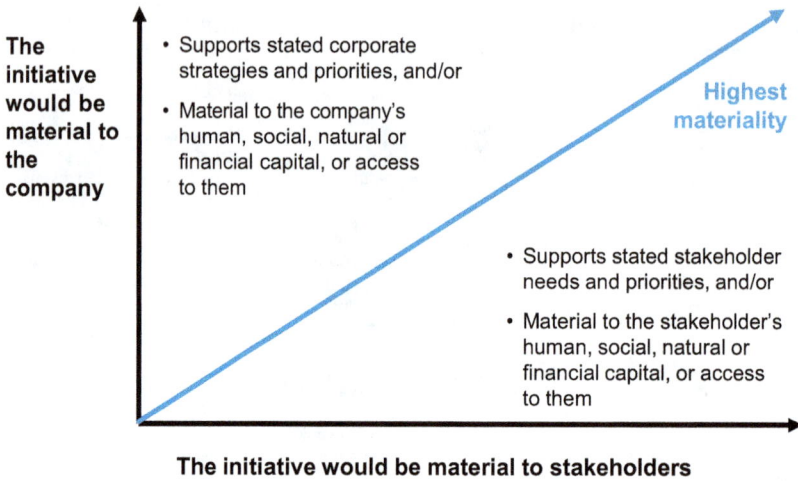

The initiative would be material to stakeholders

Source: The authors.

Figure 16 is a clear layout of the most common approach to materiality, and the one incorporated into sustainability reporting standards in Europe and Australasia. (A different approach is taken by Japan's Dai Nippon Printing, in the case study considered below.) It can be expanded on in various ways, including by noting the extent of influence the company has over the impact, and the impacts that may occur at each stage of the company's value chain.

Thule's approach to materiality

Thule is one company that integrates dual materiality in its thinking by considering impacts throughout its value chain. Thule is a Swedish-based global brand of accessories for outdoor activity: roof racks, bike racks, awnings for recreational vehicles, baby strollers and the like, with the tagline 'Bring your life'. An on-brand cycle path graphic sets out the stages of its value chain (see Figure 17), and it then assesses the extent to which it can influence environmental impacts at each stage.

Thule's assessments of its influence are:
– high, over operations in its nine manufacturing plants,
– medium for its packaging and transportation,
– medium in its customer experience (being the way customers interact with Thule and its selling agents to buy their product), and
– medium in product recycling, through its product design and instructions for end-of-life disposal.

Figure 17: Thule takes responsibility for its value chain in an on-brand graphic.

Our responsibility and impact throughout the value chain

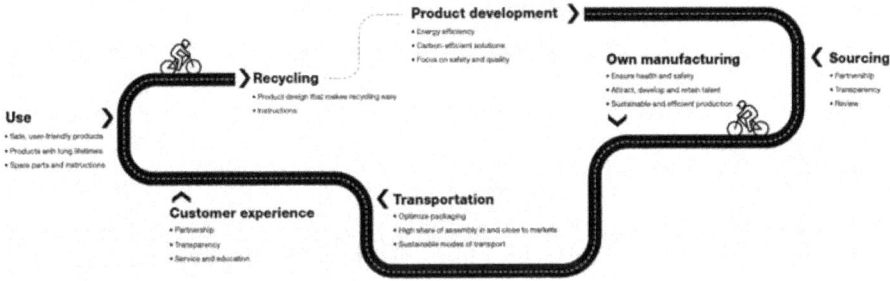

Source: Thule (2024) Annual Report, page 34.

The outlier in this responsibility assessment is the actual use of the product. Thule assesses its influence as 'low', noting that its products are used to carry bikes and outdoor equipment on cars, and they can't control the emissions from those cars. Their customers choose their vehicles and the way they use them. Thule could choose to 'nudge' those choices toward low-emission vehicles, with for example, preferential pricing and branded campaigns. It would realize that the outdoor activities that its products support would be limited by advanced global warming. Yet its influence is nonetheless less than at other stages of the value chain.

How material is ESG, generally, to the company?

For many companies, it is also worth considering how important ESG factors generally are to the business. This helps determine the resources that should be allocated to managing ESG risks and seeking opportunities to build the four capitals through ESG initiatives.

There are two sets of questions to consider in making that assessment.

1. Is a large part of the investment's customer base made up of:
    a. government at any level
    b. larger corporates themselves investing in their ESG/sustainability performance, or
    c. NGO or charitable organizations?
2. Does the investment rely more heavily or often than most on:
    a. free access to public or other resources
    b. regulatory approvals for which public consultation is required
    c. new product or service innovation

    d.   regular access to new geographic markets
    e.   high levels of employee engagement
    f.   a 'clean and green' image
    g.   third-party endorsement or
    h.   new partners to deliver products or services

Existing customer base

Firstly, consider the customer base of the investment, especially a business-to-business concern. Lurking in the client list (or client wish list) you might find a government department or entity, a large corporation, or an NGO or charitable organization. If so, then those clients are likely to be investing in their own ESG issues and may expect or *require* their suppliers to share that interest. A major bank, for example, may have minimum requirements of its suppliers, such as risk systems for ESG issues, baseline measurement,and stakeholder reporting on ESG issues, compliance with employment regulations and human rights standards, and processes to manage *their* suppliers' environmental and social performance.

Similarly, extend your scan beyond customers and clients to other stakeholders on whom the business health and growth depend. Needless to say, this might include other investors, how important are ESG issues to them and is there alignment with your approach? These assessments apply no matter the asset or, for private equity investors, what business the company is in. However, stakeholder expectations are higher if the assets or company's own offering is in the environmental or social sectors. Be it cleantech or health, transport or education, energy or food, stakeholders have heightened sensitivity to ESG issues.

Assets on which the company relies

Second, consider what assets will the investment rely on for its future, and whether they would be affected by its ESG performance? There is a host of strategic relationships an asset or company may hold or need to access that can be affected by its ESG performance. These are not restricted to a 'clean and green' image. The investment might depend on regular product, service, or technology innovation, on high levels of employee engagement or third-party endorsement, on strong corporate partnerships or privileged research and networks, or on privileged public assets. Each of these reflects the strength of its key intangible assets – its people, reputation, networks,and capacity for innovation. And each is influenced by the investment's engagement on social and environmental issues.

The higher the brand value itself, the more cautious you would be. Consider a retail clothing company and the human rights and working conditions in its supply chain. Would it be enough, for example, if the clothes are made in the same Vietnamese factory as a department store home brand? Not necessarily. If the department chain doesn't itself have strong supply chain monitoring, then risks may easily exist. And if your target investment has a strong brand, so that the shirts sell for 20 times what they cost to make, then you want to make sure there's nothing that might threaten that brand. Those with an interest in supply chain human rights will hold you to a much higher standard than the department store and can make it very difficult for you to sell to retail chains that do have a stronger interest in ESG.

Chapter 5 Summary

The first stage of building an ESG strategy in your organization is to consider the fundamentals of the risks and opportunities you are facing:

- Tangible capital is the measurable, material goods and assets that can be quantified on the balance sheet: raw or manufactured goods, real property, and financial assets. Intangible capital is the human and social capital that we can apply to that tangible capital to create more of it.
- It's the intangible capital that is the more valuable: it, along with natural capital, generates everything we might want to buy or sell. So the idea of ESG is to safeguard our irreplaceable natural capital and invest in our intangibles, or at least not run them down. Those investments may not pay back in the next quarter but should be directed to pay back in the medium term.
- ESG factors affect value in two ways: there is a risk that actions may erode the human, social, natural, or financial capital of either the company or its communities, as Rio Tinto did when it blew up Juukan Gorge. There are also opportunities to nurture those capitals, as Dai Nippon Printing has found in its focus on human capital, in the pursuit of societies where people can live safe, secure, and healthy lives, with mutual respect, in balancing economic growth and the global environment.
- The most important ESG factors are therefore those that matter to both the company and its significant stakeholders. This double materiality can be boiled down to the same two questions, asked of both the company and its stakeholders:
  - Is it relevant to what the company or stakeholders *say* is important to them, or
  - would it potentially have a material effect on their four capitals, or their ability to draw financial, human, social, or natural capital from others?

Chapter 6
Deciding what issues and actions to take on

Standing in the middle of the road is very dangerous; you get knocked down by the traffic from both sides.

Margaret Thatcher, allegedly

The four core ESG dualities – tangibles and intangibles, value and risk, double materiality, short-term and longer-term – come into play each time a company makes a decision or takes action. We see three distinct types of decisions and actions that require an ESG lens:

– **Operational decisions that are made every day.** It is a big cultural shift for people in a company to think of material ESG issues and the risks and opportunities for the four capitals, whenever they make a significant decision in their existing business activities. However, where doing so does become part of the company's day-to-day operating culture, benefits will flow.

– **Strategic decisions or initiatives to change what the business does.** These are 'interventions' into core business activities: what the company does or sells, and where. They imply an initial investment that changes the direction of both costs and revenues, to improve medium-term performance and, usually, build up long-term capital. The potential impact of ESG factors on the four capitals is critical to these decisions but often overlooked.

– **'Offline' ESG initiatives to help address a social or environmental issue.** These are specific investments a company makes in the expectation of getting greater access to more human, social, natural, or financial capital. They do not affect immediate operations – and so are not simply branding or marketing – but gain future access to more or different capital that may lead to operational and strategic shifts.

Many early ESG and sustainability reports were full of stories of the third type, but it is the first and second types that really are more important. Unless ESG is part of everyday decision-making, then risks may become real and expensive crises, and opportunities to create value will be lost. Changing business operations and strategy will better manage risks and open the window to creating more value.

Companies need to first agree on some basic principles for their approach to ESG. They can set their initial ambition, their focus on risk or opportunity, a bias to internal or external efforts, and an emphasis on social, human or natural capital.

https://doi.org/10.1515/9783111428949-009

Operational decisions that take ESG factors into account

To illustrate the significance of operational decisions, consider a firm in the financial sector, which in our experience often has large sustainability teams compared with other sectors, with very broad environmental and social initiatives. This may reflect the competition between firms on ESG ratings and awards, or a response to earlier losses of public trust in the sector.[40] They also typically have a profit margin large and resilient enough to invest in initiatives that will help develop their social and human capital; and good access to scientific and economic data on things like climate change and wage earnings, giving them a clearer picture than most on the social and environmental issues that may weaken longer-term productivity, or the ability of certain people to pay back their loans.

Financial firms with these advantages are quick to identify relevant issues, invest in things like emissions audits, financial literacy, and indigenous enterprises, and tell others about those actions. They may as a result build up strong ESG ratings and reputations. That record may correlate with better operational performance, though the results are mixed.[41] There may even be causal links between the two, for example,in reducing the proportion of nonperforming loans[42] (although that may simply be because a bank lends to fewer people in poorer districts[43]).

Yet despite these 'announceable' projects, the bank may still choose to invest in subprime mortgages, finance the companies whose poker machines are leading to their own client's loan defaults, or finance the logging of an unprotected southeast Asian forest without taking into account either its corruption of local economies and politics,or the value of potential carbon credits. Internally, it may let 'star performers' get away with bullying, or sexual harassment, or provide staff incentives that encourage credit card lending to people without the capacity to repay.

Choosing to do these things may be financially attractive, in the short term. But at some point, the immediate losses to other people will be internalized by the bank. The negative payback may come in the form of a public inquiry into the bank's conduct[44] that eats up precious management time and in the end the bank's leadership.[45] It may come silently in the loss of potential customers or government support. Or it may come powerfully in the loss of employee morale, as they hit the wall of dissonance between the expressed 'values' of the bank and its actual decisions.

A form of this dissonance is common in cases when a bank allocates sums to its branches for them to support their local communities, on application. The amount is trivial to the bank but the donations allow stories to be told internally and externally about how the bank is 'part of the community'. Meanwhile, the bank may not be supporting the community in its core business of taking deposits from some people and lending that money to other people. Head office policies may mean that good loans are called in at the smallest sign of trouble while bad loans continue to be granted to people without plans to use them. The core business of the bank is at odds with its community or ESG initiative and they may both undermine each other.

To prevent these losses and ensure the company is open to new possibilities, a few things need to exist:

- **Clear questions to ask** when making a decision to understand the trade-offs involved. These could be in broad terms: 'What impact will this have on our own human capital, the environment, and communities?' Or they could be more specific: 'Will we be comfortable if this action was reported on the front page of the national daily?'[46] This goes beyond legal considerations, as there is a big difference between actions the law allows, and actions that stakeholders would tolerate.[47] The trade-offs can also usually be understood as a function of time: a near-term cost weighed up against a longer term yet larger benefits, and vice versa.
- **Clear times to ask those questions** in the decision-making process. There's no point asking them in the final review, by which time too much time and ego has been invested in doing something that would deliver uncomfortable answers to the above questions.
- **A clear and effective policy** that secures alignment across and down the organization, sets out the questions and process and goes further to answer the 'what, why, and how' of thinking about ESG when making decisions, and the expectations for all employees.
- **An understanding of the perceived trade-offs, if and where, necessary.**
- **KPIs that take ESG performance into account**, so that the employees are rewarded for meeting those expectations, or not.
- **A communication and skills strategy** to support the policy, making people know what is expected, and giving them the skills and support to do so effectively.
- **A place to get help** with difficult decisions, to understand their potential impacts for better or worse.
- **Most importantly, leader demonstration of the policy.** None of the above will work unless people see their managers and more senior people being exemplars of the policy.

The bottom line is that ESG is treated as one of the many factors for organizational success and then explicitly integrated into its policies, decision criteria, and performance management systems.

The ultimate question to test the approach is to ask, 'Who would be accountable at the company if poor decisions were being made?' It may be the ESG specialist, who put all the policies into place. Or perhaps the head of people and culture, responsible for the skills and attitudes of the workforce. Or perhaps the line or business unit manager, responsible for all the actions in their neck of the woods. And then the CEO, ultimately responsible for all of those things.

In other words, integrating ESG into everyday decisions is everyone's responsibility. It is as hard as any other form of serious organizational change. And like any such change, it will face a lot of resistance, misinformation, and simple misunderstandings.

BOX: Dai Nippon's quest for a better future

While hundreds of companies offer ideas and inspiration for a more sustainable business model, few offer as many as the Japanese company Dai Nippon Printing. From its origins as a commercial printer, Dai Nippon now pursues an array of businesses across the broader themes of smart communication, life and healthcare, and electronics. They span anything from AI-driven editing to automotive coatings, lithium-ion battery pouches to medicine packaging, old-fashioned paints to optical films for smartphones and car displays, OLED displays to industrial glass coatings. All of them stem from the simple idea of using technology to do amazing things with surfaces.

All of Dai Nippon's activity is conceived as a comprehensive use of the six capitals. Dai Nippon's brand statement is to 'create future standards'. How does it do that? Taking the six capitals as inputs, it builds value by "multiplying the strength of its printing and information technologies by TAIWA (dialogue) and cooperation with diverse partners".[48] It then generates what it modestly calls 'output' in smart communication, life and healthcare, and electronics. Each flows from integrated business, financial and nonfinancial strategies.

The outcome of all Dai Nippon's work is a 'better future'. This would normally be left as a motherhood aspiration, but Dai Nippon goes on to define what it is. In their vision it is a society with four characteristics. A better future is one of 'four societies':
- a society where people can live safe, secure, healthy, and well-being lives
- a society where people can communicate comfortably
- a society where people mutually respect each other, and
- a society that realizes a balance between economic growth and the global environment.

Dai Nippon then internalizes this aspiration, so that each of the four societies becomes a driving force for its own business decisions. This is so much the case that, in its view, the two dimensions of materiality are whether Dai Nippon is fostering the four societies where it operates and whether its own people are experiencing those four societies in their work environment.

Dai Nippon maps out, on a large double-page spread, a causal map that flows from vision to impact for each of its human, intellectual, and natural capitals, consistent with the six capitals model that Dai Nippon uses. For natural capital, the vision is a decarbonized, circular economy through which society is in harmony with nature. Concrete initiatives are then measured, to drive intangible benefits that then drive 'sales expansion, greater profitability, and improvement of corporate value'. The causal flows for intellectual capital and human capital (considered separately) are too complex to be paraphrased or reproduced here. We can only recommend you search for their 2024 Integrated Report in all its glory. Be warned though. They have not watered down the detail or intent of their report to make it an easy read. It looks like they have applied the same rigor and discipline to these intangible elements as they do to making precision surface and information technologies, with the same engineering-style diagrams.

If you do take a peek at its Integrated Report, you will find on almost every page an approach to an element of ESG that is both fresh and rigorous. For example, the approach to human capital follows the accepted view that good practices in hiring, promotion, career autonomy, and personal health are needed to release the human creativity that adds corporate value. But one of the many objectives for its human capital is "the happiness of employees". To answer raised eyebrows, its several indicators include a measure of employee psychological capital: that is, their surveyed attitude to 'hope, efficacy, resilience, and optimism'. That is paired with a measure of psychological safety at the organization, based on the responses to questions on 'ease of communication, mutual support, willingness to take on challenges, and respect for individuals'.

This holistic approach to business reenergized the company from 2022 to 2024. The recovery followed a decade of financial doldrums as the Japanese economy was hit by the March 2011 Fukushima tsunami and nuclear disaster, then the 2019 COVID-19 pandemic. While sales rose modestly (7% over the 3 years), earnings doubled, and assets, cash flow and margins all rose markedly. Other companies may achieve these financial results by slashing expenditure, as they focus on short-term financial materiality.[49] But Dai Nippon took a different approach; see Figure 18. In the same years, employees took 12% more annual leave, injury rates dropped by 20%, training expenses rose by 41%, employment of people with a disability rose 16%, the ratio of female managers (while still low) rose 50%, and 98.7% of male employees took childcare leave, for an average of 21.4 days.[50] Its share price rose at almost three times the relevant Nikkei indices.[51]

Figure 18: Dai Nippon's positive-feedback loop of investment in human capital[52].

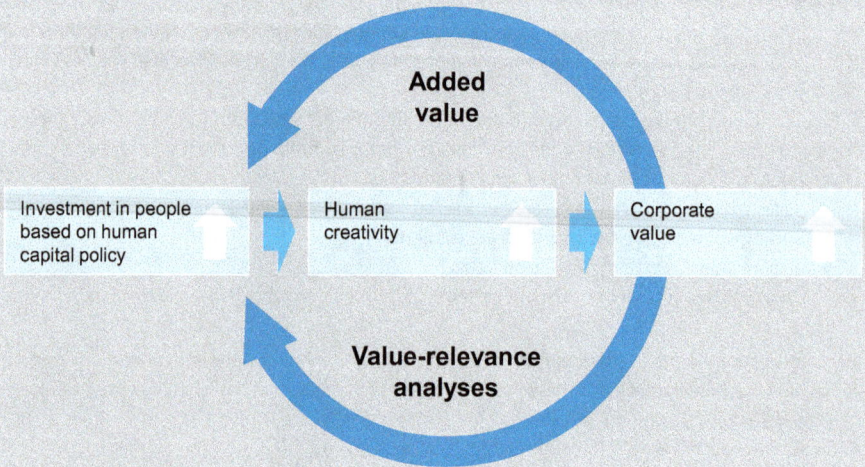

Source: Dai Nippon (2024) *Integrated Report*, p56.

BOX: Juukan Gorge and the four capitals ignored

It's hard to think of a clearer example of the value and consequences at stake – and the clash between ESG considerations, on one hand, and financial and legal imperatives on the other – than Rio Tinto's May 2020 destruction of Juukan Gorge.

Juukan Gorge was nestled in the vast iron-rich expanse of the Pilbara, near Australia's northwest coast. It was a deeply significant site for the local Indigenous Peoples for over 45,000 years – Australia's answer to France's Lascaux caves, only twice as old. As if the site's cultural value wasn't enough, it had a "high frequency of flaked stone artifacts, rare abundance of faunal remains, unique stone tools, preserved human hair and . . . sediment containing a pollen record charting thousands of years of environmental changes".[53]

Rio Tinto considered all this and then followed the letter of the Western Australian law and blew up the Juukan Gorge site – along with the eight million tonnes of iron ore it wanted. Slowly but surely, the outrage at this legal act spread around the globe, finally reaching Rio Tinto's boardroom in London. Still under legal instruction, it issued the nonapology that lawyers love: *We are sorry for the distress we have caused.* Those in distress were not impressed, and nor were the media, civil rights groups and most importantly, the investors in Rio Tinto. Before long, the CEO Jean-Sebastien Jacques stepped down 'by mutual agreement with the board'.[54] He was joined on the way out by Chris Salisbury, the head of Rio Tinto's almighty iron ore business, and Simone Niven, the global head of corporate affairs. And then, finally, by the chair of the Rio Tinto board, Simon Thompson, and another director, Michael L'Estrange, who led a widely discredited internal review of the incident.[55]

Among those most shocked by this wanton destruction were long-time observers and past employees of Rio Tinto.[56] From the 1980s to the 2000s, Rio Tinto had employed anthropologists at each of their sites purely to help understand the local Indigenous communities, and so help to act with respect for them. This started before Australia's Indigenous People had any legal right to a say on what happened on their land, and long before anyone had heard of corporate social responsibility, let alone ESG. But Rio Tinto knew how important it was to get along with the people on whose traditional lands it was mining, and to negotiate on their share of the venture, with mutual respect and good faith. In 1995, under the chairmanship of Leon Davis, the company marked 'a line in the sand for Indigenous Rights', publicly committing to engaging with Traditional Owners because it was 'the right thing to do'.[57] The highwater mark for this engagement was Rio's decision in 2000 not to mine the Jabiluka uranium site despite a legal agreement and governments being in support.[58]

However, it seems that the rot had already set in. Until 1995, Rio was operating as ConZinc RioTinto of Australia Ltd (CRA), listed in Australia with its head office in Melbourne. In 1995, however, the power base shifted to London, as CRA merged with its distant relative RTZ PLC. Soon after, operational leadership moved to London as well, including in 2006 its anthropology and cultural heritage team. They then had access to senior management, but soon after were shunted to the corporate relations division, then moved location back to Melbourne, then to Quebec, and then to Washington DC. By 2012, its PhD and MA-qualified anthropologists had gone, along with other senior archaeologists and cultural heritage experts who worked on sites. The broader team was then cut a further fifth between 2013 and 2018.[59] Arguably, the people in London didn't really understand what they were there for.

In the short term, Juukan Gorge is a lesson on the value at risk from the lack of an ESG lens. Rio Tinto had risk policies in place, knew of the risks involved, and decided the commercial value outweighed them. But while the iron ore had an estimated value of A$135 million in 2020,[60] the year-long saga that ultimately brought down a swathe of the most senior executives arguably cost Rio Tinto more. As its share price was being fueled by an iron ore bonanza at the time, it is difficult to assess the direct financial impact. But for a long time afterward investors remained concerned that Rio Tinto had lost access to capital: the natural capital (land and ore) that its business relied on, the social capital (trust and reputation) to negotiate with traditional landowners anywhere on Earth. Whatever it would have to pay to access that natural capital in the future, it would be more than it had paid in the past.

It also severely damaged its trust with investors. ESG investors look for corporate policies and management systems for assurance that the systems are in place to manage ESG issues. The Juukan Gorge made many ESG analysts in the finance sector question how much assurance they could actually place not only in the way they manage Indigenous heritage issues but everything else. It raised the question: 'Can we trust what they say and what they say they do?' For all the focus on the financial numbers by investors, trust in company management is still critical in investment decision-making.

Strategic decisions to respond to an ESG issue

We noted earlier that one of the dualities of ESG issues is looking at risks and opportunities. A focus on managing risks, or negative impacts, is where many start (and end) when thinking about ESG issues. Sound as they are, risk-based strategies are likely to capture less than the whole value of sustainability for many companies. Greater value can be found when social, human, or natural capital is being eroded, and a company applies its own assets and capabilities to find a solution.

The classic case for this in business history is DuPont's action to replace chlorofluorocarbons (CFCs) in refrigerants, aerosol propellants, and solvents.[61] Shortly after a paper on the CFC threat to the ozone layer was published in 1974, it was banned in the USA, Canada, Norway, and Sweden, effective from 1978. Other countries did not follow and a dangerous hole in the ozone layer was found in 1985. Until then, DuPont had led an industry alliance against any further regulation. When the hole was declared they changed course, and pushed governments and the industry hard toward the 1987 Montreal Protocol, which banned the international supply of CFCs. But DuPont was playing a clever dual game. Its patent protection of CFCs was expiring, so it had developed a new generation of refrigerants. With CFCs now banned, it could continue to dominate the market with its new products.

Many similar corporate strategies have been pursued since, seeking to address real social or environmental issues and benefit from that effort. Instead of a narrow inside-out product or service lens, the focus is broadened with a four capitals lens that considers major shifts in human, social and natural capital. Patagonia incorporated natural capital in its core strategy, and built lasting success from slow beginnings.[62] In 1994, Interface carpets set a goal of zero impact by 2020, setting it apart from all other carpet-makers, a goal they claimed to have reached by 2019.[63] Unilever launched its 'Campaign for Real Beauty' in 2004, recognizing that human capital extends beyond models of extremely rare dimensions, and almost doubled the sales of Dove soap, which became the biggest-selling soap in the USA.[64] Any company offering private tuition, from the oldest private school to the newest online 'AI-questioning' guide, is targeting human capital (and in the case of private schools, social capital). Car-sharing firms such as Share Now, BlaBlaCar and Moia seek to reduce the load on natural capital while building social capital.[65] The sharp rise in global investment in renewable energy responds to the threat of global heating, which in turn drives the Australian resource company AGL's shift toward the energy transition.[66] The company's success in managing the shift is driving investor support,[67] and building a brand that is then trusted to offer similar utility services, such as broadband. The same systems thinking is needed to decide what social or environmental issue a company should engage in – taking into account its impacts on *all* forms of capital.

Insurance companies around the world are a sober, methodical pointer to the social and environmental risks that business should respond to, themselves included. Starting in the 1970s, international insurers like Swiss Re, Munich Re and Allianz were among the earliest companies to recognize the likely impacts of global warming on people's lives, on the industries such as agriculture and tourism that depend on climate patterns, and on vulnerable physical and social infrastructure. They have used this information to warn governments to take action, and to adjust premiums to better reflect the cost of inaction. As with retirement funds, insurance companies are also universal stakeholders. They have a direct financial stake through their insurance they offer on almost every aspect of our property and lives. And they are immense investors in global markets as they stockpile and grow premium income to be ready for the inevitable payouts.

Allianz states this broad interest as clearly as any: "As a global insurer, investor and employer, Allianz invests to positively influence not only the present, but also the future living conditions in the communities in which we operate . . . Stabilizing society, however, also requires that we focus on addressing climate change. Its impact on individuals and businesses is profound: climate change threatens people's incomes, homes and health, just as it puts companies' physical assets and business continuity at risk. This also holds true for Allianz."[68] This principle flows through to both their insurance and their corporate operations. "Our exposure to sustainability risks is mostly indirect, through the insurance risks Allianz takes on behalf of its insured clients. We embed sustainability risk management throughout our underwriting, referral and assessment processes." Of 800 potential new clients that Allianz assessed globally in 2023, 39 were refused insurance and another 208 were asked to mitigate an unacceptable climate or other risk before insurance was offered. It leads to specific, measurable targets in its corporate operations that align with the global economy's need to decarbonize: "The share of battery electric vehicles (based on the number of passenger vehicles) in our motor portfolio will exceed the share of battery electric vehicles in the respective markets."[69]

Similarly, Allianz is in a position to monitor and evaluate the largest demographic forces of our times. They can see how improving quality of life for younger people at risk and for people with a disability adds to our overall human and social capital. Hence they invest in health, education, and work for future generations and for people with disabilities. In 2022, they launched a *MoveNow* initiative with the International Olympic and Paralympic Committees, aiming to get young people back into physical and mental activities after the 2020 pandemic. The initiative promotes accessible education and sport, both in physical camps and through digital channels.[70]

Initiatives that change the way you do business

Let's consider a clothing company.[71] It is as alive as anyone to the amount of used clothes that goes into landfill, so wants to do something about it. It may ask its procurement section whether some of the incoming textiles can be made from 'secondary material' used clothes, rather than 'virgin' materials from the cotton fields. From there on, the research and decisions are made in just the same way as any other in the company. A reasonably well-managed organization has proven methods of getting things done and these are the best starting point. There's no point reinventing the wheel just for an ESG initiative.

With a few exceptions. First, the company needs to know *all* the costs and *all* the potential benefits of using secondary stock, not just the immediate calculation of $/kg for a certain quality of material. If someone in the organization has an interest in the circular economy – more and more likely among younger generations – then this is an ideal project for them to be part of, bringing a human capital benefit. If the company connects with different suppliers, it has automatically added to its social capital. If it learns something from the inquiry, it's also added human capital – and the option value of future actions. If it tells people how it's exploring these possibilities, it's adding to its social capital. If the company can actually launch a new line of recycled clothing, there may be brand benefits and further partnerships. And so it goes.

More likely, the company will work with external partners on the problem. It may be that there is no suitable supply of the quality and type of textile it needs. So, it might consider being part of – or even initiating – an industry effort to fill that gap. Drawing on the combined standing of its own brand and supply chain partners, it can bring in researchers from the national scientific and academic institutions to get them to solve the problem. That leads to discussing other problems in which there is a shared interest. And so on.

Third, just as the company might want to consider all the costs and benefits, it will need to work out a way to measure them accurately and show them clearly. ESG initiatives typically have a heavier burden of proof than other initiatives. People are skeptical of them: they can be someone's flight of fancy, and they can be a big distraction from the main game. They are also looking for medium- to longer-term payoffs that may not be immediately obvious, nor easy to track. Even if they are successful, it's hard to show and articulate why – which is why so much ESG reporting and commentary can sound like fluff. From the outset, treat the exercise like a scientific experiment: imagine things that might happen, and record things that do. As with scientific experiments, it is important not to confuse precision with accuracy. By their very nature, some intangible assets can be difficult to measure, and so multiple proxy measures might be needed to get the overall picture, and few, if any of them, need decimal places.

Care in launching the next 'green' enterprise

A word of caution is needed at this point. The focus on ESG in strategy and risk management is continuous and needs to be holistic. Success in one area of business strategy does not necessarily guarantee success across all its business, as companies like DuPont,[72] 3M, and Johnson & Johnson[73] have found.

Monsanto was a US chemical company founded in 1901 that grew quickly after World War II. Its diverse products included treatments for Parkinson's disease, Astro-Turf, visible light-emitting diodes (LEDs), and the beta-blocker Celebrex. However, it also produced the more controversial or banned products PCBs, DDT, Agent Orange, and Roundup. In the 1980s state governments in the US promoted the practice of conservation tillage to reduce soil and additive runoff into waterways. Monsanto then promoted its product Roundup, which it had developed in the 1970s, as the 'logical complement to conservation tillage'. Sales of Roundup rose 50% in volume between 1987 and 1990, then another 50% in the next two years, and was exported to Australia and other major agricultural-producing countries.[74] Monsanto then sold genetically modified 'Roundup Ready' seeds for soy, corn, and other crops. This mutually reinforcing crop science business seemed a winner (although the combination was resisted in Europe), with annual US sales reaching over US$19 billion in 2023. Unfortunately, Roundup's active ingredient glyphosate was found to be carcinogenic when used as a broadacre herbicide in large quantities. Its new owner, Bayer, is now facing the legal consequences, with over US$10 billion being paid in litigation settlements to date.[75] What might seem to be a good environmental solution may turn out to be very much less than ideal, when all ESG risks are taken into account.

Decisions to invest in ESG initiatives

The first two types of decisions have always been made in the ordinary course of business. The evolution we discuss is that they are made by taking into account the ESG factors, i.e., the extent to which they affect the natural, social, and human capital of both the company and its stakeholders. The third type of action is different: it is being taken solely to improve natural, social or human capital, in the hope that this may lead to later financial benefits.

These are the type of initiatives that used to come under the head of 'corporate social responsibility' – not really integrated into the company's business, but an add-on to meet stakeholder expectations that companies should be part of communities and civil society and not separate from them. They are extremely common, from sponsoring an arts organization or local school event, or being a substantial partner for a charity. Some of these initiatives are really more marketing than ESG. Either way, companies would benefit from a transparent methodology to help them decide whether or not to invest in such an action, among several choices, and if so how much to invest in them.

Say a valued researcher at a pharmaceutical company wants to support a regional initiative to solve a public health issue. They have experience, insight and enthusiasm to offer, and want to lend a hand. The researcher asks the company if she can access some aggregated data to help the group decide where to focus its limited resources. The company's initial reaction is one of caution – there could be legal implications, and it may set a dangerous precedent. They check, and in-house council gives it the 'all clear', so there are no explicit barriers to making the aggregate data available.

In making its decision, the company might consider the potential impacts on all forms of its capital. First, its human capital. The researcher likes her job, but is frustrated by the very tight rein that is kept on research, and the relatively narrow group of people involved. Sure, there is valuable IP to be protected and confidentiality to be maintained, but it wasn't the collegiate experience that drew her to science in the first place. Engaging in the public health effort would be a risk-free way of widening that collegiate scope, to be part of something bigger than her immediate work's research and so – importantly – be a reason to stay at the firm.

Needless to say, the insights that she and others in the public health effort develop would also be accessible to her company. So too would the relationships that she develops, and the appreciation in that regional community that the company is lending a hand. Alongside her in the public health effort are other people in the health ecosystem, some from organizations that the company deals with commercially. Here is a chance to deepen relationships with them, outside the potentially tense negotiations on a commercial or regulatory issue.

In our view, three analyses may be taken, yet in most cases are not:

–   A **double materiality analysis**, as above, to determine what capitals may be affected by the action.
–   A **numerical analysis** to help determine how much of the firm's financial capital may be affected, as part of the materiality assessment. This may be pursued through the analysis described in "Using value driver trees to decide on and track initiatives" below. It involves a 'live' model of the firm's profitability, the value of its intangibles, and the value of its efforts (including sustainability) to strengthen those intangibles.
–   A **probability analysis**, to determine how likely it is that an initiative will be successful. Just because an issue is important to both you and your stakeholders, doesn't mean you should start acting on it. Your company should only invest in that action if there is a reasonable chance of succeeding. To consider that likelihood, you may need to consider whether there are enough people in the company who are keen to act on the issue, whether they have visible alignment with the near- or medium-term priorities, and whether the company has the assets and capabilities to make a difference.

The whole picture then looks a little like Figure 19.

Figure 19: Materiality is not enough: deciding on the likelihood of success.

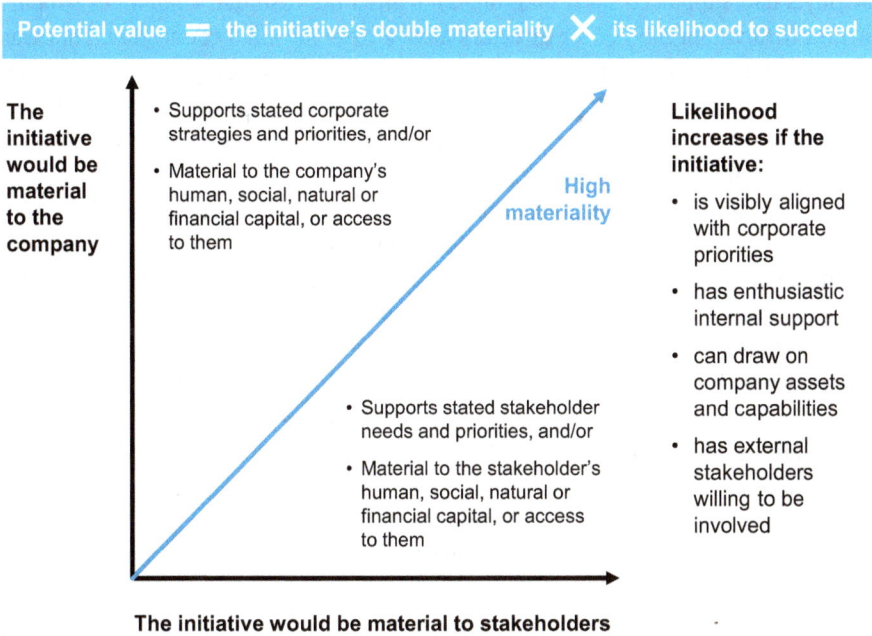

Potential value = the initiative's double materiality ✕ its likelihood to succeed

The initiative would be material to the company

- Supports stated corporate strategies and priorities, and/or
- Material to the company's human, social, natural or financial capital, or access to them

High materiality

Likelihood increases if the initiative:

- is visibly aligned with corporate priorities
- has enthusiastic internal support
- can draw on company assets and capabilities
- has external stakeholders willing to be involved

- Supports stated stakeholder needs and priorities, and/or
- Material to the stakeholder's human, social, natural or financial capital, or access to them

The initiative would be material to stakeholders

Source: The authors.

Prioritizing the initiatives

How does that work in practice? Consider Hoyts, a privately owned cinema group in the Asia-Pacific. Its cinema complexes are typically located within or next to shopping malls, where there is ample parking for their four to twelve theaters that are typically in a complex. We've all been to see the movies at these sorts of places. Apart from the films themselves, what stands out is the intoxicating aroma of popcorn, and the young age of those who take our orders and take us to our seats.

One small part of a sustainability strategy is to identify the environmental and social partnerships that the company might want to support. The company typically runs workshops to identify a list of potential options and opportunities, using a range of structured brainstorming. It can then assess those opportunities against its potential value and the likelihood that, if an initiative were launched, it would be successful.

Hoyts cleverly branded its sustainability strategy as 'The Bigger Picture', a play on the picture theme that would be easy to leverage in communicating the strategy. The brainstorming workshops identified a healthy range of ideas, starting with the charity that Hoyts had supported for a long time. It's often the case that companies support charities with whom the CEO or directors have a close personal connection. That was the case with Hoyts, and they had sponsored a charity that not only was a great social cause, but had a marathon drive through outback Australia that the directors enjoyed taking part in. Having seen some of these drives, you understand where the inspiration for the Mad Max set of movies came from.

Other suggestions were bringing movies to the young patients in specialist children's hospitals; making sure that the whole supply chain for serving that popcorn was sustainable, including its palm oil; supporting a youth mental health service; leading an initiative to improve the environment around the host shopping centers (typically the proverbial concrete jungle); ramping up employee engagement around mental and family health themes; reducing the carbon footprint of the cinemas; and supporting another favorite charity of prominent directors. Money was to be raised as it always had been – from the 'gold coin' $1 or $2 donation given by the staff as their fee to watch a movie where they worked.

All were good potential initiatives, but Hoyts could not do them all. Is it possible to prioritize such a diverse list of possibilities? Nothing is precise in assessing futures, but Figure 20 shows a simple way to consider the relevant factors, and take another step toward a decision. It assessed the materiality of the options to both Hoyts and its stakeholders, then assessed the likelihood of their being successful. However, it also decided how much weight to put to each of those criteria. That enabled a numeric ranking of the options. This combination of 'gut-feel' and structured thinking led to a shortlist of two to three initiatives, for which a business case could be prepared in the usual way. In this case, the youth mental health initiative resonated with the young cinema staff: many of them had experience with mental health issues in their peer groups, and this initiative allowed them to feel they were contributing to solutions.

Using value driver trees to decide on and track initiatives

In the first column of Figure 20 we have included the 'potential $ value' of an initiative. This is an intriguing and elusive measure, as it means getting a handle on a numeric value of the human, social and financial capital generated by the initiative.

We have developed a way to value that human and social capital in a transparent way that ties directly to the company's profit and loss statement (or P&L). It is called 'sustainability and intangibles valuation analysis', or SIVA for short, and relies on building a 'value-driver-tree' model of the firm's revenues and costs. Value driver trees just break down every branch of revenue and costs into more and more sub-branches. Traditionally, however, the branches don't go beyond tangible, numeric components.

Figure 20: Scoring and weighting initiatives (out of 5) helps to prioritise a shortlist of potential initiatives.

	Potential $ value	Company materiality	Stakeholder materiality	Materiality	X	Strategic alignment	Assets to leverage	Internal passion	External Partners	Likelihood	=
Weighting	**4**	**4**	**3.5**			**4.5**	**3**	**5**	**3**		
Youth mental health charity	4	3	3	38.5		3	4	4	4	57.5%	**22.14**
Sustainable popcorn	4	2	3.5	36.25		4	3	3	4	54%	**19.58**
Children's hospital	3	3	4	38		3	3	3	4	49.5%	**18.81**
Digital cinema	3	3.5	2	33		4	3	3	4	54%	**17.82**
Existing charity	2	1	4	26		4	3	3	4	54%	**14.04**
Waste reduction	3	3	3	34.5		2	2	3	3	39%	**13.46**
Suburban environment	4	1.5	2	29		1	2	2	2	26.5%	**7.69**
Directors' nominee charity	1	1	4	22		2	2	1	2	26%	**5.72**

Source: The authors.

SIVA digs two levels deeper. It first identifies and quantifies the social and human capital that underpin immediate financial performance. It then identifies and quantifies the ESG-related actions and metrics that influence that intangible capital. That done, SIVA can calculate how much a P&L changes with the strength of your ESG factors, and how much a specific action or initiative will influence those factors.

Building a SIVA model is quite rigorous but not as technical as it might seem. Essentially, the company's own people make their own decisions on what factors bring about a certain result – for example, more sales opportunities, and more conversions of those opportunities. It's a transparent and engaging process and reveals just how important human and social capital are to a company's outcomes. Its trick, though, is in making the transition between the hard numbers in the management accounts, and the subjective choices made by the people responsible for delivering those numbers. How this transition works, and how it can be built from your company's own management accounts, takes us too deep into the weeds for this book. The method is fully laid out in a previous article.[76]

Not surprisingly, it is the human capital – the quality and productivity of your company's people – that typically has the greatest impact on your P&L. We're talking here about how innovative and productive your people could be, and how motivated they are to bring those attributes to bear. Again, various firms have their own models for how to measure that quality and productivity. The factors typically include measures of employee wellbeing, skills and experience, values and motivation, the physical and personal work environment, and the stability and support of their family and wider community.

Chapter 6 Summary
- While deciding on the specific issues to focus on, companies might first set their overall ambition; decide whether to focus on risk or opportunity; whether to favor internal or shared external efforts; and whether to focus on social, human, or natural capital.
- With those principles in place, they can prioritize the ESG issues they face, considering both tangible and intangible capital; the risks and opportunities of action (and inaction); the impact on the company and on stakeholders (double materiality) and trade-off between short-term costs and longer-term investments.
- Decisions can be taken both strategically, to change what the company does, and operationally, to change how it does those things. It can also choose to invest in separate initiatives that bolster their human and social capital, and can be drawn upon in the future.
- In deciding what to do at any level, companies can prioritize options by calculating both its potential value and materiality to the company and stakeholders, and the likelihood that the initiative will be successful. That likelihood is determined by its alignment with corporate strategy, the assets it has to leverage, any internal passion to see it through, and the interest of any external partners.
- It is possible for a company to measure and trace their investments in social, human, and natural capital through to its management accounts. Doing so requires a collaborative effort by people from the company's finance, operations, and ESG teams, working together to break down the firm's revenues and costs into all their tangible and intangible parts. It is a transparent and effective way to engage people from across the business in the company's ESG work.

Chapter 7
Structuring roles for ESG performance

My model for business is The Beatles. They were four guys who kept each other's kind of negative tendencies in check. They balanced each other and the total was greater than the sum of its parts. That's how I see business: great things in business are never done by one person. They're done by a team of people.

Steve Jobs, Stanford University graduation address, 2005

So far, we've been talking about the issues, risks, and opportunities. As interesting as they are, they're one step removed from what ESG is all about – people. If ESG is to matter to your company, then it really has to matter to your people.

What people? The short answer is everyone. If a decent part of the Board, CEO, and executive are not on board, forget it. If people on the front line aren't interested, also forget it. However, the people who are most often overlooked are the people in the middle – the middle rungs of management who often have the highest barriers to overcome. We'll look at each of these groups, after starting with the person in your company who has an ESG-related title.

And that's to mention only the people inside your company. The people outside it matter just as much. That's the whole point of ESG and sustainability. If your company depends on other people, or has an impact on other people, then their issues are your issues.

This section suggests what people can do to assist the ESG effort, and how to get them involved. It looks at very broad groups of people, rather than individuals, and as always depends on the organization's size and circumstances.

The ESG 'specialist'

More recently, large firms in a range of industries have recognized that a senior person, with a wide brief, is needed to apply an ESG or sustainability lens across the company. That may be their sole role, or it may be combined with another. At the time of writing, Unilever and InterContinental Hotels have a Chief Sustainability Officer (CSO), Schneider Electric has a Chief Strategy and Sustainability Officer (a powerful combination which would ensure that ESG is integrated into Schneider's corporate strategies), and Siemens has a Chief People and Sustainability Officer (another powerful integration).

Being in the C-Suite means these people have a direct say and influence on the ESG agenda. Most companies are not yet at that stage. The initial push for ESG may come from anyone in the organization, on top of their day-to-day role. Once ESG is accepted as something that needs to be done, someone is appointed to look after it.

https://doi.org/10.1515/9783111428949-010

Typically, the role is placed somewhere in the corporate center, often reporting to the head of corporate affairs, and filled by someone with a background in environmental management. Never say never, but there may be a series of mistakes in this approach. Understanding why helps to get the balance and structure of the ESG function right for your organization.

First, where the role sits within the corporate center does matter. Sitting the role in either the strategy, risk management, finance, or corporate affairs group sends different messages about the role within the company and its expected influence. Companies that put the role in the corporate affairs department risk limiting it to one that supports the brand and responds to pesky questions from the public, media, or investors. The more that ESG is infused across the C-suite and throughout line management, rather than being focused in the corporate center, the more constructive it is.

Ultimately, the corporate ESG function is aiming for its own obsolescence. In the meantime, it is a supporter and influencer, building the will and capability of those with line responsibility to integrate ESG in their decision-making. Though they will have direct responsibilities (mentioned below), these might be discharged in partnership with others. Sharing these tasks enables people to talk through why particular actions are being taken, how they relate to other decisions, and how to execute them well.

Second, there have been environmental managers in line or unit positions in most corporates for up to a quarter century. Many have been shouting 'sustainability' into a headwind for much of that time, with executive committee hearing only snippets of 'toxic compliance' and 'recycle bins' between gusts. Now that a value-based ESG agenda is being set, people who have a broader view of the organization may be more likely to lead the necessary compliance, culture, and business changes. That may well be the environmental manager, but only the more adept of environmental managers are comfortable working across the range of intangible assets that can make up around 80% of company value. If another person is chosen, respect is owed to long-time leaders who may feel they have nursed something valuable in the wilderness, only to be ignored when its time has come.

With those caveats in mind, most companies now see the value in a sustainability officer (by whatever name) who is a good generalist to guide the sustainability effort. Nominally, they would be responsible for the ESG strategy and business case, identifying the issues and actions to take, engaging internally and externally, reporting to *all* the bodies that the company has committed to (or has no choice), liaising with investors, and liaising with external ratings agencies. In other words, all of the stations on our ESG cycle.

That list will clearly soak up a lot of time, with external liaison and reporting a huge burden for larger companies. The ultimate size of the team should take into account both the potential and delivered value, legitimate demands from stakeholders, available resources from other corporate functions, existing or potential environmental and social risks, and perceived opportunities. Disappointment or indifference will flow from having too few people, too flooded by immediate demands to add value to the firm. But a sustainability function that is too large may be a trap: if they don't have to draw on others in the organization, their actions, priorities, and decisions will be too insular, and any potential benefits of sustainability thinking severely dulled.

The imperative for the ESG function is to gain support from across the company, from top to bottom. Figure 21 suggests the objectives and challenges that are faced in gaining that support, and some of the approaches referred to in this book that can be taken.

Figure 21: Layering your approach to get people on board.

Communicating ESG internally

	Purpose	Resistance	Approach
Board	• Support need for investment • Support direction of investment	• Scepticism of value • Other priorities • Being out of step with peers	• Directors' duties • Risk investment • 4 Capitals
C-suite	• Support direction of investment • Treat ESG like any other investment	• Scepticism of value • Other priorities	• 4 Capitals • ESG cycle • Bind to core strategies • Hard data on returns
Middle	• Make short-term trade-offs for future returns	• Priority of immediate targets	• Value driver tree • C-suite insistence • Recognition • ESG specialist support
Staff	• Engage in idea generation and action	• Corporate action is faddish, reactive or not genuine	• Clear internal communications • Retail/social media

Sources: The authors.

Engaging the C-suite

Like everything else in your company, things that don't have senior-level sponsorship won't last long. The C-suite needs to appreciate both the risks and opportunities of an ESG lens, so that they support *some* investment in it. From there, the aim is for them to treat that investment just like any other in the company – as it proves its way, build on it.

The most common forms of C-suite resistance are skepticism of the value of ESG, and fear that any effort will be a distraction from the agreed, typically short-term, priorities of the business – especially when the business is under stress for any reason. There might also be an element of personal ideology and ego involved – being opposed to ESG because they don't like what it is asking them to do, nor the issues that it raises.

Engaging with the C-suite therefore has to address those concerns. Using the 4 Capitals framework and ESG cycle can help show what ESG is and what it is trying to do. Using the hard data examples provided in this book and elsewhere can help show that it can work. Using their own strategies, showing where ESG fits in, can help show that it can work in your company. From there it's a case of 'Well, prove it'.

Or maybe not. In the early 2000s I met with the CEO of Rabobank in Australia, talking through these frameworks and the value driver tree (see Chapter 6) to show that ESG can help his business. He laughed me off, along the lines of, 'We've been a cooperative for over a century. Our owners are our stakeholders. They have always wanted us to invest in sustainability, so we always have. You don't have to prove its value to us!'

These days, of course, there is much less argument from senior people against engagement in the ESG effort. They're the ones feeling the heat from investors – continual questions about what they're doing on particular issues and on ESG overall – so they're the ones asking those questions down the line.

A senior executive to champion the ESG effort

Since the ESG specialist is not usually part of the company's executive, they need someone there to champion its work. That person must be a genuine supporter of ESG value, with a broad view of the organization's actions and priorities, and the capacity to influence the executive team. Ideally, this falls to either the CEO or the CFO – they're the ones with the most holistic view of the company's human, social, and financial capital, and how they interrelate. Too many ESG specialists still report to the head of corporate affairs, which signals far and wide that it doesn't matter what the company *does*, but how it tells its story.

With the rising appreciation of ESG, those advocating for the value of a CSO claim that 66% of their small sample of new CSOs reported directly to the CEO.[77] Diageo had a good model when it was getting its effort underway. With brands including Johnnie Walker, Guinness, Smirnoff, and Baileys, its approach to ESG is understandably grounded on responsible drinking. The CEO chairs an ESG Committee, with another 12 members selected on rotation. The rotation ensures all corners of the organization get direct exposure to the citizenship deliberations at the highest levels. All functional and geographic units are represented through their executive. That way, all units contribute to and learn about the major sustainability initiatives — 'communication' isn't left to the communication team.

Another successful option is for the CSO to report to the CFO, as Schneider has arranged it. Having the CFO as a thought partner for sustainability actions is a real benefit. The CFO typically has superb support and inquiry skills. Their appreciation of business value can help identify opportunities for sustainability to assist the firm's more immediate priorities, and for sustainability proposals to appeal to the executive committee. So too will the CFO's responsibility for financial rigor.

Alternatively, ESG may be a shared responsibility. Unilever's executive Corporate Responsibility Council ensures resources are available to the sustainability effort, to identify and overcome bottlenecks, and to judge where influence alone is not enough to make things happen between business units. Involved executives can also represent the firm on sustainability partnerships. While senior executives have deep contacts with peers in their industry, sustainability offers rewarding relationships to prosper outside the industry, and in other circles.

Oversight from within and without

Consistent with the inside-outside nature of the ESG lens, there needs to be both internal and external oversight of how the company is treating its human, social, and natural capital. An existing or specialized board committee works for the inside, while companies can be quite innovative in the way they might draw on an external advisory group.

Oversight by the Board

The Board of a company is responsible for setting the strategy and overseeing the risk management of the company, as well as employing the CEO and setting their remuneration structure. Once upon a time, it was possible to act credibly on ESG with limited board involvement. The British telecommunications firm BT and Australia's IAG were two companies in the 2010s who had no board-level committees, with the sustainability strategy or matters raised at board level 'at least once a year' as a fait accompli.

That's no longer the case. Many companies these days might have a Board 'Sustainability Committee'. That sounds good until you look at the remit of the committee and it's all about compliance with laws or managing brand or community trust. While it is good that the Board has sustainability on their agenda, sustainability is more than compliance and brand management.

Companies have started to recognize that while climate change is an environmental issue, for the company, it is a strategic risk and needs to be addressed in the same way as other strategic risks, which is not within the Board Sustainability Committee but with the Board itself. The potential impact of public policy and sustainability issues on a firm's value makes board oversight essential. Many boards allocate the role to their risk (or risk and audit) committees, who help ensure that ESG risks are reviewed with the same rigor as other business risks. Reports may also be assured under similar oversight as the familiar audit of the annual accounts and reports.

However, other board committees may have a more holistic view of the company's reputation. In the USA, Procter & Gamble's Governance and Public Responsibility committee oversees organizational diversity, sustainable development, community and government relations, product quality assurance and corporate reputation. The Coca-Cola Company similarly appoints a Public Policy and Corporate Reputation Council from its board because it recognizes the extent to which its brand value makes up its total worth.

Dai Nippon Printing has taken the holistic approach even further. While its board has four independent directors, it also engages with an external advisory committee with a broad representation of stakeholders. Following deliberation with that advisory committee, the board resolved to restructure its committees in 2022. "Due to recent rapid changes in the social environment, factors that may affect our business are becoming increasingly diverse and widespread. The Company's Board of Directors believes that appropriately assessing risks in this environment, incorporating these assessments into our medium- to long-term management strategies, and strengthening the process of converting the risks into business opportunities will allow us to more significantly contribute to a sustainable society." The lead committee is now the Sustainability Committee, chaired by the board president, to "manage medium- to long-term risks, identify business opportunities and integrate them into management strategies".[78] It regularly reviews material management issues, which it discusses with the board and management to "appropriately integrate risks into our medium-to long-term management strategy." The Business Continuity Committee then works to ensure the safety of employees and maintain the continuity of production activities even in the event of emergencies such as natural disasters. The Corporate Ethics Committee then "seeks to reduce risks by increasing employees' awareness of legal compliance, which is the foundation for business continuity." The firm's audit department reports directly to the board, rather than through a committee.

There are other questions about how the Board addresses sustainability. Many boards are made up of older males, who while bringing great expertise and experience in operations or finance or other fields, may yet be a product of their times, where sustainability was not a strategic focus for companies, beyond complying with the law. Does this mean there should be an ESG or sustainability specialist on the board to balance the skill set? The jury is still out on this. The key is whether the person or persons, and in fact the board as a whole, can translate sustainability into the company's strategy and risk management.

Oversight by external advisory groups

For some time, mining companies like BHP that have been at the pointy end of managing ESG issues have had external advisory committees reporting to the board or the CEO, to ensure they get the broad stakeholder perspectives on material issues. Every company investing seriously in its ESG performance will ask whether it needs an external advisory group. Individuals in this group may be drawn from NGO, professional service and academic ranks, as well as government and other links of the firm's value chain. It can have a formal role in reviewing the firm's ESG actions and board committee proceedings (as in the UK retailer Tesco) or in reviewing its ESG report (as in BT, the UK telecommunications firm). The public disclosure of this external feedback adds to the firm's ESG credentials. Inclusion of feedback in the ESG report is highly regarded by rating agencies, as are any responses to that feedback, so long as they are credible.

An external advisory group offers more than review. BT's Sustainability Panel supports 'the work BT is doing in . . . scoping and developing new business opportunities based on people living more sustainably'.[79] As with IAG's Expert Community Advisory Committee, it can help disseminate the firm's own sustainability agenda and performance, as well as an appreciation of the hurdles it may face. The panel can also be drawn on for advice on particular issues or initiatives.

The most effective meetings of the external group are those with the firm's executive committee, or a sufficiently large part of it. For a long time, the European cement company Lafarge has put aside an annual day at which questions can be put, understandings raised, and ideas generated at the most important levels, with perspectives put without the usual internal pressures, drawn from the broadest expertise and experience.

Panel members can also give feedback as individuals, as a group, or both. For example, Alistair McIntosh, a member of Lafarge's stakeholder panel, acknowledged that the industry's competitive pressure to 'buy cheaper and cheaper' has worked against Lafarge's commitment to sustainable development in and around its plants, and against its vision of developing more sustainable buildings.[80]

These groups can differ in their degrees of external inclusion, reporting, cross-unit collaboration, and board involvement. There is no universally perfect combination, as each element is designed to reflect the firm's existing structures and culture or meet its desired ones. A balance can be achieved between existing structures that have proven their effectiveness for the firm and introducing new combinations for their energy and potential.

In summary: a RASCI chart

So, that's a lot of people involved. As with a lot of other collaborative endeavors, it's worth setting out clearly who is responsible for what. A 'RASCI' chart does this well, capturing on a page who is:
- **R**esponsible for doing the work
- **A**ccountable for the work they do
- **S**upports that work
- **C**onsulted on that work, and
- **I**nformed about that work.

Figure 22 lays out a typical RASCI chart for the ESG effort in a medium-size company. As always, the Board and CEO have the ultimate say on that effort. The executive leadership team is responsible for setting the ESG strategy, identifying the core actions, and engaging internally, with one of that team taking particular responsibility for its implementation. They would be supported throughout by the head of the ESG team, who would consult with the company's operational or site leaders. Roles are allocated in line with the company's normal operating approach. While this example represents an actual set of decisions, each company will make its own choices.

Figure 22: Indicative RASCI for the ESG effort in a typical company.

RASCI Model defines who is **R**esponsible for the project, who they are **A**ccountable to, who would **S**upport them, and who they should **C**onsult and **I**nform

	Board and CEO	Executive team	Exec ESG owner	ESG lead	Site GMs	ESG site champions
Set ESG strategy	A	R		S	C	I
Lead implementation		R	R	S	C	C
Identify actions		R	A	S	C	
Engage internally		R	A	S	C	
Specific actions		C	A	S	R	S
Measure performance			A	R	S	S
Report performance	I	I	A	R	S	
Engage externally		C	A	S	R	

Source: The authors.

Henkel's purposeful growth agenda

Henkel is an example of a company that has welcomed external review of its operations. Henkel is a leading European company in consumer brands (hair and body care, detergents, and cleaners) and industrial markets (adhesives, sealants, and functional coatings). It has for many years focused on innovations that would step us closer to a more circular economy with reduced emissions. For example, Henkel has set the simple targets of 100% of its packaging to be recyclable or reusable[1] by 2025, with fossil-based virgin plastics in that packaging being reduced by 50%. To that end, its EcoFloat® packaging sleeve for PET bottles, which is easier to remove in recycling, won the AWA Award for innovation in 2023. Digital information and innovation through the supply chain is essential for these targets and technology is making that possible.

Henkel understands as well that its biggest source of carbon emissions is not in making its products but in their use. These are the Scope 3 emissions that are so difficult for companies to measure and manage. The most extreme example is in the extraction of oil for energy. For example, Chevron declares that 5% of a barrel of oil's emissions are from its initial extraction, another 7.5% from its refining, 2% from moving it around the world, and the remaining 85.5% from burning the oil, usually for heating or transport.[81] Similarly, Henkel has found that the use of its products accounts for just over two-thirds (67.6%) of their total emissions. The raw materials, transport, and disposal account for another 30.7%. That leaves just 1.7% of emissions from manufacturing the products – yet that is the area over which Henkel has the most control. It's a good example of how reducing emissions, like any other ESG issue, is often an industry- or economywide issue, not one that companies can solve by themselves.

To that end, Henkel tries to engage its stakeholders at every opportunity. It tells people who use its laundry detergents that using cold water will do the job just as well, and would reduce their emissions by about 30%.[82] It partners with organizations along the packaging value chain to improve the infrastructure needed for recycling, aiming for "no unregulated disposal of packaging waste".[83] It partners with the Circular Valley Foundation to help develop the Rhine-Ruhr region into a hub for young companies and researchers wanting to play a part in the circular economy. Most of all, it sits down with almost everyone who would have an opinion on its operations: opinion leaders, professionals, academia, rating agencies, sustainability analysts, and the like. "We welcome these external assessments of our sustainability performance, as they lead to greater transparency in the market and show us how our performance is assessed."[84]

That sense of transparency underpins another noteworthy aspect of Henkel's approach to ESG. Many companies struggle with finding meaning for the 'Governance' element: the G of ESG. For Henkel, performance on governance comes down to one question and one metric: Do you trust us? It wants to be a trusted partner for those pursuing the return to a sustainable planet. All of the compliance, culture, and disclosure elements of governance are directed to "ensure business success with integrity, promoting performance, transparency and collaboration".[85] In turn, that trust can be monetized: Henkel has raised about 1370 million euros in sustainability-linked bonds.[86] Investors in those bonds trust Henkel to achieve its sustainability targets – and to repay its loans.

Chapter 7 Summary
–   The more people who understand and participate in the ESG effort – both inside and outside the company – the more valuable that effort will be.

- The person with the responsibility to lead the effort in the company will be passionate about its success. They also need to be systems thinkers, able to see multiple perspectives on the same issue, good communicators and influencers, and have a full understanding of the priorities and financials of the business. Then they'll need the full support of someone on the executive who also has all those qualities.
- The company board has ultimate responsibility but will assign it to a committee that makes sense – there is no one right answer. However, they will need to be supported by a panel of external representatives who can offer them unfiltered views with which to test the management's intent and record.

Chapter 8
Reporting to engage on ESG performance

We make quality shit in classic styles that will look good your whole life if your kids don't steal it first – not the kind of trendy shit you throw away in a year.

Sailor Jerry environmental statement, 2007

By this stage, you will have considered the risks and opportunities in ESG performance, decided on the issues to prioritize, and set actions in motion. You'll now need to engage with people on that ESG performance, both inside and beyond the company. After all, the whole point of the exercise is to make sure your company has access to the natural, human, social, and financial capital it needs – and all of those assets are in the hands of other people.

This engagement is kept in view from beginning to end around the performance-and-engagement cycle. Maintaining focus around the cycle – through measurement, reporting, building a narrative and engaging with stakeholders – is difficult, as the distractions and pitfalls are many. Performance is shared indirectly through reporting and ESG ratings, and directly through conversations or shared experience through and outside the value chain. Engagement, rather than raw data, determines the outcomes.

While the most effective form of engagement is a face-to-face discussion, the baseline is a clear and coherent report on your ESG or sustainability performance. That becomes the reference point for all conversations as needed, and helps confirm that the company has a clear and coherent strategy for its ESG performance. Formal reporting may need to meet mandatory reporting requirements, but most reporting is voluntary and the bigger choices are about the optional frameworks and narratives the organization chooses to use.

In this chapter, we look at ESG or sustainability reporting as the basis of engagement. For many companies, this is a necessary but difficult task. While there may be mandatory elements, there is a lot of discretion in how a company might engage with its stakeholders through its reports. Understand you have choices. In deciding them, we suggest you may need to:

1. Stick to your strategy to decide what matters are worth reporting on.
2. Adopt measures on those matters that are both insightful and meaningful to people.
3. Do what mandatory reporting requires you to do – the rest is voluntary
4. Invest in a workable system solution to track and report on measures.
5. Decide on standalone or integrated reporting.
6. Decide who is going to be the arbiter of your performance: your Board, a ratings agency, your most important stakeholder, or all three.
7. Prioritize a rigorous and honest narrative.

https://doi.org/10.1515/9783111428949-011

Let's tease out these suggestions a little more.

Voluntary and mandatory reporting

Since the 1990s, many companies have carefully shared some of these measures externally, in the form of corporate sustainability or CSR reports. It was entirely up to them what they reported. Over time, some helpful voluntary standards were developed, notably the Global Reporting Initiative or GRI, with standard metrics to enable comparison across and within industries. A number of different voluntary standards were consolidated by the International Sustainability Standards Board (ISSB) in 2023. These standards for the 'disclosure of sustainability-related financial information' are now mandatory in an increasing number of countries.

The launch of the UN PRI in 2006 lifted the bar substantially, as discussed in Part A. The initial 20 and now over 3,000 investing institutions agreed that they would "seek appropriate disclosure on ESG issues by the entities in which we invest". The investors wanted as much information as they could gather on those listed companies, and preferably enough to compare one company's profile and actions against others in their sector.

The companies were initially skeptical. Perhaps naively, many thought that investors wouldn't care if they reported or not, so they didn't. But investors took that to mean that the company either didn't care about the ESG risks they were facing, or weren't doing anything about them. That may have been true of many companies, but most companies actually were treating at least some of the risks as important, and addressing them. The nonreporting companies may have saved some bother in the short term, but were penalizing themselves in the long run. In any case, pretty soon listed companies were fielding question after question from nosy investors. It made a lot more sense to pull all that information together and report on it publicly.

A significant step forward occurred in 2014, when G20 Finance Ministers and Central Bank Governors assessed and acknowledged the potential impact of climate risk on the financial system. They requested the global Financial Stability Board (FSB) to set up a Taskforce on Climate-related Financial Disclosures (TCFD) to help keep on top of those risks. The TCFD was spearheaded by former FSB Chairman and (then) Bank of England Governor Mark Carney (now Prime minister of Canada) and chaired by Michael Bloomberg, three-term mayor of New York City and founder of the financial information, software, and media firm that bears his name. Again, it is worth noting, the agenda was being set by central and determined figures in our capitalist institutions.

The TCFD took company disclosure to another level. Global financial regulators were saying that global warming is not only an environmental issue but a material financial issue for companies, and companies needed to assess and report on the potential financial impacts. The TCFD asked companies to disclose their governance structures for managing climate risks, as well as their emissions and targets. It also required companies to test the resilience of their business to a range of scenarios that reflected how the physical world might be affected by global warming, and how governments might take action to reduce greenhouse emissions.

The third set of comprehensive standards were those set by the International Sustainability Standards Board (ISSB), an offshoot of the International Financial Reporting Standards Foundation. The ISSB was tasked with developing, in the public interest, a high-quality, comprehensive global baseline of sustainability disclosures focused on the needs of investors and the financial markets. It published the General Requirements for Disclosure of Sustainability-related Financial Information (IFRS S1) in 2021 and the Climate-related disclosures (IFRS S2) in 2023. The IFRS standards have been adopted by over 140 jurisdictions for all or most publicly listed companies.

Table 2 sets out reporting frameworks that your company may be required to comply with, or may choose to be guided by. The main mandatory reports are the European Union's Corporate Sustainability Reporting Directive (CSRD) and elsewhere the International Financial Reporting Standard S2 (Climate-related disclosures). By October 2024, 30 countries or states are taking steps to introduce these standards as mandatory, with these jurisdictions representing about 57% of global gross domestic product and more than half of global greenhouse gas emissions.[87] Other regulations require disclosure on gender pay and representation, on greenhouse gas emissions, or on health and safety performance. That's just standard compliance, part of a company's legal and risk management regimes.

For now, nothing is required by federal law in the US. The closest that country has come to mandatory reporting is the SEC's proposal for listed companies to report on their climate risks. California has required climate risk reporting for certain companies, but that is the only mandatory provision in the US for broad climate or ESG reporting. Indeed, as discussed in Part A, many states have sought to *ban* their pension funds from considering ESG factors, a remarkable constraint on the market's consideration of risk.[88]

Integrated or standalone reporting

The IFRS standards give companies the option to report their sustainability data in a standalone report that accompanies their annual report, or to integrate them both into a single document. It is as good a sign as any that a company is treating sustainability seriously if it chooses an integrated report. It helps them build and share a single narrative for all their financial and nonfinancial reporting. That is useful since, as we will see in Part C, the combination of data offers investors a number of good proxy indicators of the company's quality of management. It's not always clear how a company manages risks in its business environment or its workforce, but strong ESG reporting offers insights into how the company manages similar risks, and how it thinks of itself as just one part of the economic system in which it operates.

Table 2: Mandatory and voluntary ESG reporting standards.

This standard . . .	From this agency . . .	Applies . . .	Since . . .	Covering . . .
Mandatory reporting				
International Financial Reporting Standards (IFRS)	International Sustainability Standards Board (ISSB)	In adopting countries, globally	2023	The two International Financial Reporting Standards are IFRS S1 (Sustainability-related Financial Information) and IFRS S2 (Climate-related Disclosures). These were adopted in part or whole as mandatory standards by Europe (from 2024), the UK (2024), New Zealand (2024), Canada (2025) and Australia (2025).
Corporate Sustainability Reporting Directive (CSRD)	EU Government	EU	January 2023	About 50,000 large public and private companies, including non-EU companies generating more than €150m in the EU. Reporting must comply with the European Sustainable Reporting Standards (ESRS).
Corporate Sustainability Due Diligence Directives	EU Government	EU	January 2024	The same companies as the CSRD, requiring reporting on due diligence initiatives internally and through the supply chain on material human rights and environmental impacts.
Climate Risk Disclosure Rules	Securities and Exchange Commission	USA	Implementation pending	The SEC finalized the rules in March 2024, but litigation is holding up implementation, which may be affected by the change of US government from January 2025.
	Workforce Gender Equality Agency	Australia	2013–	Almost 5,000 agencies report gender-related employment, pay and discrimination data, claimed to be the most comprehensive such data reporting in the world.

Table 2 (continued)

This standard . . .	From this agency . . .	Applies . . .	Since . . .	Covering . . .
Voluntary reporting				
Carbon Disclosure Project (CDP)	CDP	Global	2000–	More than 23,000 companies globally complete the CDP questionnaires to allow global tracking of corporate emissions.
Task Force on Nature-related Financial Disclosures (TNFD)	UN Financial Stability Board	Global	2023–	First global standard for environmental metrics beyond carbon emissions, including land clearing and other impacts on biodiversity. Being considered by the ISSB as the basis for a new IFRS standard on biodiversity disclosures.
UN Global Compact	UN	Global	2000–	Promotes 10 principles on human rights, the environment and governance, with more than 24,000 organizations submitting an annual 'Communication on Progress', linked to the UN's Sustainable Development Goals (SDGs).
Workforce Disclosure Initiative	ShareAction	Global	2016–	Reporting on workforce practices and management including health and safety, and employee wellbeing, used by 50 institutional investors.
Superseded frameworks				
SASB Sustainability Standards (Sustainability Accounting Standards Board)	Sustainability Accounting Standards Board	Global	2018–2022	Sustainability information that is reasonably likely to affect a company's financial performance, with specific guidance for 77 industries. Merged with the ISSB standards in 2022.

Table 2 (continued)

This standard . . .	From this agency . . .	Applies . . .	Since . . .	Covering . . .
GRI (Global Reporting Initiative)	GRI	Global	2000–2023	The global standard for voluntary reporting for over two decades, with comprehensive frameworks for specific sectors and topics. Guided reporting on over 120 measures of a company's impacts on the economy, environment and society in which they operate. Merged with the ISSB standards from 2024.
Task Force on Climate-related Financial Disclosures (TCFD)	UN Financial Stability Board	Global	2015–2023	Reporting on climate-related governance, strategy, risk management, metrics and targets to help maintain stability in global financial markets. Merged into the ISSB Standards from 2024.

Measures that are relevant, meaningful and actionable

ESG ratings agencies track up to 1100 different metrics for a listed company, every one of them an indicator of its impact on and access to natural, human, social, and financial capital. Nobody is interested in all of these measures, least of all the company. The decision to measure and report on one will eat up resources.

The short answer might be to track and report on measures that the board asks for. They represent the shareholders after all. Some boards carry people with the expertise to ask for the most useful measures, but most are guided by management. So the long answer is still needed.

There may be some mandatory ones, but otherwise you need to be selective, to save resources on what you don't have to do, and free up resources to perform well on the things you should care about. Your measures should track the performance you want to achieve and can be accountable for on the issues you choose. So, they're just like anything else in your company that you want to measure and improve.

Some of those mandatory measures and many other ones will represent your performance on the things that matter. We've covered before what is material to both the company and its stakeholders. Which of the asked-for ESG data on natural, human, and social capital would correlate most with your own business priorities? In other words, which would indicate progress as a necessary or constructive input to an immediate priority or a strategic goal? As well, what ESG data would indicate that state of natural, human, or social capital on which your business depends in the long term? That capital might be either held by the business or held by the community and accessible to the business (assuming it continues to exist).

One of the measures that companies most often report is the money and time they've donated to community causes. For example, a company valued at $389 billion and a reporting-year profit of $11.5 billion tells us that they have invested $24 million in community organizations, and allowed their people a day a year of company time in support. Too often, the value of this metric is unclear. If it is to show the communities in its market that 'they care', there will need to be a strong narrative on the purpose, nature, and durability of this generosity. The $24 million may be made up, in part or whole, by company employees through a workplace giving program, which is not bad in itself but needs to be part of a bigger picture. More importantly, the $24 million might not go far across the markets of a company that size. It could be spread across a thousand small organizations, or a hundred, or just ten – and each one would have a very different impact. While the output of the donation to community causes is measured as $24 million, it doesn't measure the outcome or impact of the community investment.

Instead, the metrics might focus on what is to be achieved with that money. It may have alleviated human suffering in some way, or improved educational outcomes, so that there is a net increase in human capital. That may be the primary purpose of the company's efforts, as it is partnering with governments and other companies with which it wishes to strengthen relationships and so its social capital. Or it may be that its employees have expressed the wish to help out on the issue, so it is more about engaging those employees, and so strengthening the company's human capital. The point being that once there is clarity on why a company is investing in a community initiative, there is also more clarity on what it measures, reports and engages on.

ESG ratings agencies and other arbiters of performance

When you report on your performance, who will decide whether you are doing well or not? Will it be your own Board, an ESG ratings agency (see Chapter 10) or your most important investor or customers? A possibility is to engage all three: you can identify the ratings agency that takes an approach to ESG and intangible value similar to your own, and engage with your Board and investors to treat their assessment as an independent 'mark' of your performance.

It is a little unnerving for public and many private companies to be continually ranked on their ESG ratings scores. They might take comfort from the view that there is nothing at all conclusive about these ratings. Some are from the same experts who issued AAA ratings for subprime mortgages in the lead-up to the financial crisis of 2007, so their assessments might be taken with a sizable rock of salt. Discrepancies between ESG ratings on the same company are a natural part of competition in the ratings market (see Chapter 10). But the variance has been great enough as to discredit the whole exercise for many;[89] these views which have been readily adopted by those who oppose ESG actions on political grounds.

Nonetheless, ESG ratings remain a powerful influence and help determine the allocation of investor money by ESG funds who have taken a quantitative approach, for better or worse. In Chapter 10 we discuss how many large institutional investors sidestep the noise of ESG ratings. Companies themselves might also sidestep that noise and focus on their own targets and progress.

A rigorous and honest narrative

For any report (as with any other form of engagement), the need is greater than ever to tell a consistent, verifiable story on how an organization takes natural, social, and human capital into account in its decisions, and how that approach plays out in specific examples. Such a narrative helps protect against isolated facts and events taking on greater meaning than they have, or being used against a company in social and other media. While the narrative is needed for all stakeholders, it will be tested by institutional investors, employees, and activist NGOs in particular, so they are the ones with whom direct and honest engagement is needed.

Such a narrative would span a holistic view of all capitals. Investors want more than the company's financial story. They want to understand more about the natural, human, and social capital the company has with which to generate next year's financial story and the year after that. ESG disclosures and ratings are a useful basis but direct conversations with institutional investors count more. Fundamental equity investors use them to understand how the company manages its valuable intangible capital. They will push and probe on the narrative to make sense of it, alongside the financial reports and the CEO's insights on them. If these stories all support each other, with the data supporting the narrative, confidence rises. The flipside, of course, is that capital may be withdrawn if they don't like what they see. Getting corporate signoff on an honest narrative able to foster capital is no trivial endeavor, with so many corporate agendas to meet.

There are a few things to avoid in building a company report, so that investors and other stakeholders retain confidence in the company.

– **Telling a 'good story' without the data to back it up.** It took a while for stakeholders to understand what ESG was all about, and some companies took advantage of that lag to try a narrative greenwash. Now, unless a story has click-through transparency to the verified data behind it, it is likely to be counterproductive, if not noncompliant.[90]

- **Telling no story at all.** Equally, it is counterproductive to pull the narrative back so far as to be 'graywashing' ("setting of a strategy and policies which appear aligned with ESG principles but which are too unambitious, ambiguous or qualified by exceptions and loopholes to result in meaningful change").[91] Simply reporting raw data for stakeholders to make sense of it all would seem a lost opportunity, since the sole purpose of a company's ESG disclosure is to engage with others more deeply.
- **Glossing over the bad news.** A transparent report needs to disclose when things go wrong. This requires acknowledging what went wrong and the impact it has had on key stakeholders, and committing to rectify the issue, report back on progress, and change operations to minimize the chance of it happening again. It can be painful to hang out the "dirty washing", but demonstrating accountability without scapegoating is more valuable. Nor does it work to hide the bad news in the footnotes or trivializing it compared to the good things the organization has done. Unfortunately, fatalities do occur in mining, agriculture, and heavy industry. Deciding where to mention them signals to all stakeholders what is important (and what is not) to the organization.
- **Peppering absolute numbers**, without reference to a ratio that offers a meaningful measure of relative year-on-year performance. Absolute numbers disguise shifts in the underlying realities. Water usage may indeed have gone down, but if revenues and output went down faster, then something is wrong. Material usage may have gone up, even faster than revenues, but if the investment switched its product lines from light-framed scaffolding equipment to heavy, energy-intensive capital equipment, then the performance may still be impressive. You may be comforted to read that a large company made 89 factory visits in its supply chain, but less so if this was only 10% of suppliers visited, and only 5% of those visits were unannounced.
- **Trends without analysis**. Many reports and interviews can state performance records but have not gone far in explaining the trends or taking on responsibility for avoidable causes.
- **Policies and management systems** proudly declared but with no accountability or reported incidents and no operational changes when something is reported. Things do happen, and a clean slate is more likely to signal a lack of transparency than a perfect record. Policies may have been written, with no budget or intent for their implementation.

Finally, one could imagine a 'narrative blue rinse', which attempts to pitch an attractive story but seemingly misses the point. Accessing social capital is often about partnering with other institutions and 'brands' to access their social capital by association. A company may find it difficult to conduct research or run a pilot project in a certain area, but the local university is usually trusted to do so. If they could do so in concert, commercial benefits and social capital may flow. Yet a university may not be impressed by a list of corporate donations to local good causes, if its own research reveals that the company has more questionable impacts on social, human, or natural capital.

Graywashing or blue rinsing both include elements of 'dishonesty by omission' – skipping over things that go wrong or that might put the company in a less than glowing light. An honest narrative will tell things as they are, including the things that went badly. It will not hide them under a footnote or appendix, particularly for mistakes that lead to fatalities. It would acknowledge that fact and the impact on stakeholders; and it would say what they will do differently to reduce the risk of the error happening again. While it may be painful to 'hang out the dirty washing', it is essential to maintain or restore trust with stakeholders. If there's been a problem that isn't acknowledged, people will notice and trust is lost. Life is complex and people make mistakes. Demonstrating accountability, without scapegoating anyone in particular, is all that people ask.

* * *

As outlined in Part A, the term 'ESG' is the latest in a long line of terms that recognize that a company's success rests on more than its financial capital. The term is less important than the recognition itself. Managerial prowess and investment acumen go a long way, but ultimately come across factors they cannot control: that is, human beings, the relationships between them and the environments in which they live and work. These systems are so complex that the company will be pitched on their tides. The more it can access human, social, and natural capital, the greater its chance of a long and successful journey.

The long-term ESG performance-and-access cycle is a way of appreciating how a company navigates its way through those systems and accumulates capital as it goes. It makes room for all the ESG-related terms used in the market and uses them to paint a more complete picture of both the company and of its ESG performance. It is useful both in introducing people to both ESG and to the 4 Capitals and in planning an organization's journey with them.

Chapter 8 Summary
- While the most effective form of engagement is a face-to-face discussion, the baseline is a clear and coherent report on your ESG or sustainability performance. That becomes the reference point for all conversations, as needed, and helps confirm that the company has a clear and coherent strategy for its ESG performance.
- Some form of ESG reporting is mandatory in Europe, the UK, Canada, Australia, and New Zealand. In most countries it remains voluntary. Fortunately, most of a range of voluntary guidelines have now been consolidated into a single set that deliver the information that stakeholders need.

- Either way, the report is an opportunity to lay out the company's story on how it engages with its world. It has to build its own story, just like it does for any other part of its business. It just has to be rigorous and honest, otherwise it may be self-defeating.
- Measures must be a meaningful part of that narrative, outlining why they are important and how they are used. Printing them in superlarge fonts do not make them meaningful. Rather, reporting on measures should reveal a trend or comparison that relates to a target, and so is a meaningful indicator of progress on the company's ESG strategy.

Part C: **The investor view: Improving outcomes with ESG**

In Part B, we saw how companies can manage risk and create value by selectively investing in ESG actions.

Investors of various types have a keen interest in how companies are conducting their ESG efforts and the data reported in doing so.

Part C is all about those investors. It will be a useful read if:

- you're in a company and want to know what investors are interested in, and how to engage with them,
- you're in the finance sector and want to know what your colleagues are doing on the ESG front, and why, or
- you have hard-earned money sitting in an investment, pension, or superannuation fund, and want to know how or if they're taking ESG factors into account. (There's more on this in Chapter 14.)

We'll touch on a great many things of interest here. Why mainstream funds are taking ESG factors into account, not just the specialist labels. What investors are signing up to, and demanding the ESG data they need. How a whole new industry of ESG ratings agencies is really just a new trade by old players. How investors become active on ESG issues, and use their influence to bring about concrete change on issues as diverse as climate, health and safety, board governance, and, well, diversity. How some investors have muddied the waters by claiming to be sustainable or responsible, when they're really just greenwashing.

As we've seen in Part A, a political backlash against ESG and investor activism has led to a quieter approach from investors. But don't let that fool you – the work on making ESG an everyday part of investing is continuing as strongly as ever.

Before we get into those deep waters, let's first have a quick look at who those investors are, and what's made them think about ESG.

Who's who among investors

In many quarters, it's really quite cool to say you work in 'investments', looking after other people's money and helping them to attain their financial security or dreams. In others, not so much. In both, it's like saying you work in 'tech', or 'retail' or 'religion'. It really could mean anything, so you're hoping there's a follow-up question.

Figure 23 presents our best attempt at mapping out the different people who work in 'investing'. It focuses only on the actual investors and doesn't include the numerous other people who depend on investing – the ratings agencies, service providers, advisers, intermediaries, and regulators.

Everyone in the diagram is dealing with a portion of your money. From the top left, 'asset owners' are the people who look after the money you have paid into insurance, your pension or superannuation fund, or even part of your taxes. They're looking to safeguard and grow that money and can do so in many ways. They allocate the money

https://doi.org/10.1515/9783111428949-012

to the people on the diagram's next level down: either their own internal fund managers, or one of the great variety of external fund managers. Those fund managers are also more than happy to take money directly from you, calling you a 'retail investor'.

At the next level down, we see all the things that the fund managers actually invest in. When it's all boiled down, they can invest money in entities like companies, governments, and supranationals, or in specific assets like infrastructure, property, or asset-backed securities.[92] Any of these 'underlying assets' are looking for money to provide a public service or create more wealth for all concerned. The fund managers may be investing in companies and sharing in their future outcomes as shareholders, or just lending to them and expecting a fixed return as bondholders. Loans could also be made to governments or banks, who also issue bonds. If any of these shares or bonds are traded on public exchanges like the DAX or the NYSE, they are 'listed' or 'public'; if not, they are 'unlisted' or 'private'. Finally, the fund managers may invest in aggregated assets through index funds, exchange-traded funds, debt aggregators, or simply other fund managers.

Figure 23: Who's who among investors.

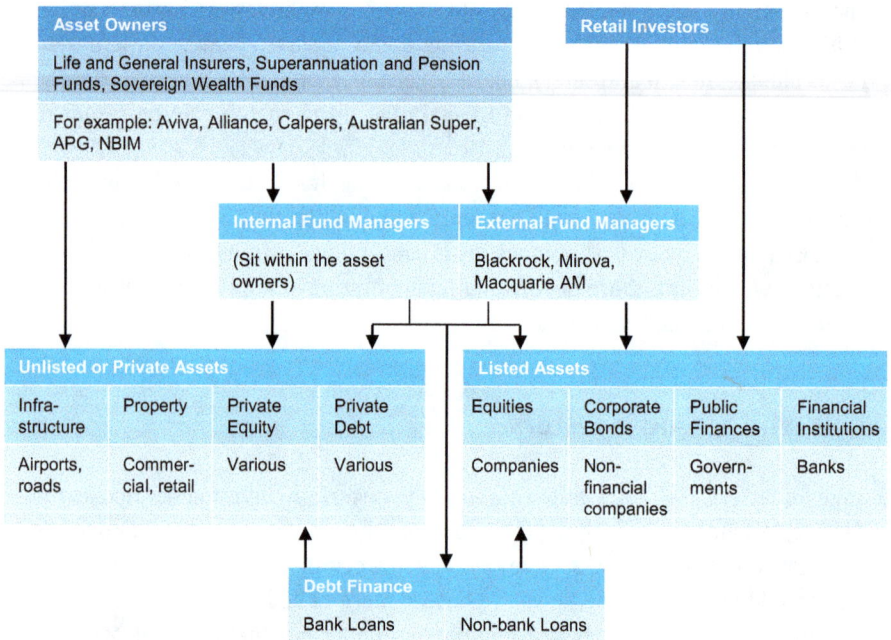

Source: The authors.

Every fund manager tends to have a specialty, preferring to invest in or lend to companies, infrastructure or property, or a mix of all three, while looking for a different balance of risk and reward.

Chapter 9
Wake-up calls to investors

In Bakersfield, California, a Mexican strawberry picker with an income of $14,000 and no English was lent every penny he needed to buy a house for $724,000.

Michael Lewis, *The Big Short*

Most fund managers now take ESG factors into account, to a greater or lesser degree. This was not always the case. The history of ESG becoming a mainstream reality is given in Part A. Until the mid-2000s, the prevailing view was that giving environmental or social issues a place in investment theory was inconsistent with the fiduciary duty of investors to focus on returns. Environmental disasters like the Exxon Valdez hitting a reef in 1989 and spilling 11 million gallons of crude oil into Alaska's Prince William Sound were considered one-off events that did not suggest the need for systematic analysis. That all changed when a series of diverse events challenged investment theory: the global financial crisis, the Deepwater Horizon oil spill, and the introduction of carbon markets, to name a few.

These events suggested very strongly that fund managers have a fiduciary *obligation* to consider ESG issues that may, directly or indirectly, affect investment returns. In both their causes and impacts, they support the systems view of capitalism: that companies operate in complex systems that are infused with the four capitals, and that their decisions and actions must take environmental, social, and governance factors *and implications* into account.

Lehman Brothers, the GFC and ESG

We'd like to take you through the collapse of Lehman Brothers and the resulting global financial crisis (GFC), which was so bad it has its own acronym. What we'd really recommend though is seeing *The Lehman Trilogy*, a masterfully staged play that tells the whole story with levels of humor, speed, and insight we can only aspire to. And we're also mindful of what the economist Paul Samuelson said of the GFC: "What we know about the global financial crisis is that we don't know very much".[93]

The Lehman Brothers collapse in 2008 stands forever as a reminder that a pure focus on making money does not guarantee a good long-term investment. Lehman Brothers certainly didn't collapse on its own. It took many actors and actions, and many other financial companies would have failed around the world if it wasn't for government support. In many respects, Lehman Brothers was both an example and a victim of the culture within the US finance sector.

Late in the 20th century, the US government promoted the idea of home ownership and relaxed long-standing regulations to make it easier for people to take out a

https://doi.org/10.1515/9783111428949-013

loan. That also made it easier to lend to people who didn't really have the income or wealth to pay it back. Salespeople were rewarded for doing just that; the number of these 'subprime' loans took off, and with them the US housing market.

Then, the lenders did what they always did: bundled up hundreds of loans and sold on the bundles as 'mortgage-backed securities' or the more complex 'collateralized debt obligations' or CDOs. That made some sense, because even if one or two borrowers defaulted on their home loan, the risk was costed into the whole bundle and, according to the theory, that diversified risk was a good investment. Surely, they can't all go bad.

The trap for buyers though was that if you bundled up the subprime loans with just a few 'A grade' loans, you could call the whole bundle 'A grade' and sell it on. Worse still, the ratings agencies such as Standard & Poor's and Moody's were happy to endorse the bundles as 'A grade'. So, to the debt market, these bundles seemed 'as safe as houses'.

Banks like Lehman Brothers became very adept at trading in these bundles, and going a few steps further. They took advantage of weak financial standards, developed some complex structures and sophisticated financial products, and applied creativity to their accounts.

If you're finding this hard to follow, that is the point. No one really knew the full picture, not those who developed the products, certainly not regulators or rating agencies, and definitely not the original bank managers and borrowers. There was no incentive to look too hard. While conflicts of interest abounded, share prices were running hot, stock options were worth a fortune, and bonuses were great. Everyone's a winner.

Until they weren't. When people couldn't afford the home loans anymore, they just walked away from the houses. The bubble in the US housing market had burst. Whole suburbs had 'mortgagee sale' signs, with nobody wanting to buy. The loans were greater than the houses were worth. The mortgage-backed securities and CDOs were then next to worthless, and the GFC had begun.

Banks who had booked these 'assets' in their accounts for billions of dollars were suddenly in trouble, and other banks knew it. They stopped lending to each other and started calling in existing loans, because they didn't know whose balance sheets were okay and whose relied on now-worthless CDOs. This flowed quickly across the US banking system, and then onto the Asian and European banks they were trading with.

In the year from September 2007, the US banks NetBank, Delta, and Washington Mutual all went bankrupt. Fannie Mae, Freddie Mac, and AIG were taken over by the Federal Reserve. Bear Stearns and Merrill Lynch were sold for peanuts, and Goldman Sachs and Morgan Stanley depended on government guarantees to survive. All up, from the end of 2007 to the end of 2010, federal debt held by the public increased from roughly 36% of GDP to roughly 62%.[94]

Lehman Brothers, thought to be too big to fail, was actually too big to be saved. When it filed for bankruptcy on 15 September 2008, it was the fourth-largest investment bank in the United States with 25,000 employees, $639 billion in assets, and $613 billion in liabilities.[95] From humble beginnings, it became the symbol of the excesses that led to the 2007-2008 Financial Crisis.

The GFC became known as the Great Recession, the biggest since the 1929 Great Depression. Globally, an estimated $10 trillion was lost in economic output.[96] The social implications were worse.

What does ESG have to do with all this? It goes back to the original lending. Alan Greenspan, the Chair of the Federal Reserve, said that "The big demand was not so much on the part of the borrowers as it was on the part of the suppliers who were giving loans which really most people couldn't afford."[97]

Where traditional investment analysis would look at the volume of lending, ESG analysis would look at the quality of the lending: who were the loans to, would they be repaid, and how were they being treated in the accounts. Where traditional analysis would consider whether a loan passed regulatory hurdles, ESG analysis would consider whether it should have been made in the first place, or whether the sales methods were predatory.

More broadly, the GFC highlighted the culture and governance risks that ESG analysis is interested in: the nature and impact of incentive schemes, and the risk of unacceptable and significant social impacts. Ten years later, Australia held a Royal Commission into Financial Services to look at the same issues.[98] Though the financial products were different, the culture and governance failings lived on.

BP in deep water

Just after the GFC, the interest of ESG analysts was again piqued by a wholly different set of numbers. In late 2009, Matthew Kiernan of ESG advisory firm Innovest noted an alarming discrepancy in health and safety disclosures by major oil companies in the USA. One of them, BP, had been issued 734 notices over three years from safety regulators for 'egregious breaches'. BP was an extreme outlier – the other oil majors had, collectively, only one such notice. It showed that BP had done nothing to address the safety culture that had led to a fire at its Texas City refinery in 2005, the death of 15 people, and the sacking of its previous CEO. Innovest alerted its clients that BP was still shaky, even if its financial reporting looked solid.

Innovest was right to be concerned. On 20 April 2010, BP's oil drilling rig Deepwater Horizon exploded in the Gulf of Mexico, resulting in the immediate death of 11 workers. Four million barrels of oil then flowed from the damaged well over 87 days, the largest offshore oil spill in US history. The spill contaminated about 400 square miles of the sea floor and 1,300 miles of shoreline, stopping commercial and recreational fishing, and damaging beaches and coastal wetlands, along with sea birds, sea turtles, marine mammals, oysters, and other creatures of the sea.[99]

The economic cost to the community was enormous. The US Department of Industry estimated that the fishing losses alone amounted to 25,000 jobs, US$2.3 billion worth of industry output, US$1.2 billion gross regional product, US$700 million labor income, US$160 million state and local tax revenues, and US$160 million federal tax revenues.[100]

The cost to BP was almost as great, estimated at US$65 billion.[101] That included an unprecedented US$5.5 billion penalty under the US Clean Water Act penalty, and up to US$8.8 billion in natural resource damages.[102] Mainly though, it was the fall in BP's share price, which dropped by over 50% immediately following the accident. Unlike the other major oil companies, BP's share price in August 2024 was still less than what it was just before the incident 14 years ago.

The BP Report 2010,[103] the Commission Report 2011,[104] and the Joint Report 2011[105] concluded that though multiple parties were involved, BP had the prime responsibility. The spill happened because the cement at the base of the 5.5 km-deep well failed. When it did, hydraulic jaws were supposed to clamp shut the base of the well, but instead the hydraulics operated in reverse and jammed open. The drilling program was behind schedule and over budget, and shortcuts had been taken. BP had decided to check and maintain the hydraulic jaws, rather than engage the company that had installed it at greater cost. Unfortunately, when the disaster struck, BP was already preparing to pause operations at the Deepwater Horizon well and move onto another site.

BP's failings continued with its poor leadership, poor contingency and response management, and poor (to put it politely) communication.[106] CEO Tony Hayward attempted to apologize but fell short: "We're sorry for the massive disruption it's caused their lives. There's no one who wants this over more than I do. I would like my life back". Shortly after, he did get more time to enjoy, being sacked by the BP board in June 2010.

Putting a Price on Carbon

A very different type of market shock occurs when, quite deliberately, a company has to pay to pollute the environment *before* any damage is done.

Very, very few companies or investors put a price on the natural capital they rely on, and most assume it is infinite. Limitations on the use of or impact on natural capital are typically set by government regulation, and for most companies 'compliance' is the start and end point of their care for natural capital. The natural capital is an 'externality': external to micro-economic equations of profit and loss, and so none of its concern. Unless constrained by specific regulation, a company could pollute as much as it liked.

Economists in the 1960s and 1970s thought there might be a better way. The economic line starts with Ronald Coase, who saw the possibility of trading in externalities through property rights.[107] When economists realized that pollution was an externality worth recognizing, economists thought a price on that pollution might help.[108] This novel idea was wrenched from academia and into the policy sphere by World Bank economist Herman Daly.

Governments could put a nominal value on natural capital and then require companies to buy permits to use it, that is, to pollute. The permits would be tradeable, but limited to the natural capital that the environment could spare (i.e., the pollution it could handle). In so doing, governments would be creating a market for that scarce commodity. Companies would be the demand side of the equation: they would pay for permits if they needed to pollute or sell the permits if they did not. Governments would be on the supply side: they would assess the state of the environment, and either reduce or increase the number of available permits to ensure the use of the natural capital was sustainable. The theory was quickly tested in a number of schemes for managing environmental resources, notably clean air,[109] fisheries,[110] and rivers.[111]

The granddaddy of all emission trading schemes was the US Clean Air Act 1990, brought in to stop sulfur dioxide emissions from US coal plants, which were polluting parts of North America and drifting over the Atlantic to cause acid rain. When the scheme commenced, the cost predicted for reducing emissions was between $700 and $1500 per ton. The coal plants screamed blue murder against the scheme, and then got to work on technology that would stop the emissions. Within months, the market price of emission allowances stabilized at $100. Within 6 months, the scheme was redundant – the acid rain was finished, and the permits were all but worthless.[112] Given a direct financial incentive, companies will act.

Climate change is a far more complex problem, and nobody suggests an emissions trading scheme (ETS) is the certain or only answer. In the United Nations, where they were negotiating over the 1997 Kyoto Protocol, the Europeans were skeptical. They wanted to just set regulations to limit the amount of greenhouse gases that any process or company could emit. But the Americans argued the case for the market. It had worked for acid rain and Hudson River pollution, so it was worth a shot. The Europeans agreed to put an international ETS as a *potential* mechanism to help reduce global greenhouse emissions and address climate change. They then ratified the Protocol, along with 192 individual countries, and waited for the Americans to do the same.

While they were waiting, the EU decided to give an ETS a try. They launched their scheme in 2005, the world's first and among the largest greenhouse gas trading schemes. It had a rocky start but ultimately worked. By 2023, the EU ETS had helped bring down emissions from European power and industry plants by approximately 47%, compared to 2005 levels. As of 2024, there are 36 emission trading schemes in force around the world, covering approximately 18% of global greenhouse gas emissions, a third of the world's population, and 58% of global GDP. A further 14 trading schemes are currently under development and 8 more are under consideration.[113]

These carbon prices don't instantly solve the pollution problem. Instead, they change the business case equation for what technologies are commercially viable, and what are not. When high-emission products and services become, say 5% more expensive, then low-emission technologies and energy-saving solutions become that much more cost-competitive. They become that little bit more attractive for investment. As investment flows, the scale of production increases and distribution channels improve. As prices to customers then fall and margins for suppliers rise, there is further investment in low-emission technologies. This results in further innovation, continuing the cycle. Before long, in a real economic timeline, renewable energy has become cheaper than coal. An investor totally reassesses the value of a company that operates coal-fired generators.

None of these markets are perfect, and vested interests can and do influence the design of their market for their own gain. But the market is our society's most powerful agent for change, and a carbon price is a market kick-starter. By putting a price on the environmental resource, the EU and similar environmental trading markets have significantly changed the technologies, business models, and investment decisions right through our financial markets and will continue to do so.

All these are ESG issues and are intrinsic to economics and investment. It is somewhat bewildering then when a company board considers ESG to be about wokeness, public relations, or exclusion. That board view in itself might prompt investors to consider whether that particular board is up to the task. It seems not to admit a systems view of capitalism, and the many stakeholders that are part of it.

The main questions for investors though are 'How do you determine what issues are material?' and 'How do you factor them into investment decision-making?' And it is to these that we now turn.

Chapter 9 summary
– Major financial, political, and real-world events will continue to remind investors of the real risks of ignoring ESG-related issues. Chapter 2 lists several of those events: the governance debacles of Enron and WorldCom, the destruction of environments and livelihoods by BP's Deepwater Horizon, the global financial crisis, the explosion of Union Carbide's chemical factory in Bhopal, the Rio Tinto's destruction of Juukan Gorge, the abuse of law and people at Murdoch's *News of the World*, climate change, and the COVID-19 pandemic.
– Most if not all of these events have in turn been caused by a chain of decisions that have placed short-term financial capital before long-term natural, human, and social capital.
– For example, the GFC was enabled by US legislation that promoted easy lending for housing, by predatory salesforces who wrote loans that could never be repaid, and by banks and ratings agencies who represented that debt as AAA when it was far from it.
– Similarly, the Deepwater Horizon explosion was enabled by a lax regard to safety and health, and by short-term decisions in the maintenance and monitoring of safeguard mechanisms.
– Placing a price on carbon emissions is a different type of market shock. While we are now experiencing the painful physical realities of global warming, scientific awareness of the threat goes back many decades, and government responses go back to the 1990s. How corporates will respond to both the physical and regulatory changes remains to be seen.

Chapter 10
The ESG information that investors seek

Rarely are opportunities presented to you in a perfect way. In a nice little box with a yellow bow on top. 'Here, open it, it's perfect. You'll love it.' Opportunities—the good ones—are messy, confusing and hard to recognize. They're risky. They challenge you.

Susan Wojcicki, CEO of YouTube, 2014

Different investors need different types of ESG information. As their needs differ, there is no 'one-size-fits-all' way of meeting those needs. This is a challenge for companies when it comes to reporting relevant ESG information to investors. Nonetheless, the role of the four capitals and the relevance of ESG disclosure for investors is being increasingly recognized in regulation and by standard setters.

What investors are looking for

Investors are on the other side of what can be a very extensive data pool, particularly when ESG ratings agencies produce thousands of potentially relevant morsels on each listed company. The PRI's Investor Data Needs Framework (IDN),[114] developed with support from Chronos Sustainability, sets out the type of ESG information that different types of investors are looking for, at different points along the responsible investment process. The IDN Framework:
- assesses the type of ESG data needed for different types of investors, covering 19 activities along the responsible investment process, for research, valuation, portfolio construction, stewardship, and investor reporting
- identifies the different types of company data that investors use: inputs (e.g., processes and management systems), outputs (e.g., operational data, quantity of material used), and outcomes (impact on stakeholders)
- calls for data on both past performance and future objectives and targets, both qualitative and quantitative
- insists that data is accessible, comparable, verifiable, a fair representation, and relevant.

With this guidance, the Framework assists companies and regulators to better understand how investors use ESG information and the different needs of different investors and to improve their corporate reporting and other communication with investors.

True, that's all pretty demanding on companies who are already striving to meet international disclosure standards. The problem is that companies may be tempted to disclose 'near enough is good enough' data, just to get the job done. But that backfires in two ways: first, it means those companies are not taking the opportunity to tell a

https://doi.org/10.1515/9783111428949-014

compelling story about their performance with the evidence they need to back it up. Investors fill in the gaps with their own skepticism and beliefs, and more questions. Second, it only extends the process as investors continue to ask those questions and insist upon answers. The IDN Framework helps bring both sides together more efficiently.

As to expectations on the content to be covered by companies, that is mercifully being consolidated into just one set of standards: the IFRS Sustainability Disclosure Standards (see Chapter 8). Though still voluntary in most countries, regulators and accounting bodies in many are making them mandatory. Before the IFRS Standards, there were six or seven different frameworks that companies could use to support their ESG or sustainability reporting. In 2024, the International Sustainability Standards Board (ISSB), the International Accounting Standards Board (IASB), and the Global Reporting Initiative (GRI) joined forces to consolidate their efforts.

There are two IFRS standards:

–   **IFRS Standard 1** requires companies to set out how they manage sustainability-related risks and opportunities: the overall strategies they use; the methods to identify, assess, prioritize, and monitor the issues; and the governance processes to manage them. Then it calls for companies to declare their performance on sustainability-related risks and opportunities, referring to targets set either by themselves or by regulation.
–   **IFRS Standard 2** is more specific, seeking information on how entities identify and manage their climate-related risks and opportunities. It supersedes the Taskforce for Climate-Related Financial Disclosure (TCFD) framework, launched in 2015, whose leaders declared at the G20 Finance Ministers and Central Bank Governors Meeting in October 2023 that "they had done their job".

The Taskforce for Nature-related Financial Disclosure (TNFD) builds on the success of the TCFD and asks companies to think about and disclose their impact on natural habitat and biodiversity. While the voluntary TNFD is still being developed and adopted by investors, it is highly likely that it too will be taken up by regulators and made mandatory.

All the company reporting standards discussed in Part B are intended to solicit performance and forward-looking information that can be included in mainstream financial filings. That would make them more useful than many traditional company disclosure requirements but there are problems beneath the surface.

While the IFRS standards are gaining acceptance globally, they may be inconsistent with regional reporting standards. For example, the IFRS standards are content with a single materiality lens (what may have an impact on the company) while the European Sustainability Reporting Standards (ESRS) insist on double materiality reporting (adding impacts to the environment and other stakeholders).

Another issue is that the data is limited to the company's issues and impacts. While that may be useful for company-specific investment risk, it may disguise real-world impacts that universal investors are also interested in. The classic example is when a company sells an asset or business that is emissions intensive. That may reduce the climate risk of the company, but nothing has really changed in the global quest to reduce emissions. In fact, the sale may be to a company with less concern and controls on emissions. Instead of selling the polluting asset, the company may have invested in new technology or processes to reduce its emissions. By doing so, the company would have shown itself to be taking responsibility for the emissions, garnering support from investors who have set targets to reduce emissions in their portfolio.

Ownership and operational control differ on ESG liabilities

The true state of affairs may also be hidden within the layers of 'entities' that are covered by a company's reporting. Historically, companies have reported ESG information on operations for which they have *operational* control, consistent with many environmental compliance requirements. However, financial accounts usually report on a company's *ownership* of operations. It's quite common for a company to operate a plant in which it has only a slice of ownership, say 20%, and still have operational control. Conversely, a company may have significant ownership of a facility, without actually operating it (a 'nonoperated entity').

The greenhouse gas emissions reported on an operational basis will be quite different from those reported on an ownership or equity basis. To give you a sense of how far apart they can be, let's look at BHP Group, the world's largest miner. For the 2024 financial year, BHP reported its total operational Scope 1 and 2 greenhouse gas emissions to be 10,080,000 tonnes CO_2-e. To their credit, BHP also reported emissions on an ownership basis, with reported equity emissions for the same financial year of 8,620,000 tonnes, nearly 15% lower than the operational emissions.

Investors want to match the share of revenue or profit from the operation with the share of potential liability associated with the emissions, both of which are calculated on an ownership basis. If an investor puts a price on emissions that are calculated on an operational basis, they may end up with a materially different assessment of the carbon liability.

Similarly, ESG reporting and analysis seek to reflect the costs and risks in a company's value chain on which the financial statements are silent. A company may have no operational control or even influence over parties to whom it buys and sells but may bear consequences if something goes wrong. If a retailer gets its garments made overseas under conditions that verge on modern slavery, ESG investors will know of the liabilities that may flow. Modern slavery legislation makes it clear that such conditions are a clear and material risk for all the wholesalers and retailers downstream, irrespective of their financial exposure. Similarly, under climate legislation, fossil fuel companies may also have to calculate and report on the 'Scope 3' emissions generated when customers use their products. Again, as investors look to manage climate change–related investment risks in their portfolios, fossil fuel companies become less attractive.

BOX: The Fundão tailings dam: another BHP dam fails

Another example of just how a nonoperated entity can headline a company's ESG risk was shown when the Fundão tailings dam in Brazil failed on 5 November 2015. The breach sent 32 to 40 million cubic meters of minerals, water, sands, and clays down the River Doce to the sea more than 600 km away, taking with it 19 lives and countless villages. It left hundreds homeless and ruined the livelihoods of thousands, flooding agricultural plots and killing off fish and aquatic life.

The mine and the tailings dam were operated by Samarco Mineração S.A., a joint venture between the Australian company BHP and the Brazilian company Vale. As neither company actually operated Samarco, neither was required to report on its activities and ESG performance in its operational reporting. Both companies could have let Samarco bear the whole cost of the cleanup and remediation, arguing they were not legally liable for the losses downstream. To their credit, both companies recognized the reputation risk and accepted that they were morally responsible to support Samarco. In the end, courts also held the two companies liable for damages as a result of the accident, irrespective of the ownership structure. As a result, their financial accounts now report their shares in US$7 billion in compensation to date,[115] a $66.3 million fine from the Brazilian government, with numerous class action lawsuits to come.

For BHP, this was a very uncomfortable echo of a similar disaster in Papua New Guinea. In 1984, the tailings dam in its Ok Tedi copper mine collapsed, leading its contents to flow down the Ok Tedi river and then into the Fly River system – the largest in Papua New Guinea. It was 15 years before BHP reported in 1999 that the mine was discharging 90 million tonnes of waste every year, to be deposited along over 1000 km of downstream rivers. In the end, BHP walked away from the mine, which continued to operate, leaving it to the Papua New Guinea government on condition that two-thirds of the mine's proceeds would compensate the Ok Tedi and Fly River communities and fund sustainable development throughout the country.[116]

These mining accidents are extreme examples of the materiality of environmental, social, or governance issues to a company's value. In response, risk management policies and processes have been tightened against a great range of potential harms in the mining and other sectors. They recognize that harm to natural or human capital beyond the company, bad enough in itself, will also come back and harm the company's social and financial capital. The lessons from these events are lasting. But elsewhere in this book, we show how a holistic look at the same ESG issues can lead to innovation, new services, technologies, and investment opportunities.

ESG data and ESG ratings agencies offer their opinions

The MSCI All Country World Index has over 1800 companies in it, and many managed funds invest from that universe. If investors use an ESG lens, they face the daunting task of trying to keep track of all the ESG data from all of those companies. As a result, many investors rely on ESG data aggregators and firms to interpret and summarize ESG performance with an ESG score or rating. They may provide scores or ratings on a company's overall ESG performance, or on specific aspects of the company's performance, such as its emissions profile or its performance on diversity, equity, and inclusion. These 'ESG ratings agencies' and data providers therefore play an important role in integrating ESG into investing. But each agency has its own take on how to rate ESG, none of which is perfect, and so you need a way to pick a path through the distractions they create for both companies and investors.

ESG ratings agencies are a response to the tidal waves of information that come with sustainability reports. When combined with media reports and third-party analyses, that wave of information becomes a massive analysis exercise for investors. Rather than individual investors reading individual reports, they can subscribe to an agency that will do it for them and assess each company's performance against others in their sector and in other sectors.

Innovest Strategic Advisors in New York prepared the first global and comparative 'ESG ratings' way back in 1995. Several agencies followed, but it took another 10 years before their ratings were getting broader attention from companies and investors. These ESG agencies then fossicked for more and more data on the companies, so that they weren't all issuing the same ratings from the same data. After everything in the public domain was included, the agencies probed companies again with their *own* surveys, seeking data they could apply to their own competing frameworks for rating companies.

Indeed, Daniel Cash has analyzed the ESG ratings market using a 'signals theory' approach. In his view, ESG ratings intervene in the feedback loop between the company and investors, complicating the signals that are being sent. "Under the current ESG system, that signal is massively noisy because there are so many ESG rating agencies vying for position, it is inherently inefficient because of duplication costs and poor relationships between issuer and agency, and ultimately it contributes to a depressed system."[117] For the large institutional investors, Cash says, "research has been quite clear that the informational content of ratings is extremely low."

Accordingly, many ESG investors do not use the ratings. Others believe that they should be more like credit ratings, where there is usually very little difference between different agencies' ratings of the same company. The expectation is that the ratings methodology should be transparent, that the methodologies should be consistent, and that therefore the ratings should be consistent. As a result, jurisdictions are regulating[118] or setting industry standards[119] for ESG rating providers.

Arguably, though, there should not be uniformity in ESG ratings and the variations are easily explained. Each agency applies its own subjective philosophy of how ESG performance reveals the value, risks, and opportunities in a company, so they weigh different aspects of performance differently. Some may weigh leading indicators (such as investment in renewable energy) more highly than lag indicators (past emissions from fossil fuels). Some may weigh governance and ESG management systems or a company's response to a negative event, more importantly than a related performance metric or even the impact of that event.

As well, ratings agencies use different data sources. While most use the company-supplied ESG data as their primary source, they will also use other legitimate sources, such as regulators, industry associations, customers, social media, and civil society. There should be some consistency in objective data like Scope 1 emissions, which are calculated by the companies themselves and verified or audited by qualified third parties. To the extent the data varies between ratings agencies, the frustration may be better directed toward companies who haven't accurately disclosed their Scope 1 emissions.

So, a better analogy for ESG rating companies is that they are like the opinions expressed by equity research firms on a company's value. No one expects or necessarily wants all analysts to come up with the same valuation or opinion. Transparency of both ratings methodology and sources is far more important than ratings uniformity. Therefore, some ratings agencies go to extraordinary lengths to set out their methodologies, on their websites, through reviewed and published articles, and through industry conferences.

Investors learn to appreciate the different approaches that are reflected by different ESG ratings for the same company, just as they value differences in opinion by equity research analysts. They will better understand the basis for the ESG ratings, and decide which approach is best aligned to their own investment philosophy – which ESG rating best reflects the investor's concerns and ESG philosophy. Just as a wise company would identify the ESG rating that best aligns with its own strategy (see Chapter 8), so too will the canny investor.

Nonetheless, ESG ratings remain a powerful influence and help determine the allocation of investor money by ESG funds that have taken a quantitative approach, for better or worse.

Chapter 10 summary
- Investors want data that reveals trends in a company's inputs, outputs, and impacts on stakeholders, both past performance and future objectives, both qualitative and quantitative, in a way that is accessible, comparable, verifiable, fair, and relevant.
- Sourcing and reviewing that data is complex. Different types of investors look for different types of data, for different purposes. The most relevant data varies between industries. And the data for what a company owns is different from the data on what it manages.
- To make it easier, ESG ratings agencies sift through all the data, including from non-company sources, for example, regulators, NGOs, and competitors, to rate companies on their performance. However, they do so in their own ways. While people who issue credit ratings look at similar data and produce similar ratings, the ESG agencies assess a wider range of data to produce a wider range of ratings.
- In fact, ESG ratings are similar to the opinions expressed by equity research firms on a company's value. No one expects or necessarily wants all analysts to come up with the same valuation or opinion. Transparency of both ratings methodology and sources is far more important than ratings uniformity.

Chapter 11
The basics of investing with ESG

The best way to navigate the complexities of the market is to focus on long-term goals and strate-
gies, rather than getting swayed by short-term fluctuations.

David Solomon, CEO, Goldman Sachs

As we saw in the introduction to Part C, there are many different types of investors. To understand how they use ESG to improve their investment outcomes, we'll reorganize that picture to reflect the degree of influence an investor has in the underlying asset. That's significant, as the more influence an investor has, the more their ESG approach will impact on what a company does and ultimately affect real-world outcomes.

Four levels of investment curiosity and commitment

The investors with the most riding on a company's performance are those that have a **direct stake in an unlisted (or private) company, or property or infrastructure asset**. They may own the whole asset, or a significant share of a consortium or joint venture ownership, with relatively few co-investors. Investors may also provide private debt to these companies or assets. They are committed investors with typically quite a long-term holding in the company. Whether their stake is equity or debt, their main concern is understanding how the company preserves and grows its value over the long term. Therefore, they need to be comfortable that the ESG risks are acceptable, the asset is managing them well and, for equity investors, that ESG opportunities are grasped. ESG factors are an integral part of the due diligence they perform both before and during their investment.

On the next level are investors in listed assets, either debt or equity. The so-called **fundamental investors** in listed companies, property, or infrastructure may be one of thousands of investors, and while they may have a shorter-term focus, they seek a deeper understanding of what determines their asset's current and potential value. They trade on the public market after closely examining the company's strategy, the markets it operates in, its assets and capabilities, and how well it is doing. ESG factors can loom large over these issues, so the investors want the relevant data and many engage directly with companies to get it. Yet because they invest in so many companies, they may not be able to do a thorough ESG analysis, so many lean more heavily on the ESG data agencies.

On our third level are investors who hold interests without necessarily too much fundamental analysis of the underlying asset and typically have a much more shorter-term focus. The first type is the so-called **quant investors**, who look for nu-

https://doi.org/10.1515/9783111428949-015

meric data that might correlate with outperformance against a benchmark or for events that might indicate the best time to buy or sell (e.g., short-term price and earnings momentum, 'quality', 'growth'). ESG factors may well be included in these factors, but only if the math reveals that correlation. They inhale the raw data from ESG analysts or ratings agencies but are rarely if ever interested in what that data represents. So, while fundamental investors look for causation between ESG management and company performance, quant investors are content with any correlation between the two. Deep in quantitative analysis and with their shorter investment timeframe, many quant investors step back from actual engagement with companies (or other investors for that matter).

Finally, **passive investors** avoid looking at specific companies at all. They set up a portfolio of companies that will mirror a particular index, and then let that portfolio run with minimal interference. The index could be either national (the FTSE 350 or S&P 500), regional (FTSE Russell Asia Pacific), or global (MSCI All World, FTSE Russell All World), and it could be either market-wide or limited to a particular sector. In this way, what matters is the larger macroeconomic issues facing a country, region, or sector, rather than what is happening with specific companies. ESG factors, such as systemic poor corporate governance or poor attention to climate change, matter to the extent they might affect the whole portfolio, but the passive investors do not review the comparative ESG performance of particular companies or assets.

Yes, it is subjective

For fundamental investors, the approach to analyzing ESG issues is really nothing new. Before ESG was mainstream, they might consider 'quality of management' as an X-factor, and an analyst's expertise in assessing that quality was both critical to the investment approach and a potential competitive advantage in investment markets. It was their subjective judgment that made all the difference. ESG factors are now added to that assessment of management quality, as declared ESG management and performance are often a good proxy for assessing how the business gets things done behind the scenes. For example, investors might be interested in whether the company can drive performance to achieve stretch goals and whether there is a culture of accountability. An investment analyst can tell a lot about whether that culture exists within a company by looking at the way they set ESG goals and report on ESG performance, especially when things might not have gone as the company would have liked.

Direct investing in companies, property, and infrastructure

ESG analysis and direct investing really do go hand in hand. As direct investors are typically long-term holders, they will still be there when ESG strengths and weaknesses play out, for better or for worse. They have a strong incentive to keep an eye on ESG risks and opportunities, and to steer actions that will improve their long-term risk and reward. When they own a significant share of a company, often majority or wholly owned, they have a real ability to do just that.

The long-term nature of direct investing aligns with the timeframe over which many ESG issues can materialize. ESG issues, such as climate change, can represent almost existential threats to some forms of infrastructure and property. The physical risks of climate change may fundamentally challenge property valuations due to an increase in major flood frequency and coastal inundation. Transition risks of climate change may fundamentally challenge the valuations of energy infrastructure.

In recent years, the value of deals (mergers and acquisitions) in the private market has exceeded those on publicly listed markets, and pension funds are allocating more and more funds to private equity managers. Once the money is allocated, the private equity manager is termed the 'general partner' in the fund, as they are empowered to make the investment decisions and manage the 'portfolio companies' that the fund then owns. The pension funds and others who are investing our money are called the 'limited partners', as by agreement they have fewer powers and are not involved in the management of the portfolio companies.

Figure 24 sets out the end-to-end process for private equity investment and the key questions from an ESG perspective at each stage. Obviously, each investment is unique with specific issues to be considered, in line with the fund's mandate. Private equity and direct investors consider ESG factors before they invest, through the due diligence process, and in managing the assets they then own.

The deal sourcing and screening stage has typically focused on the red (or at least amber) flags, for example, is it a business aligned with our principles and values? How much does it take advantage of environmental or social costs that are left to others?

Aside from clear environmental or employee liabilities or inoperable reputational damage, it would be rare for ESG issues to knock an acquisition cold. It's more a question of identifying risks that may, alone or collectively, be taken to the negotiating table. Conversely, there may be opportunities identified that have not been factored into valuations, and which may reassure the buyer to make that additional bid.

Most investors in direct property and infrastructure consider many ESG issues in their due diligence process as a matter of course, for example, consideration of soil or groundwater contamination, or the impact of physical climate change on the business and its operations. There are well-established guidelines or tools, such as the Global Real Estate Sustainability Benchmark (GRESB), that assist them in identifying what's material and assessing them in a systematic way. High measures of employee engagement may indicate that the company is a prized employer for talented people with strong word of mouth from the existing teams.

Post investment, similarly, direct investors will typically focus on the oversight of risks, asset performance, and potential growth areas. In many respects, they may take

Figure 24: ESG questions for private fund investments.

Deal sourcing and screening	Due diligence and valuation	Investment approval	Portfolio company management	Exit
• Is the proposed investment in a sector acceptable to both general and limited partners? • Are there any obvious ESG issues with the company? • Are we comfortable with the other investors with a stake in the company?	• How material are ESG issues to the company? How vulnerable is it to them? • What ESG and risk management policies and practices are effective? What are not? • How does our ESG analysis affect the buyer negotiating position?	• Are the ESG issues incorporated into investment documents? • What issues can be incorporated in investment documents to create ESG obligations? • What ESG issues need to be managed in a post-investment review and with new practices?	• Are there action plans and accountabilities on ESG issues? Are they being met? • How does the company respond when limited partners and other stakeholders raise ESG issues? • How are we reporting to stakeholders on ESG issues?	• Are there any ESG skeletons being left that may affect the fund's reputation? • Might the potential buyer affect the fund's reputation? • Is the ESG value recognized?

Source: The authors.

the same approach as both fundamental equity investors and the company itself: identify and manage material ESG issues that are relevant to the execution of their strategy and the management of risks. The due diligence, valuation, and management of the company mirror the issues raised in Part B: the double materiality of issues, an assessment of risks, and the potential to build social, human, and financial capital through ESG initiatives.

Doing a little due diligence on Myer

So how might an investor try to digest the ESG data that companies and others provide? Until recently, companies or private equity firms on the verge of a listing, merger or acquisition would rarely consider the target's culture and performance on ESG issues. Matters of legal compliance, yes, and perhaps the risk of soil or groundwater contamination, but not all that loose ESG stuff.

A good example was the sale of Myer, a large retail chain in Australia, that was listed by its private equity owners in 2009. The prospectus indicated the extent to which the PE firm had considered ESG in its six-year holding of Myer. All it offered was half a column on Myer's philanthropic activities. That proudly shared information is unlikely to indicate to an investor how the Myer business may be affected by ESG issues.

There were hints in the prospectus that ESG issues might have been reviewed further. The prospectus confirmed that 'The reputation and prominence of the Myer brand are considered fundamental to its ability to attract and retain customers, which in turn drives sales.' Three of its five supporting attributes are 'supporting the community', 'trusted reputation', and 'committed to sustainable practices' (the last mention of those practices in the prospectus). The implication is that if the brand drove sales, and ESG issues helped underpin the brand, perhaps they were worth a look.

More important to consider are the six 'key investment risks' disclosed in the prospectus. They were that economic conditions might deteriorate, Myer's growth strategies might not achieve their objectives, IT failures might occur, Myer's competitive position might deteriorate, customer preferences might change, and Myer's brand name might diminish in reputation and value. Other risks were that Myer's relationships with key brand owners, designers, concession operators, landlords, and suppliers might deteriorate, Myer's flagship store rebuild might be delayed, loss of key personnel might occur, Myer might be unable to attract and retain staff, and Myer's marketing campaigns might be unsuccessful.

Aside from economic conditions and IT, each of the risks is directly affected by ESG issues, and by Myer's approach to them. If you were looking to buy such a company, a large part of whose value is its brand, those issues are intrinsically and explicitly relevant. It's a timely reminder of the ESG due diligence needed if you are thinking of raising capital or investing in a company.

Investing in listed companies

As we saw in Part A, human imagination has delivered us the opportunity to buy shares in a public limited liability company. That imagination has also created many ways to take up that opportunity. Professional investors may do so by assessing its fundamentals, by searching for numeric clues in its data (quant investing), or by letting their money ride on an index of which the company is a part (passive or index investing).

Fundamental investing

Fundamental investors assess a company's underlying value and compare that with its market price. That's a puzzle for which different investors consider different factors, which is why there are usually both buyers and sellers in a market. The assessment takes into account the company's current tangible assets, but more importantly, its potential for growth in earnings and returns, and the risks to that growth. So, they might adopt an extended SWOT analysis (strengths/weaknesses/opportunities/threats), looking at:

- **the company's strategy** and how it will affect earnings growth (in their opinion, not just as declared by the company)
- the external **opportunities and threats** in the company's operating environment that may either reduce or accelerate that growth
- the company's **strengths and weaknesses** in its assets and capabilities that will enable it to pursue its strategy, respond to opportunities or address threats, and
- **any uncertainties**, in any of the above, that may reduce confidence in their analysis.

Adding ESG pieces to this puzzle might make it more complex, but it is essentially the same problem. The ESG analysis considers ESG issues that are a material risk to the company's strategy, to the tangible and intangible assets upon which future earnings depend, and how the company is managing those issues.

Opportunities and threats that shape the operating environment

Traditional investing sees a market as a relatively closed system. The leading framework for analyzing that system is Michael Porter's Five Forces Model. That model first considers a company's competition, both existing players and the potential for new entrants into their market. Then, it looks at the wiggle room for cutting a profit in that market: the negotiating power of both suppliers and customers. The fifth force is the revolutionary possibility that customers might not want that product at all, that there is a potential substitute product or service that fulfills the same need. Surprisingly, that's as far as traditional market and strategy analysis went. Back in the day, an investor who held shares in a thermal coal mine or a predominantly coal-fired electricity generator, might have looked at the substitutes for coal in generating electricity and seen no immediate threat.

An ESG lens opened that field of analysis right up, looking at all the environmental and social issues that shape the broad business environment and the specific markets in which companies operate. It considers such things as demographics (including an aging population), attitudes to privacy, and changes in how we work and move around. This expanded analysis even has its own acronym, PESTELE:

- P – Political
- E – Economic
- S – Social
- T – Technological
- E – Environmental
- L – Legal
- E – Ethical

While many of these trends are considered in traditional investing, ESG integration broadens and deepens the analysis, typically picking them up earlier. For example, the above investor would take into account the science of global warming, the role of fossil fuels in that science, the likelihood that governments may regulate markets to put a price on carbon, the opportunity that would create for renewable energy companies and minerals used in batteries, and the accumulated threat to fossil fuel businesses. They would see the rise of cheap renewable energy (economic and technological) changing the competitive landscape in the electricity market, decreasing the price in the energy market, and increasing the price volatility, both of which are the focus of traditional mainstream investment analysts.

One may argue that considering the impact of global warming on fossil fuels and electric utilities *should* be part and parcel of mainstream investment analysis. But the reality is that it was only in about 2014 that mainstream investors started to focus on that impact. When they did, it was clear to them that global warming was going to lead to major structural changes in the energy and electricity generation markets. That view reinforced the decline of the fossil fuel–dominated energy sector, as a percent of the S&P 500, since 1980. It also prompted a rethink of the utilities sector, which had typically offered stable if unspectacular long-term returns. Figure 25 shows the total return (share price and dividends) for the global energy and utility sectors since 2014. It highlights that other sectors that weren't subject to the threat of climate change policy provided better returns.[120]

Figure 25: There have been better investment sectors than energy and utilities.

Energy and utility sector, total market total returns
October 31, 2014 = 100

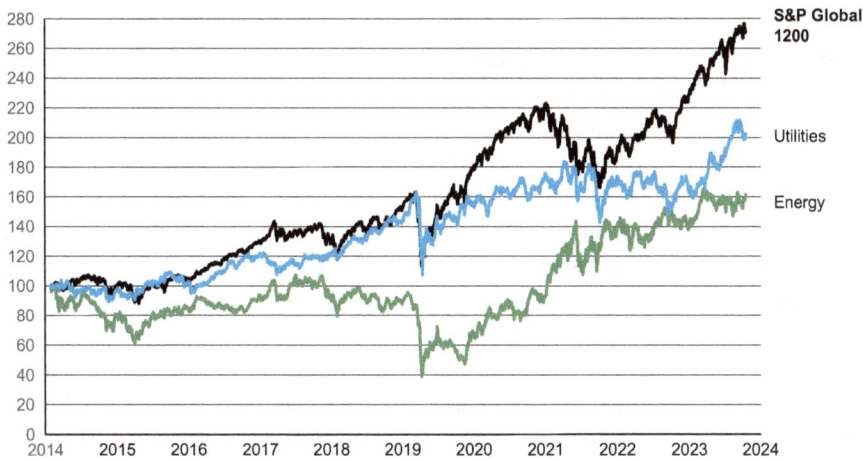

While such ESG trends are not critical for all companies, companies in the same sector tend to face the same issues, and some are better positioned than others to benefit from those trends. It is now the orthodox approach for fundamental investors to take a harder look at ESG trends, and to consider their threats and opportunities for a company's earnings growth.

Strengths and weaknesses: the Four Capitals return

Taking an ESG lens to a company's operating environment or market reveals the opportunities and threats it faces. An investor might next consider the company's strategy to both be resilient and then prosper in that market (that is, grow its earnings), and what strengths or weaknesses the company may have to execute that strategy. With this in mind, investors might look at the strengths and weaknesses of the company's four capitals. The company's growth in earnings is a measure of the financial return on all its capital, and will depend on the state of those capitals, how they are nurtured, and how well the company applies them toward its strategy and in managing risks.

An alternative way to look at all this capital is the stakeholder view of the company, as different capitals align with different sets of stakeholders. For example, human and intellectual capital encompass the relationship with employees, natural capital is the relationship with the environment, and social capital is the relationship with customers, suppliers, the community, or joint venture partners. Taking this approach, the investor might consider the role and materiality of each stakeholder relationship to its strategy, the quality of those relationships, and the systems or structures by which the company manages the relationships.

It may seem hard to measure the quality of these relationships or assets, but there are many direct and proxy indicators. For example, an investor might consider the human capital of a mining company by looking at metrics on staff turnover, staff engagement, safety performance, and the strategies it uses to attract and retain the people it needs. A retail phone company might need to create unique relationships with its customers, as it competes in a market where all retailers offer similar phones and service coverage. Again, metrics on the quality of the customer service or the number of complaints can be instructive. A metric such as the Net Promoter Score (NPS) will take dissatisfied customers into account. The cost to acquire customers is often a negative proxy for a retailer's reputation: the better the word-of-mouth, the less they need to spend. Similarly, metrics on the rate of customer churn are a negative proxy for the strength of customer relationships. And for all such metrics, as always, the question is not the actual number, but how it compares with competitors or other benchmarks, and whether the trend is to the good or otherwise.

Investors (and company executives) will consider the relevance of these metrics to both the company's strategy and the underlying capital or relationship. These may overlap with metrics for issues that are important to stakeholders, but they are not necessarily aligned. What a company needs to execute its strategy may not be material to its stakeholders, and vice versa. Nonetheless, and increasingly, the sweet spot is where doing well on a metric is important to both: the 'double materiality' we considered in Chapter 5.

Again, it is not enough to assess the strengths and weaknesses in its management of the four capitals. It requires an assessment of how the management of the four capitals will impact the company's ability to execute its strategy and manage risk. This needs to be reflected in the investment analyst's assessment of a company's earnings growth and risk and ultimately the analyst's assessment of the financial value of the company.

Considering Uncertainties – how confident is the investor in their analysis

The SWOT analysis described above identifies factors – such as climate change – that may impact a company's future earnings. An investment analyst may assess those factors to create a range of future earnings 'profiles', which are contingent on how the factors play out. The analyst then decides how confident they are that a factor may play out or not, which in turn leads to a level of certainty for a certain earnings profile and its implied company valuation. As the analysts consider more factors – climate change, trade tariffs, employment markets – they will create their own distribution of implied valuations. If the distribution is skewed to be higher than the current market price, the investor may decide to buy more of the stock, or go 'overweight' in the stock against the benchmark index. This process is exactly what is recommended in the TCFD guidelines for assessing the potential impact of climate change. It would be surprising if a fundamental investor chose to ignore its own assessments to align with the political zeitgeist of the day.

Quant investing

While fundamental investing sees a causation between ESG performance and financial performance, quant investing relies more on a correlation between the two. It seeks factors that are correlated to outperformance against a benchmark, for example, short-term price momentum, 'quality,' and 'growth'. ESG is just one of a range of factors the fund may target to seek outperformance at the portfolio level.

Again, a number of approaches have been taken by quant managers to integrate ESG. Some may 'tilt' their portfolios toward overall ESG performance, using data from ESG ratings agencies. Others may target one of the environmental, social, and governance scores, or even a particular E, S, or G characteristic, such as the number of women on company boards. They may also construct a portfolio where the greenhouse gas emission intensity of the portfolio, measured as tonnes CO_2-e/\$ market capitalization, say, is a given percent less than the fund's benchmark.

One of the challenges for quant investors, especially if they want to investigate a specific ESG characteristic, is finding ESG characteristics that are relevant across the whole market. It is rare that data for companies is comparable and that there is enough history to identify a statistically significant correlation between the ESG characteristic and company financial performance. For example, occupational health and safety performance may be a significant ESG issue for mining and industrial companies and, therefore a correlation worth investigating. However, it may not be as relevant for a software company, say. This does not mean that OH&S issues are not relevant to software companies, but that those metrics are not useful for investors.

Passive or index investing

Rather than selecting particular companies, passive investors focus on the larger macroeconomic trends of a country, region, or industry sector. Those trends are reflected in the performance of a particular index, for example, the FTSE350 or the MSCI Emerging Markets Index. A fund manager can then construct an investment portfolio of companies that, in aggregate, will match the performance of the relevant index. To match that performance and also allow people to buy and sell into the fund, the portfolio takes into account the size (market capitalization) of companies, their liquidity, and other factors. Once set, these passive (or index) funds can use relatively simple automated systems to trade shares in the portfolio so that the fund tracks the index. Since both the analysis and the trading are automated, the fees charged to invest in these funds tend to be relatively low.

This passive investing means you are investing in 'the good, the bad, and the ugly' from an ESG perspective. If the company meets the size and liquidity criteria, it will stay in the fund. Even if there are obvious governance issues, such as a dominant shareholder who overrides minority shareholder interests or a history of poor capital investment decisions, the index funds will keep their stake. Similarly, such funds ignore a company's exposure to climate change risks, both to their core business (fossil fuel companies) and to their operating assets (healthcare and tourism companies).

Now, indices are being developed that do consider climate change risk, as well as size and liquidity, to narrow the selection of companies in a fund. The EU has developed criteria to enable fund managers and index providers to develop funds or indices that are consistent with the EU's Paris Aligned Benchmark (PAB) and Climate Transition Benchmark (CTB). For example, the aggregate company emissions in a PAB index fund need to fall 50% faster than in the fund's parent index (all companies) in the first year of tracking and then fall 7% year-on-year. An index fund might require companies to adhere to the EU 'Do No Significant Harm' (DNSH) requirement or similar exclusion criteria. These benchmarks also benefit active investors who have Paris-aligned climate objectives, as they can assess their investment performance against a more relevant benchmark than the whole market index.

Over the long term, these more selective indices can be extremely useful for investors, despite shorter-term fluctuations, as they have different exposures to particular companies or sectors. Consider again Figure 25, this time looking at the period when the energy stocks almost caught up to the other stocks in 2022. When oil and gas prices rise, as they did as the global economy emerged from the COVID-19 pandemic and when Russia invaded Ukraine in 2022, oil and gas companies perform well. But over the longer term, as both regulation and innovation bite to help address climate change, a lower exposure to oil and gas companies may secure better returns – as well as direct capital to less polluting companies.[121]

Investing in debt

The approaches discussed above for equity investing can also apply to fixed-income investments. To date, though, investors in corporate debt have not developed their ESG approaches to the same level of sophistication as equity investors.

It is easiest to apply ESG principles in lending either to companies (corporate bonds) or to projects (structured finance). The lender may assess the ESG risks to these companies and projects in the same way as an equity investor might. However, as they have a fixed return on their investment, and no upside, they have less incentive to assess the ESG-related opportunities for the company to grow their business or revenues.

The more complex ways to invest in debt may demand a slightly different ESG assessment. Take, for example, securitized fixed income or asset-backed securities, such as bonds issued by banks to finance their lending portfolio. Typically, investors rely on credit rating agencies to assess the credit quality of these instruments, which usually means rating the credit quality of the bank.

As the global financial crisis showed (see Chapter 9), credit ratings may not fully disclose the underlying risks involved. Investors need a deeper ESG understanding of the companies or the assets to which the loans are being made. The GFC was triggered by housing loans made to people who could not afford to pay them back, secured by houses whose values fell below the amount loaned. Debt investors may benefit from a similar inquiry on climate change risk. A bank may have very limited greenhouse gas emissions from its operations, but may lend heavily to the resource and materials sectors, and so will have significant exposure to climate change risk. For debt investors to assess those underlying risks, they need to assess the bank's loan book – which not many banks are open to.

Similarly, bonds are issued by sovereign, supranational, and agency borrowers (such as the World Bank) to finance government debt or economic development. Again, ratings agencies issue credit ratings for these borrowers. Traditionally, they have focused on governance issues, such as the rule of law, the strength of legal and government institutions, and the level of government corruption. More recently, environmental and social issues have been considered when assessing sovereign bonds, especially for terms of 10 years or more. These issues include a country's reliance on fossil fuel royalties, exports, or imports,[122] its reliance on imported food, or its income and education inequality – all being indicators of risks to its long-term economic performance.

It is worth integrating ESG into investing

In Chapter 4, we noted a number of studies that confirmed how ESG considerations improved risk-weighted investment returns. This has held true across the different types of funds we have considered in this chapter. The best way to evaluate that performance is not to consider just one piece of research, but to draw on studies that have aggregated all the available studies into the subject.

One of the first of these 'meta-studies' was conducted back in 2015 by specialists from Deutsche Asset & Wealth Management and the University of Hamburg,[123] and offered an exhaustive, quantitative study of the entire universe of 2,250 published academic studies on ESG performance spanning four decades of data from 1970 to 2014. The analysis concluded that ESG correlated positively to corporate financial performance in 62.6% of studies and produced negative results in less than 10% of cases, with the remainder being neutral. The analysis of investment portfolios showed a less clear correlation between ESG and investment portfolio performance. However, it did identify a correlation for North America, Emerging Markets, and in nonequity asset classes.

Similar findings were produced by academics from New York University, Johns Hopkins University, and the Wharton School[124] in a 2022 meta-study. They surveyed 1141 primary peer-reviewed papers and 27 meta-reviews (based on ~1400 underlying studies) published between 2015 and 2020. They found the correlation between corporate ESG and financial performance to be positive in 60% of those studies, neutral or mixed in 34%, and negative in 6%. However, the correlation in investment performance was weaker: Of the studies, 38% found a positive correlation, 49% were neutral or mixed, and 13% were negative.

One of the challenges of meta-studies is distinguishing between the different types of funds that might be labeled as ESG Funds. As discussed further in Part D, there are funds that integrate ESG analysis in the way we have outlined in this chapter (assessing the performance of a company on several ESG factors), and there are funds that simply exclude or 'negative screen' companies and/or sectors for moral or ethical reasons. These negative-screen funds were the more typical of ESG funds prior to 2005, and their performance depends heavily on the companies or sectors they excluded. The 2022 meta-study specifically considered this distinction. It excluded studies on negative screen funds, and found that 59% of the studies on integrated funds, showed a positive impact on portfolio investment performance and only 3% showed a negative impact. The remaining studies found a neutral or mixed impact on investment performance.

Chapter 11 summary
  – To boil a complex market down to the essentials, investors invest in private (unlisted) assets or they can invest in public (listed) assets. They can invest in debt or equity. These ways of investing correspond to different levels of control and investment risk, and therefore different levels of interest in ESG factors.
  – Direct investors such as private equity firms and the founders and their families are typically long-term holders with the incentive and capacity to keep an eye on ESG risks and opportunities and respond to them.

- There are three main approaches to investing in listed assets: fundamental, quant, and passive. Each takes and uses ESG information differently.
- Fundamental investors look at a company's strategy, its strengths and weaknesses, the threats and opportunities it faces, and the uncertainties in their markets. ESG factors influence all of these aspects, so are typically part of their analysis.
- Quant investors try to find correlations between share price performance and other company factors. Increasingly, their computers look for correlations with ESG factors.
- Passive investors select and then follow an index by automatically buying and selling shares to maintain the number of shares in their portfolio that would track the chosen index. Unless the index itself is ESG-driven, passive investors have little interest in using ESG information in deciding what they will invest in.

Chapter 12
Money can talk if it wants to

Shareholder activism is not a privilege – it is a right and a responsibility. When we invest in a company, we own part of that company and we are partly responsible for how that company progresses.

Mark Mobius, Mobius Capital Partners LLP

In 2008, ExxonMobil was by far the biggest company in the US S&P 500, with a market capitalization of over US$455 billion.[125] By 2016 – which happened to be when 196 parties bound themselves to the Paris Agreement on limiting climate change – ExxonMobil had lost 25% of its market capitalization to be only the fifth largest company. By 2020, it had lost 60% of its heady 2008 valuation and was no longer in the top 20 companies. Its shareholders were far from impressed.

One of the best-known shareholder revolts against a company's board was hatched. A small investment firm, holding only 0.2% of ExxonMobil's shares in the name of 'Engine No.1', started a campaign to replace four directors. It made its case to larger shareholders in an initial letter in December 2020, citing:

- failure to position ExxonMobil for long-term value creation (particularly with respect to impact of climate change)
- rhetoric not addressing long-term business risk from greenhouse gas emissions
- lack of capital allocation discipline
- little reason to trust (the then) newfound spending discipline
- lack of successful and transformative energy experience on the board, and
- misaligned incentives.

Engine No. 1 kept gathering support in the lead-up to ExxonMobil's 2021 annual general meeting. The directors led what was undoubtedly one of the world's most influential oil and gas companies, able to have a say in global climate, economic, and development outcomes. However, the shareholders voted three of the four target directors off the board and replaced them with directors who were more alive to the scientific realities and corporate risks of climate change.

While ExxonMobil may still have a long way to go in addressing the threat of climate change, the 2021 shareholder revolt is a taste of what will continue to happen to companies that don't respond to investor concerns, and the power investors have to change the direction and strategies of even the largest of companies – if they so choose. This is just one example of how investors assert pressure on companies to limit or cease activity that erodes natural, social, or human capital, as well as poor governance practices that erode financial capital. They may wield that power with more or with less vigor, depending on the political mood and governance of their countries. But the power will remain.

https://doi.org/10.1515/9783111428949-016

In this chapter, we look into how investors assert pressure: by engaging with companies one-on-one, by engaging collectively with other investors, and by proposing and voting on shareholder resolutions. Ultimately, if there is no sign of the change they're looking for, they will sell or 'divest' their interests. That may be easy when the company is small, or its returns are poor. But it is happening even to larger companies, who represent a material share of an exchange's index, and are doing well financially.

Money has reason to talk

What would prompt investors to take such actions? As we saw in Part A, there are a number of potential drivers.

The first is investor enlightened self-interest. If they identify an ESG issue that is likely to have a material effect on the company's value, they will want the company to be managing it well. It makes sense then to engage with the company on how they are managing that risk, to improve or protect the return on their capital. On the whole, investors don't wish to be associated with harmful activity, as that directly erodes their own social capital.

The second is that large institutional investors such as superannuation or pension funds, with diverse investments across all asset classes, are 'universal investors' who are exposed to the entire national or global economy. Broad socioeconomic and environmental issues, therefore, will ultimately affect their long-term returns. Social cohesion, human rights, and inequality are such issues, as are access to affordable education, healthcare, and housing. Any of these ESG issues involve systemic investment risks or opportunities that require action across investments. Even if an issue seems immaterial to any one investment, it's liable to affect medium- to long-term portfolio returns across the portfolio. So it makes sense for institutions to make a stance across their investments.

Universal investors are also conscious that if a company saves money or pursues revenues in a way that leads to harm elsewhere, it is really just shifting the cost onto another investment, or simply degrading the four capitals available across a market. An extreme example is BP cutting costs in the operation of Deepwater Horizon (see Chapter 9), but the principle is commonplace among gambling, fossil fuel, alcohol, tobacco, and sugar drink companies, and companies in any industry with a culture of, for example, bullying, discrimination, or pollution. These activities directly erode the community's access to natural, social, and human capital.

Climate change has become the standout issue of interest to investors. As institutional investors have a fiduciary duty to their beneficiaries, they must manage material risks and opportunities in their investments. The material risks from climate change include risks to human health, immigration and security, coastlines, infrastructure, the environment, and agriculture. All of these may directly affect investment returns, not to mention the natural, social, and human capital on which those returns depend. Managing those risks is likely to mean changes in corporate behavior, and not acting may trigger additional regulatory and financial risks.

Similarly, large investors rely on the rule of law, without which market-based economies cannot operate, and so will fight against bribery and corruption that undermines that rule of law. An example is the listed Brazilian oil company Petrobras that paid kickbacks to politicians and executives of 3% on each major contract between 2004 and 2012. In 2015, it had to announce an impairment charge of US$14.8 billion to reflect the decreased value of its assets and a US$2 billion charge for costs related to corruption.[126] Its share price dropped by over 80%.

Petrobras wasn't the only Brazilian company allegedly involved in bribery and corruption this century. The construction company Odebrecht admitted in a plea agreement with the US Department of Justice that it and its co-conspirators had paid some US$788 million in bribes, on 100 public infrastructure projects in 12 countries.[127] What came to be known as Operacao Lava Jato (Operation Car Wash) and overlapping investigations led to prison sentences for top executives and politicians, mass layoffs, and billions of dollars paid in fines. The scandals undermined efforts to revive the economy amid Brazil's worst recession in more than a century. As the political crisis worsened, investment levels and consumer confidence suffered, leading to a 3.9% drop in GDP in 2015 and another 3.6% decrease the following year.[128]

These are exactly the type of crises that universal investors are keen to avoid, hence their enthusiasm for legal compliance, and their engagement with companies to ensure the rule of law is not undermined. Some ESG investors engaged with their fund managers as the Petrobras-Odebrecht scandals grew and divested from the key players. Other investors inflicted more pain on the companies by participating in class actions against them.

One may argue that it's the role of government to address these issues. Indeed, governments have a duty to protect their people against human rights infringements by nonstate players, and to establish ways to defend against or in the end prosecute against those breaches. These obligations are laid out in the UN Guiding Principles on Business and Human Rights.[129] However, it's usually much cheaper to avoid a harm in the first place than to remedy it later. When governments and societies have to allocate money and time to bear the cost, they miss opportunities to fulfill their ambitions and obligations elsewhere, which in turn reduces economic growth and overall investor returns.

Accordingly, global investors will engage with governments to ensure that appropriate policy and regulation exist to protect human rights and the rule of law, and to take action on climate change. With those regulations in place, companies have the direct legal duty – on top of their ethical and long-term fiduciary duties – to build the cultures and structures needed for compliance, wherever they may operate.

Engaging one-on-one

Increasingly, listed equity investors engage with companies on a one-on-one basis, either as part of periodic briefings or to dig deeper into a particular ESG issue. **Equity investors** have the opportunity in many countries to have regular meetings with company boards and management to monitor progress, identify issues, and ensure that the governance processes are in place to manage them. Sometimes, investors in private companies have seats on the board. ESG issues will be on the table throughout those discussions.

The success of these one-on-one engagements may be difficult to assess and may depend on other investors engaging on the same issue. Changes in company practices are rarely if ever attributable to engagement by one investor. But they can drive real results. CCLA is a relatively small UK fund manager, with GBP 14.9 billion assets under management. Since 2021, it has benchmarked 100 leading global companies on how they are managing the mental health of their employees and contractors, and engaged with those companies on their progress.[130] This effort has successfully raised mental health as an investment issue, provided a framework for companies and investors to assess and track company performance, and a structured approach for investors to engage with companies on mental health. By May 2024, the benchmark was used by a coalition of investors, representing US$9.4 trillion of assets, who are signatories to the CCLA Corporate Mental Health Benchmark.

For **passive investors**, engaging with companies, or investment stewardship, as it is also called, is one of the few levers they have to influence companies. The approach they take can vary significantly. Take, for example, the big three passive fund managers. Vanguard[131] sticks to traditional corporate issues like board composition and effectiveness, board oversight of strategy and risk, executive compensation, and shareholder rights. State Street[132] and BlackRock[133] may engage on broader issues such as climate and natural capital. Whatever the scope of the engagement, the focus of all three is the same. Engagement, through letters and meetings with management and the board, seeks to focus on the issues that, if not addressed, reduce the investors' ability to deliver long-term financial returns and so meet their fiduciary role as asset managers. They prefer to engage diplomatically, as an owner, and not with a megaphone. They may not support action on every ESG issue raised by stakeholders, nor blindly support everything the company does. As a result, they have been called the 'meat in the political sandwich' during the antiwoke debates of the 2020s.

Pension and superannuation funds also engage with companies one-on-one. Like passive index managers, they are typically long-term owners of the company and see engagement as an important part of their fiduciary duty to look after the long-term returns of their members. This is true irrespective of what their underlying fund managers may do.

Debt investors generally have less access to the issuing company and they and **quant investors** do not tend to engage with them directly on ESG issues, but this is also changing over time.

Engaging alongside other investors

Needless to say, the thousands of shareholders on a listed company's register are not a homogeneous group with the same interests and expectations. (As an aside, that fact makes the director's duty to act 'in the best interest of shareholders' quite a challenge, as there is no single 'interest of shareholders'.) There are, however, issues on which many investors share a common view. It is more effective for both the company and shareholders if like-minded investors work together and send the company a common and consistent message.

One of the largest collective engagement initiatives is Climate Action 100+ (CA100+), launched in 2017.[134] The 700 institutional investors in CA100+ engage with over 170 companies in the MSCI All Country World Index that are responsible for up to two-thirds of all carbon dioxide emissions from the companies in that Index. The initiative asks these companies to:

- implement a strong governance framework that clearly articulates the board's accountability and oversight of climate change risk
- take action to reduce greenhouse gas emissions across the value chain (including engagement with policymakers) in line with the Paris Agreement's goal of limiting global average temperature increase to well below 2°C above preindustrial levels, moving toward net-zero emissions by 2050 or sooner, and
- share their plans to deliver on those targets, in line with the Task Force on Climate-related Financial Disclosures (TCFD) recommendations.

Investor signatories of CA100+ can either lead or support engagement with a particular company to encourage them to act on climate change.

Why do so many institutional investors worry about climate change? As mentioned earlier, institutional investors have a fiduciary duty to manage material financial risks and opportunities, including medium- and long-term financial risks. Pension and superannuation funds have members with a range of ages. The investment returns of those in their twenties or thirties, expecting to retire in another 30 or 40 years, will be affected by global warming, one way or another. Companies are changing their operations, and countries their economies, to meet commitments to act on climate change. Those actions will materially change investment returns, for better or for worse, depending on how investors take them into account. If, on the other hand, there is no action on climate change, there will still be material financial risks from the physical impacts of climate change. So, climate change is a systemic investment risk. Large institutional investors cannot manage the systemic risk simply by selling shares in companies that are most exposed to climate change impacts. They have to address the underlying risk itself, and that is best done collaboratively.

Signatories to CA100+ and similar initiatives develop expertise and processes to make that collaboration and their engagement with companies more effective. For example, CA100+ has developed a Net Zero Benchmark to assess company performance on emissions reduction, governance, and disclosure. It looks at the company's climate-related accounting practices and disclosures, and whether their climate policy actions (both direct and through their industry associations) align with the Paris Agreement goals. It sets specific expectations for sectors such as electric utilities, steel, food and beverage, and aviation. These approaches give both investors and the companies a deeper understanding of climate issues, and what might be done about them.

Investor collaboration is not limited to climate change. Broad alliances have been formed nationally and internationally to take effective action on specific issues, or indeed on any ESG issue of investor concern. For example:

- The Australian Council of Superannuation Investors (ACSI)[135] engages with ASX-listed companies on material ESG issues such as board diversity, workforce and corporate culture, and corporate governance.
- EOS,[136] part of Federated Hermes, provides engagement and stewardship services to global asset owners, engaging on their behalf with companies around the world on material ESG issues.
- The Farm Animal Investment Risk and Return Initiative[137] (FAIRR) raises awareness of the ESG risks and opportunities in the global food sector.
- Mining 2030[138] seeks to define a vision for a socially and environmentally responsible mining sector, and to develop a consensus about the role of finance in realizing this vision.
- Advance[139] seeks to advance human rights and positive outcomes for people through investor stewardship.
- The Global Investor Coalition on Workplace Mental Health[140] works on improving corporate approaches to workplace mental health.

Engaging with governments

Investor engagement isn't limited to companies. The PRI leads the Collaborative Sovereign Engagement on Climate Change, aiming to engage with national governments, regulators and authorities, and subsovereign agencies on climate change. Apart from the obvious role of governments creating a policy environment that supports climate action by the private sector, investors hold nearly US$60 trillion in sovereign debt. The ability of a sovereign government to make interest payments and repay the debt depends in part on a country's economic performance and credit rating, which in turn depends in part on its effective action on climate change.

The evidence is that this collective engagement action works, and so institutional investors continue to launch and join collaborative efforts. For example, the 2023 Progress Report of CA100+ reported a significant two-year increase by focus companies in the three target areas:

- 77% now commit to net zero by 2050 or sooner across at least Scope 1 and 2 emissions
- 93% have board committee oversight of climate change risks and opportunities, and
- 90% explicitly commit to aligning their disclosures with the TCFD recommendations.

The US political environment in 2025 has meant that investor appetite to join collaborative actions has eased. It is unlikely to cease, as it is an effective and efficient means of engaging in critical issues.

Another example of effective collective engagement followed the tailings dam collapses in Brazil in 2015 and 2019; see Chapter 9 above. At the time, there was no global public register of these tailings storage facilities (TSFs), so the nature and scale of risks to communities and investors were unclear – there was no way of easily knowing which companies were responsible for which facilities. The Church of England Pensions Board and Swedish Council on Ethics for AP Funds took the initiative to write to 655 publicly listed mining companies asking for details of their TSFs.[141] The mining companies responded, because the English and Swedish bodies were backed by the UN PRI, whose members manage over $25 trillion in invested funds. The letter led to companies identifying over 18,000 TSFs worldwide, of which 3500 were currently active, then to a public global database of those TSFs, and finally to a Global Industry Standard on Tailings Management. Eighty-one mining companies have committed to that Standard, and a further 23 to a similar standard.[142]

Working together is legal

Part of the backlash against ESG is a claim that this collaborative engagement is actually anticompetitive, breaching long-held rules against corporate collusion. In most countries, laws prohibit practices that intend to prevent, restrict, or distort competition, or have that effect. The most serious breaches involve companies exchanging competitively sensitive information and coordinating their strategic behavior to keep out competitors or deceive consumers.

In general, collective engagement on ESG issues does not breach these rules. It is no different from other areas where an industry considers a policy or economic issue that is relevant to all players. The PRI (which hosts numerous collective engagements through its website)[143] has obtained legal opinion to confirm that collective engagement would not trouble competition laws – if it did, then so would the activity of any industry association. The constraint, as always, is that participants do not ask for or exchange confidential market-sensitive information about each other's businesses.

As there is always more to do, institutional investors will continue to pursue changes to protect and nurture economy-wide social, human, and natural capital.

Proxy voting and shareholder resolutions

A listed company's annual general meeting (AGM) provides a unique opportunity for investors to engage. They can hear from and directly question the Board and the CEO on ESG issues, and they can vote on company resolutions, director elections, and in many cases the CEO's remuneration structures. However, AGM voting can be a very blunt engagement approach for investors, so they typically combine their vote with other action.

Having a say on 'standard' resolutions

The resolutions put to AGMs are usually drafted by the Board and are limited in scope: for example, on director elections, or on capital raises, or mergers and acquisitions. By voting against the Chair's recommended view on a resolution or director, the investor may publicly signal that directors are not representing the views of their shareholders. As a result, the Chair and other directors may seek to spend time with investors, to understand and address their concerns before they're aired at the AGM.

When investors do vote, the limited voting options restrict and may sometimes disguise what the investor really means. A 'Yes' vote may not necessarily mean investors are completely happy with what is being proposed. An 'Abstain' or 'No' vote may mean that investors aren't happy with what's being proposed, but gives no message to the company about why they've voted that way, nor what they really expect of the company.

To make their intentions clear, investors might engage with the company or even make public how they are going to vote on a resolution, and why. And while it's possible to try and raise the issue at the AGM, the very nature of the AGM makes meaningful dialogue all but impossible. Investors may also choose to write to the company on why they voted the way they did, and what their expectations are, but none of these actions, of themselves, are likely to shift the company dial.

Shareholder resolutions on governance issues

A more direct proposition is for investors to propose their own AGM resolutions on specific ESG issues. These resolutions are difficult for companies to handle if they have significant support and can be devastating if they have majority support.

In March 2023, a number of North American investors put a shareholder resolution to the Starbucks AGM, asking the company to undertake an independent assessment of its labor practices. In particular, the investors wanted to confirm "Starbucks' adherence to its stated commitment to workers' freedom of association and collective bargaining rights as contained in the International Labour Organization's Core Labor

Standards and as explicitly referenced in the company's Global Human Rights Statement."[144] The resolution received 52% support.

Starbucks engaged with those filing the resolution and prepared a report for the AGM. If the company thought that would be the end of the matter, they were mistaken. The investors were not impressed, noting that the report had no input from workers and therefore lacked credibility. In November 2023, a union-backed investment fund (SOC Investment Group) announced it was seeking to get three directors onto the Starbucks board. These included the former chair of the US National Labor Relations Board, the independent agency safeguarding employee rights to be represented by unions and remedying unfair labor practices in the private sector.[145] These directors really knew what 'freedom of association and collective bargaining' meant, and how to enforce them.

Starbucks had no choice but to write a letter to the union acknowledging that they had reached an impasse over how to even conduct collective bargaining, let alone any substantive issues. They wanted to restart collective bargaining negotiations with the union, 'in good faith and with mutual respect'.[146] As a result, SOC withdrew their nominees.

One might think that shareholder resolutions such as these are a new phenomenon – a fresh challenge to usurp the responsibilities of the board or company management. Yet the USA has a long history of shareholder resolutions, particularly on governance-related issues. They took off after the 2002 Sarbanes-Oxley Act was passed after financial scandals involving publicly traded companies like Enron Corporation, Tyco International plc, and WorldCom shook investor confidence in US corporate governance. As with many business and legal trends, what started as a US practice is becoming more common in Europe, Asia, and Australia.

Just putting forward a shareholder resolution is a strong signal to the Board that the company is not addressing an issue adequately. A majority vote in favor of the resolution is an even stronger message. Many resolutions are not so strongly supported – shareholders may well agree with the intent of the resolution, but not with its specifics, and may abstain or vote against it.

Yet even less well-supported resolutions can and do create change. Having similar resolutions on the same issue over a number of years and across a number of companies can bring about awareness, discussion, and eventual acceptance of an issue. As a result, it is not unusual for shareholders to campaign until their particular expectation has been adopted broadly, either voluntarily by most companies or by law. These include having a greater say on CEO remuneration, securing an independent chair, preventing 'poison pill' provisions that deter takeovers, and allowing for special resolutions and meetings with supermajority voting; see Figure 26.

One example is the many resolutions that eventually led to a majority vote being the standard for the election of directors in US-listed companies; see Figure 27. Before this, directors were elected using plurality voting – meaning the nominees who receive the most 'for' votes are elected to the board, until all board seats are filled. This

Figure 26: Consistent volumes of shareholder proposals have led to better governance.

Volumes of filings of select governance shareholder proposals

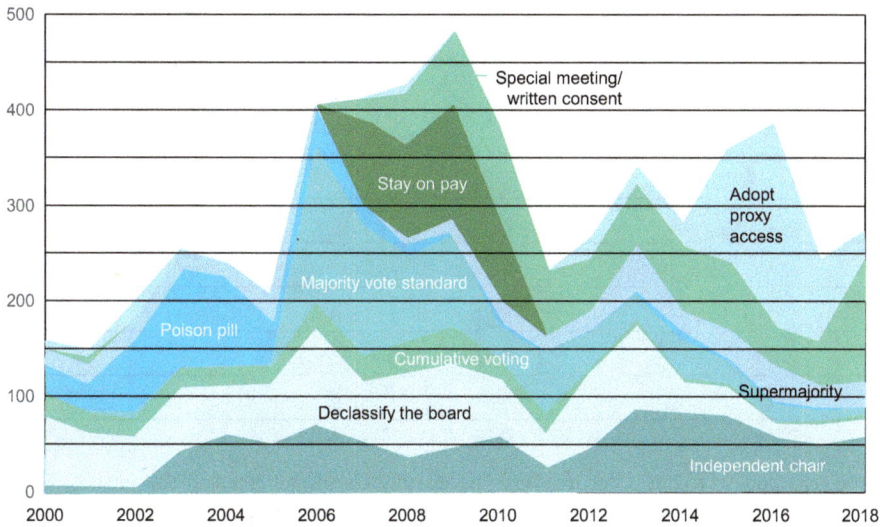

Source: Papadopoulos K (2019), 'The Long View: The Role of Shareholder Proposals in Shaping U.S. Corporate Governance (2000-2018)', Harvard Law School Forum on Corporate Governance, https://corp gov.law.harvard.edu/2019/02/06/the-long-view-the-role-of-share holder-proposals-in-shaping-u-s-corpo rate-governance-2000-2018/ accessed 19 November 2024.

is an issue where the number of nominees and available board seats are the same – every nominee can be elected after receiving just one vote! That's not a great sign that the directors would represent all shareholders and act in the best interest of the company.

As shareholder resolutions are not proposed by the company, directors prefer them not to be put to a vote. Some get withdrawn by negotiation between the company, 'activist' shareholders, and other shareholders. If the shareholders are satisfied that the company has, or promises to, act in a way consistent with the intent of the resolution, they may withdraw it, as was the Starbucks resolution above. In the USA, companies can also appeal to the SEC to get no-action relief so that a resolution can be omitted from the AGM. The number of shareholder resolutions omitted in this way has decreased over time but varies from year to year, in part due to political influence placed on the SEC. Nonetheless, most shareholder resolutions do get put to shareholders.

Figure 27: The majority vote becomes standard in less than a decade.

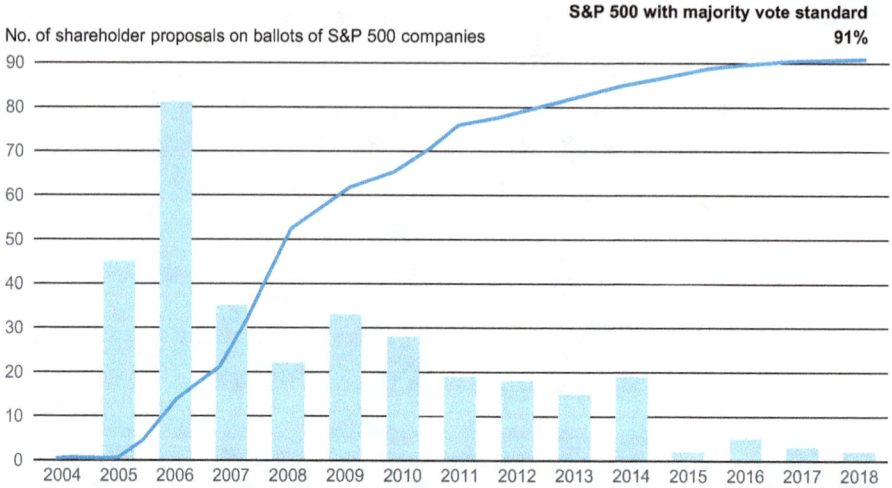

No. of shareholder proposals on ballots of S&P 500 companies

S&P 500 with majority vote standard
91%

Source: Papadopoulos K (2019), 'The Long View: The Role of Shareholder Proposals in Shaping U.S. Corporate Governance (2000-2018)', Harvard Law School Forum on Corporate Governance, https://corp gov.law.harvard.edu/2019/02/06/the-long-view-the-role-of-share holder-proposals-in-shaping-u-s-corpo rate-governance-2000-2018/ accessed 24 November 2024.

Shareholder resolutions on environmental or social issues

The USA also has a strong history of shareholder resolutions on environmental or social issues, which typically require the company to report to shareholders on how it manages risks, a trend which saw 607 such resolutions being proposed in 2022 in the USA; see Figure 28. Climate change and political influence are outstanding issues, though human rights, working conditions, and workplace diversity are each becoming as common. If a resolution is put to a vote, the board typically recommends that investors vote against it. Increasingly, however, the resolution may be advisory; larger institutional investors may support it, and the company will take that advice on board. Of a record 282 ESG-focused proposals voted on in 2022, thirty-four won majority support.[147]

Elsewhere, the placement and negotiation of resolutions reflect the prevailing relationship between institutional investors and companies. For example, Asian and Australian institutional investors typically have had far greater access to company boards and management, and have less confrontational relationships with them. Issues are raised behind closed doors by individual investors wanting to work with the company to address an issue. In Europe, investors are a little more willing to push for a resolution, but issues may also be more likely to be raised on the board by independent and stakeholder representatives.

Figure 28: Workplace conditions now outnumbering environmental resolutions.

Total, and breakdown of the number of proposals filed (as of 1 August 2023)

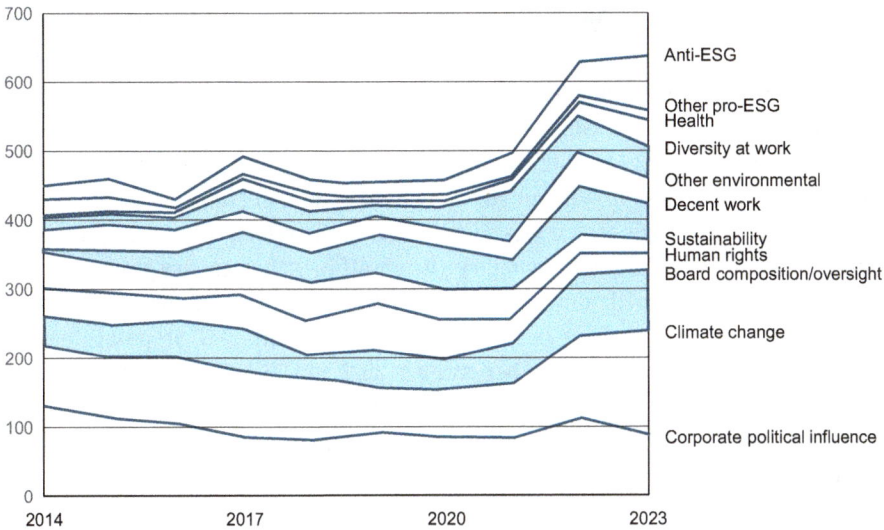

Source: Welsh H (2023), 'Assessing Anti-ESG Efforts in the 2023 Proxy Season', Sustainable Investments Institute, https://siinstitute.org/reports.html accessed 25 November 2024.

In response to shareholder pressures, companies are now putting their own environmental resolutions to AGMs, particularly on carbon transition plans, to get the approval of shareholders on the company's proposed approach. Since 2021, companies might present a climate action transition plan to outline their proposals to align with the Paris Climate Change Agreement. These resolutions are typically well supported by shareholders, reflecting the previous engagement between shareholders and the company, through initiatives such as CA100+. However, there have been some notable examples where the company has seriously misjudged shareholder expectations. For example, in 2023, over 30% of shareholders voted against Glencore's Climate Report,[148] and in 2024, over 25% rejected Sasol's climate report.[149]

The Australian oil and gas company Woodside Petroleum has had a continuing debate with many of its investors, starting with the 2022 surprise 49% vote against its Climate Report.[150] By 2024, over 58% of investors voted against its Climate Transition Action Plan (CTAP) and 2023 Progress Report.[151] Two triggers for shareholder disapproval were over emission reduction targets: Woodside's use of carbon offsets to meet Scope 1 and 2 targets (rather than reducing emissions in operations), and the lack of any substantive target to reduce Scope 3 emissions. A third trigger was more problematic, with Woodside's plan including continued investment in new oil and gas fields, inconsistent with the International Energy Association's assessment that, if the world is to reach net zero by 2050, no new oil or gas fields should be developed.[152]

While casting a protest vote together, investors had differing reasons. Some took the holistic view of the risk that climate change poses to the world economy and recognized that each fossil fuel company needed to demonstrate they are acting to help minimize that risk. Others took the harder-nosed view that Woodside's CTAP did not demonstrate the effective management of climate risk: the carbon credits were not seen as an effective long-term solution. Without effective management of risk, these shareholders didn't know whether their capital was going to attract the returns expected from an oil and gas company, or whether they would be better off with their money elsewhere.

There has been a reaction to the increase in ESG-related resolutions to companies. As seen in Figure 28, there have been a small number of 'anti-ESG' proposals to company AGMs since 2014 with the number rising in 2022 and 2023. The Si2 report[153] identified that most of these 'anti-ESG' resolutions questioned the wisdom of encouraging racial and ethnic diversity on boards and in the workplace. However, the resolutions secured less than 2% support; see Figure 29.

Figure 29 also shows the average support for 'pro-ESG' resolutions has decreased since the peak in 2021. There are a number of reasons cited for this. One is that investment managers are deciding to be less activist in their voting as a response to the ESG backlash and threats against fund managers, by some US states, to withdraw investment mandates. This is discussed in more detail below. A second reason, and one espoused by the large US fund managers Vanguard and BlackRock, is that some resolutions have become overly prescriptive. Whatever the reason, shareholder resolutions still remain an important part of the way shareholders engage with companies.

Divesting

There are regular calls for investors to divest of (sell their shares in) companies with clearly negative environmental or social impacts. Nongovernmental organizations in particular call for divestment and some have a specific objective of galvanizing divestment of companies involved in particular industries.

Tobacco Free Portfolios[154] advances tobacco-free finance to bring an end to the world's greatest cause of preventable death. Their Tobacco Free Pledge has over 210 signatories, that collectively manage US$18 trillion in assets, lend over US$2.6 trillion, and write over US$268.5 billion in insurance premiums. Another organization, 350.org, describes itself as an international movement of ordinary people working to end the age of fossil fuels and build a world of community-centered renewable energy for all. Its "Go Fossil Free" divestment campaign is designed to "systematically challenge the political power of the fossil fuel industry, create uncertainty about the long-term financial viability of the industry, and move money away from dirty energy towards

Figure 29: Despite the backlash, pro-ESG resolutions still gain 10 times the support of anti-ESG resolutions.

Average support for pro-and anti-ESG resolutions, US listed companies
Percent of votes

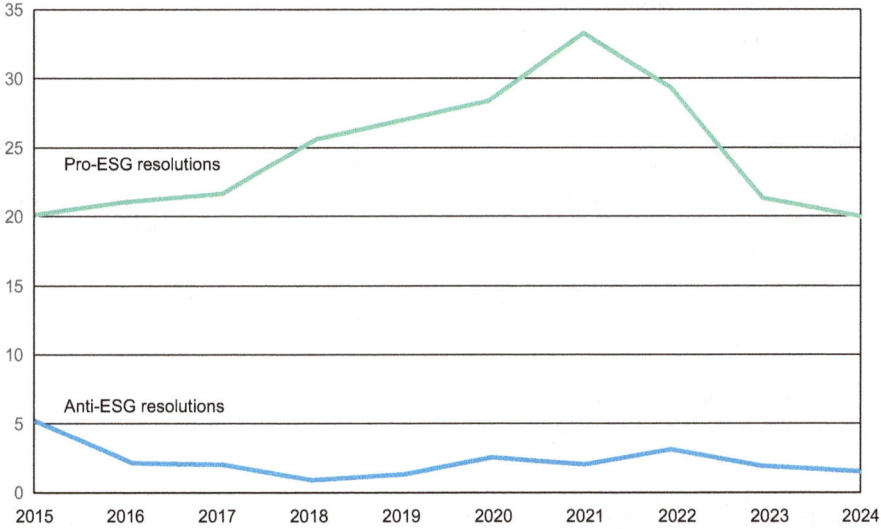

Source: Welsh H (2024), 'Long-term Trends for Pro-and Anti-ESG Shareholder Proposals', Sustainable Investments Institute, https://siinstitute.org/reports.html accessed 25 November 2024.

climate solutions."[155] It cites, with enthusiasm, Norway's Sovereign Wealth Fund, the largest single owner in the world's stock markets, which excludes "mining companies that derive 30% or more of their revenue from coal or produce more than 20 million tonnes of thermal coal per year, and power companies that derive 30% or more of their revenue from coal-based power generation or have coal-based power generation capacity of more than 10,000 MW."[156]

The fact that the Norwegian Sovereign Wealth Fund divests a company – or in this case an industry – certainly makes headlines. But does it really change anything in the real world? It depends. Of itself, selling shares in a coal mining company does nothing to reduce greenhouse gas emissions or reduce the amount of coal mined; all that has happened is a change in ownership of the shares. However, if enough investors sell that puts downward pressure on the share price, raises the cost of capital, and makes it more difficult to attract capital. That means there's less money available to fund activities that cause real-world harm.

Similarly, buying shares in a company shown to have a positive environmental impact does not in itself cause a positive impact. However, if a large number of investors do so, the share price will likely rise. The higher share price can make it easier for the company to raise more capital, and to invest in more activities that may lead to real-world benefits.

For many ESG investors, while divestment is a last resort, the preferred action is in retaining ownership. That way, they can raise questions directly with the company, engage with other shareholders, press for resolutions, and directly influence how that company operates in the real world. Once they have sold their shares, all of that influence disappears.

Chapter 12 Summary
- Institutional (or large) investors engage with companies and industries to prevent any unnecessary erosion of natural, social, or human capital. They have a financial interest in doing so, as that capital underpins their investments across the whole economy; any erosion of it reduces the potential for their future returns.
- Mostly, these investors engage one-on-one with those companies. They approach it diplomatically, as an owner of the company, and not with a megaphone. Sometimes, however, they will be more vocal, or even take legal action to ensure that a company responds to an ESG issue it is facing.
- Often investors find it more efficient and effective to work collaboratively to change the practices of a company or a sector. Some of the largest collective engagement initiatives are facilitated by the UN Principles of Responsible Investment and Climate Action 100+ (CA100+).
- Large and small investors can express their views on a company's approach to an ESG issue by filing a resolution to be put before a company meeting, by voting and speaking at such a meeting, or by voting out directors who have not taken appropriate action. These resolutions become more common when there are large-scale failures of governance in a company – such as occurred through the GFC.

Chapter 13
Crossing the line: Greenwashing and the ESG backlash

Greenwashing is a problem. That's why the practice of just sticking a label like ESG on a company or a project isn't good enough.

Hendrith Vanlon Smith Jr., CEO of Mayflower-Plymouth

The global consultancy PwC estimates that the amount of money investors will be prepared to place in ESG-related funds will reach US$33.9 trillion, up from US$18.4 trillion in 2021, at a compound annual growth of 12.9%.[157] Naturally, more and more funds seek to make themselves eligible for these flows. Some may gild the lily of their ESG credentials. That's the natural rhythm of capitalism: an opportunity arises, and it's pursued by both innovators and opportunists.

That natural rhythm then predictably split into several counterpoint beats. First to join in was the regulator section of the band, keeping an eye on the ESG claims being made. When fund managers made false claims about the sectors excluded from their portfolio, or on the social or environmental impact they had, regulators were bound to act against this 'greenwashing'. They were supported by PRI-member investors who were doing the right thing, who also support extending broad 'misleading and deceptive conduct' to explicit regulation against greenwashing.

For example, in June 2022, German authorities raided the office of Deutsche Bank and its subsidiary DWS over greenwashing of its ESG financial products. The DWS CEO resigned the day after the raid and, over a year later, DWS agreed to pay the US Securities and Exchange Commission (SEC) US$19 million to settle charges of making misleading statements about their ESG products – greenwashing.

Not surprisingly, the finance and investment sector is not the only one accused of greenwashing. RepRisk has looked at the number of companies, not just financial or investment companies, linked to misleading the public about their environmental impact since 2019.[158] In 2024, the banking and financial services sector made up approximately 10% of identified companies at risk of greenwashing, with companies in the oil and gas sector responsible for the most identified cases.

There's some evidence that the extent of greenwashing has plateaued as a result of greater regulatory scrutiny, though concerns have not gone away. In 2024, most of the companies (70%) identified as being at risk of greenwashing were private companies. RepRisk found that over 1100 companies were at risk of greenwashing in the EU in 2023, about double those in the USA or Asia; see Figure 30.

https://doi.org/10.1515/9783111428949-017

Figure 30: Companies are being penalized for misleading communication.

Companies at risk of greenwashing
No. of companies

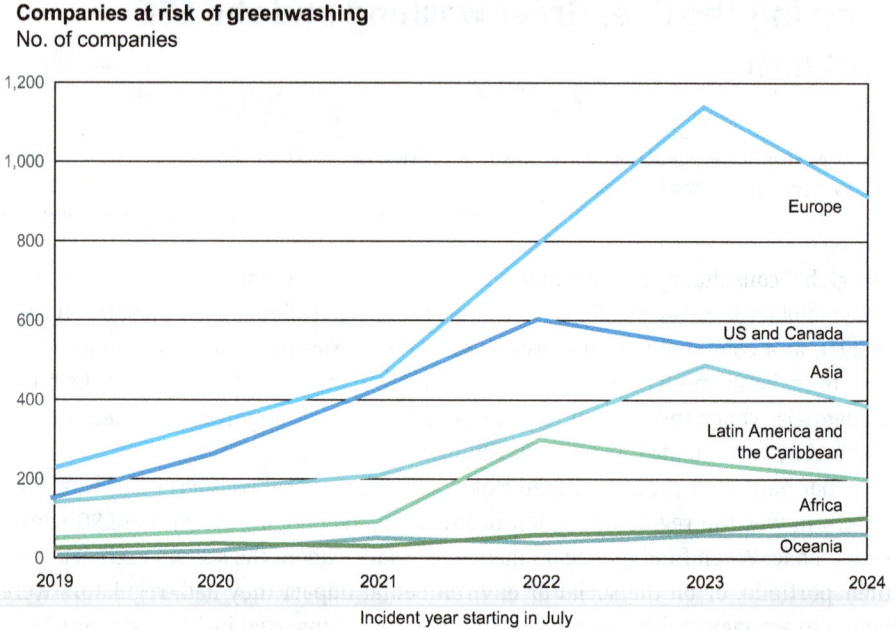

Source: RepRisk (2024), 'A turning tide in greenwashing? Exploring the first decline in six years', https://www.reprisk.com/research-insights/reports/a-turning-tide-in-greenwashing-exploring-the-first-decline-in-six-years#ix-banking-and-financial-servicessector-sees-a-20-global-drop-in-climate-related-greenwashing accessed 25 November 2024.

Common forms of greenwashing

Simply put, investment greenwashing is to misrepresent the extent to which a financial product or investment strategy is environmentally friendly, sustainable, or ethical. From a legal perspective, it is no different from a company making incorrect claims about a product and is typically covered by laws dealing with misleading and deceptive conduct. We'll look at the different types of greenwashing here.

Misleading claims in portfolio construction

A negative screen is one in which a fund manager says to its investors that it will not allocate funds to a particular type of company. While that may seem straightforward, you only have to scratch the surface to see how greenwashing may arise.

Say a fund claims that it doesn't invest in tobacco. That claim would obviously be misleading if the fund invests in companies that grow tobacco or market cigarettes. But what about a company that markets vapes, or transports cigarettes, or a retailer that sells cigarettes – even if that trade represents less than 1% of its total revenue? To overcome this, a fund may say that the screen only applies to certain parts of the value chain (e.g., production) or where the involvement is nontrivial, amounting to more than 10% of revenue, for example. In these cases, the fund's small print can clarify expectations.

There are more challenging examples, perhaps a fund claiming to be 'fossil fuel free'. Its fine print could similarly limit investments to companies that extract or process fossil fuels. However, does it remain 'fossil fuel free' if it invests in pipelines to transport natural gas, or tollways or airports that depend on fossil fuel combustion, or even banks that lend to fossil fuel companies? In such cases, clear communication should again be the answer, allowing investors to make their own decisions on where to draw the line. But you can see the challenge for fund managers in trying to communicate a key characteristic of a fund without having to rely on pages of small print.

And then there are the clear-cut cases of misleading conduct. The Australian corporate regulator ASIC launched court action against Mercer Superannuation (Australia) Limited for "allegedly making misleading statements about the sustainable nature and characteristics of some of its superannuation investment options". The fund was marketed as suitable for members who 'are deeply committed to sustainability' because they excluded investments in companies involved in carbon-intensive fossil fuels like thermal coal, alcohol production, and gambling. However, ASIC found that the fund invested in 15 companies involved in the extraction or sale of such fossil fuels, 15 companies that helped produce alcohol, and 19 companies involved in gambling. ASIC won the court action and Mercer was required to pay an A$11.3 million penalty, plus legal costs.[159]

Overstating the impact

Another area of greenwashing is where a fund in listed equities overstates the positive impact it's having, for example, on climate change or in support of one of the UN Sustainable Development Goals (SDGs). The implication of the claim is that money invested in the fund is creating an impact. As noted earlier, investments in listed equities give the share owner a small slice of the company. Money is transferred from the buyer to the seller of the share. This transaction in itself changes nothing; there has been no impact in the real world. There could be, if the fund uses its shareholding to engage with the company to change its ways, but that is a different matter. It's not inappropriate for an investor to communicate that it has an exposure, through their share portfolio, to a company making a positive impact. However, the 'exposure' is the keyword rather than the 'impact' of the investment.

The RepRisk report[160] cited above identified that, for 2024, climate change and greenhouse gas emissions were the environmental issues most linked to greenwashing, with impacts on landscapes, ecosystems, and biodiversity coming in second. On a more positive note, the number of these misrepresentations decreased significantly in 2024 compared to 2023.

Responses to greenwashing

In all new markets, there are genuine businesses who look to establish a long-term brand and build up market structures, so that their business and the market itself are sustainable. Opportunists are those who seek to cut corners and mislead people before a market is properly understood, and they are the ones who damage the market the most. They can expect a strong response from regulators, especially from the bona fide industry, which is exactly what is happening in response to the problem of greenwashing. This is in addition to standard consumer protection laws, under which fund managers can be prosecuted for misleading and deceptive conduct in their dealings with retail investors.

The resulting pressure is for investment firms to report on their ESG approaches, increase their accountability for ESG claims, and enable consumers to make an informed investment choice. For institutional investors, these disclosures are very effective. It remains to be seen whether retail investors – who are guided more by marketing materials and financial product disclosures – are similarly protected.

Regulatory responses to greenwashing

Since 2010, there's been an explosion in the regulatory requirements for investors to disclose ESG information, mainly in the European Union but increasingly elsewhere. The PRI has a database of these sustainable finance regulations and policies, which reached 59 in October 2021; see Figure 31.[161]

The EU's Sustainable Finance Disclosure Regulation (SFRD) is the leading regulatory attempt to guard against greenwashing, in a way that helps both retail and institutional investors, and both equity and debt investors. It's linked to a taxonomy of activities that outlines activities considered to be environmentally sustainable.[162] Under the SFRD, asset managers reveal how and the extent to which sustainability (read ESG) is integrated into their funds. They must first label themselves as either an Article 6 fund (no integration at all), an Article 8 fund ('environmentally and socially promoting'), or an Article 9 fund (targeting sustainable investments, with an index as a reference benchmark). They must then disclose how sustainability risks might impact financial performance, how the product considers those risks, and how they monitor, measure, and assess their sustainability impact. To do this, the mandatory Principal Adverse Impact (PAI) statement consists of 18 indicators and two extra ones chosen from 46 options.

Figure 31: ESG reporting instruments rise to counteract the threat of greenwashing.

Corporate and investment-related instruments
No. of instruments

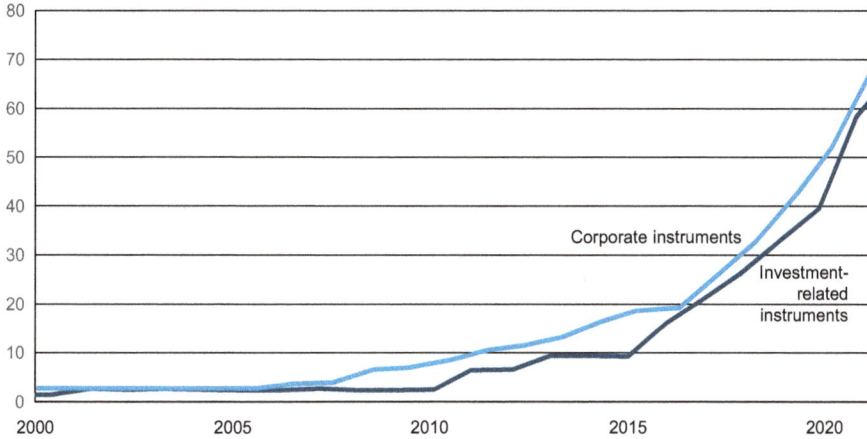

Source: Principles of Responsible Investment (2022), 'Review of the trends in ESG Reporting Requirements for Investors' https://www.unpri.org/driving-meaningful-data/review-of-trends-in-esg-reporting-require ments-for-investors/10296.article.

The disclosed information allows both retail and institutional investors to consider how the fund's integration of ESG issues might affect their risk and returns. That in turn depends on whether they are only interested in the financial risks and returns, or they're also interested in any real-world impacts from their investments. For example, say the fund invests in the renewable energy sector, including companies in which there may be human rights or modern slavery violations in the supply chain for their solar panels. Those violations would mean a great deal to the workers involved, but investors may not see them as material to their investment returns. The SFRD will help investors decide what's important to them, and what action they'd expect the fund manager to take: ignore, engage, or divest.

Even for investors only interested in the financial equation, a debt investor and an equity investor may regard the same information differently. Typically, an equity investor has a greater tolerance to risk than a debt investor, and may have different investment timeframes. Again, each may have a different tolerance to real-world impacts, with different corporate investment policies. The SFRD and the EU taxonomy help ensure investors have the information they need to meet their mandates and policies – assuming of course that the fund disclosures are accurate.

Jurisdictions following the EU's approach include Australia, Canada, China, Mexico, Russia, and Singapore. They've sought to learn from the EU experience, both from the taxonomies themselves and the process for developing them. The challenge is that taxonomies are slightly different in each jurisdiction, so a particular activity may be seen as sustainable in one jurisdiction but not in another. Often, the final taxonomies will depend on policies or politics. For example, the EU taxonomy considers nuclear power as sustainable and natural gas as a transition fuel, while the proposed Australian taxonomy does not.

ESG certification of investment products

The finance sector in multiple jurisdictions has set up regimes for the certification of ESG funds and investment products. For example, the Responsible Investment Association of Australasia (RIAA) has had a responsible investment product certification scheme in place for nearly twenty years. The certification, which has evolved over time, certifies that a product or service has implemented an investment style and process that systematically takes into account ESG or ethical considerations, and that this process has been verified by an external party. The product or service also needs to meet certain operational and disclosure practices.

Voluntary commitments to increase accountability

Investors have also signed themselves to commitments to take action on broad ESG performance or particular ESG issues. These initiatives typically call for greater and more transparent disclosure, as the investment firms hold themselves accountable to meet their commitments. Doing so again helps protect against greenwashing.

The broadest of these initiatives is the Principles for Responsible Investment (PRI), discussed in Part A. The PRI requires signatories to report on their responsible investment activities using the PRI's Reporting Framework. For example, asset owners report on how ESG issues might affect the fund managers they use, and listed equity managers' report on how ESG issues might affect the stocks they invest in. Both the reports and the PRI's assessment of them are publicly available, so that investors have a clear guide on their ESG practices (more so than marketing materials may allow).

Another example is the Net-Zero Asset Owners Alliance (NZAOA)[163] and its counterpart, the Net-Zero Asset Managers Initiative (NZAMI).[164] In both, signatories commit to transition their investment portfolios to net-zero GHG emissions by 2050 – consistent with the 2015 Paris Climate Agreement. Signatories also commit to tracking and communicating their progress by setting and publishing intermediate targets and publicizing their annual progress. Globally, the number of investment policies and corporate policies to strengthen ESG disclosures now both exceed 400, according to the PRI; see Figure 32.

Figure 32: ESG disclosures are being formalized by voluntary and mandatory codes.

Cumulative number of global ESG disclosure policies

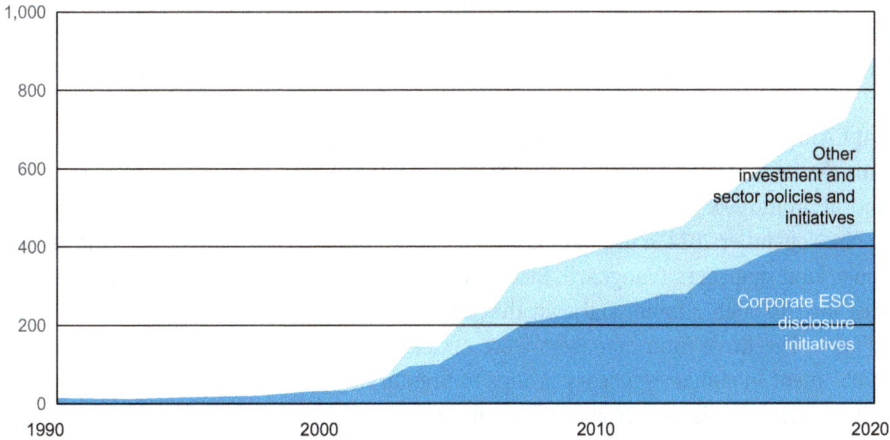

Source: Principles of Responsible Investment (2021), 'Regulation database update: the unstoppable rise of RI policy', https://www.unpri.org/pri-blog/regulation-databaseupdate-the-unstoppable-rise-of-ri-policy/7352.article accessed 20 November 2024.

The 2023–24 ESG Backlash

Change can be hard to adjust to, especially if it challenges fundamental beliefs. Some want to fight back, and this has been the case for companies, politicians, think tanks, and wealthy individuals for whom the whole notion of ESG is repellent. As we saw when considering the emergence of anti-ESG resolutions, there are professed free-marketeers who would prevent companies from even considering ESG to get a competitive edge in an open market, or prevent investors from analyzing ESG factors and asking questions to reduce risks to their investments from those factors.

This has been particularly so in the USA. In 2023, there were more than 165 proposed bills in state legislative sessions, which resulted in new anti-ESG laws in 16 states.[165] The trend continued with over 100 proposed bills in 2024. Most of the bills haven't passed into law. In resisting the bills, lawmakers noted that the bills would restrict investment officials from fulfilling their fiduciary responsibility or, rather ironically, they would interfere with the free market.

Also in 2023, Republican Attorneys General in 21 states wrote to 53 of the biggest US mutual fund firms saying the firms' actions to support GHG emissions reduction efforts were contrary to their clients' financial interests; they argued the firms should not support climate-change shareholder proposals. The firms replied, again, that not to consider something that may be a material risk was contrary to their fiduciary duties.

The anti-ESG agenda continued in 2024, with Republican lawmakers on the House Judicial Committee sending a letter to more than 130 US-based investor CA100+ signatories, demanding information on action they planned to take as part of the initiative. The ideological agenda of the group of lawmakers was reflected in comments made by some of the committee members, saying that CA100+ was a "climate cartel" and that CA100+ members were "a group of left-wing activists and major financial institutions that collude to impose radical ESG goals on American companies".[166] A rare collaboration indeed.

In November 2024, a group of eleven US states attempted to sue three of the largest global fund managers (Vanguard, BlackRock, and State Street), alleging violation of antitrust law through climate activism that reduced coal production and boosted energy prices.[167] The three fund managers were accused of exploiting their market power and involvement in climate advocacy groups to pressure coal companies to slash output and reduce carbon emissions from coal by more than 50% by 2030, driving up consumers' utility bills. The fund managers have said the case is baseless and defies common sense.

Some companies have also taken legal action against investors. In February 2024, ExxonMobil sued Arjuna Capital, a US-based wealth manager, regarding a shareholder proposal that Arjuna had sponsored. The proposal related to ExxonMobil's greenhouse gas emissions and its alleged contributions to anthropogenic climate change, as had several resolutions that Arjuna had submitted in previous years. The sight of a company suing an investor over a shareholder resolution was new and alarming for other investors. Many who may not have agreed with that specific resolution expressed concern about ExxonMobil's approach and voted against one or a number of ExxonMobil directors as a result. In the end, Arjuna withdrew its proposal, and ExxonMobil's litigation was dismissed by the judge.

In another case, the New Civil Liberties Alliance (NCLA), representing the National Center for Public Policy Research, filed a petition with the US Court of Appeals requesting review of the Securities and Exchange Commission's (SEC) new rules that would require public companies to disclose their climate-related business risks and mitigation procedures. The NCLA argued that the SEC had exceeded its statutory authority and demanded an immediate end to the "illegal SEC pursuit of climate activism at the cost of civil liberties".[168] The National Association of Manufacturers (NAM) took it one step further and filed a motion to intervene in the case, arguing that the SEC has no authority to regulate the shareholder proposal engagement process at all.[169] At the time of printing, the case was continuing.

The consequences of this ESG backlash have been varied but ultimately very limited. It may have had some short-term success: a number of US-based fund managers have not renewed their membership to groups such as Climate Action 100+. However, the statement of Franklin Templeton was typical of many of the fund managers who left. "Over the last two years, we have grown our internal capabilities significantly and invested heavily in climate-related data and tools around the analysis of and engagement on our climate-related risks and opportunities in our clients' portfolios."[170] And, notably, Climate Action 100+ announced in October 2024 that its total membership had increased over the previous year.

While the ESG backlash may have led investors to be more cautious in expressing how they incorporate ESG into their investment processes and stewardship activities, it is highly questionable whether it has or will change anything investors actually do. Climate change, for example, still represents a material risk to returns. Environmental and social issues are still shaping the markets in which companies are operating. Not considering them would be contrary to fund managers' fiduciary duty.

Regulations against greenwashing and the ESG backlash are both indicators that the push to ESG may have 'crossed the line', and together have given pause to the patient rise of more responsible attitudes to investing. The regulations will stand, as they should. The backlash may be extended through the term of the 2025–28 US presidency but will not last. As we argued in Part A and repeat here, incorporating ESG factors into investment analysis is really a conservative extension of risk assessment that reflects the complexities of the 21st-century economy. It may be resisted, but will not be stopped.

Chapter 13 summary
- With over US$20 trillion invested globally in funds that claim to be ESG-related, it is inevitable that some of those claims are misleading. Prospective investors should read product disclosure statements carefully to see exactly how funds take ESG factors into account.
- Some funds may mislead investors on the sectors they invest in or avoid, or may overstate the social or environmental impact of their investments. Holding shares in 'greener' companies does not, in itself, act to safeguard the environment.
- Investment markets have helped negotiate regulations, certification schemes, and voluntary codes to build more understanding and confidence in this relatively new market. They align with similar efforts for the trade of carbon and nature offsets.
- Nonetheless, Republican lawmakers in 16 US states have acted to restrict investments in ESG-related funds. Their argument cited the prevalence of greenwashing and the unnecessary restraint of shareholder primacy. Similar laws may be expected in the Trump administration from 2025.
- Meanwhile, US investment firms operating internationally continue to press companies for the same ESG-related information as before, as it is relevant to their portfolio risk and opportunity assessment.

Part D: **Choices for the individual**

In the previous two parts, we've seen how ESG makes sense for both companies and institutional investors. We've also seen how both companies and investors are improving their ESG disclosures so their people can make better, more informed decisions.

These ESG disclosures give us much clearer information for deciding how we should participate in our economy – as consumers, shareholders, employees, and voting citizens. In particular, they enable us to consider whether we can align our interests and values in all those roles. How can we bring to our work and our investing the same values we aspire to have at home? And can our choices influence the nature of our economic system and the impacts it has?

Our every decision and action matters. We can't make a difference as individuals alone, but without our individual actions, things will stay the same. Our voluntary actions won't by themselves stop companies from eroding the social and natural capital on which we all depend. Instead, governments and investors will have to demand that they do.

For that to happen, they need evidence that people care. If we're all happy to see the status quo continue, then why would a government be bold enough to change it? If we're all happy to keep buying and selling things without regard to the social or environmental cost, then why would companies and investors take the lead?

Often, governments and investors do act before there's majority support for their actions. But they can't do that unless there's at least solid minority support, which is where we come in. And they'll fail unless they can explain to everyone why they are doing it. Again, that's where we come in. We need to have conversations with people. That's not to bombastically declare what needs to be done. But it does mean asking appropriate questions at appropriate times, learning from others' point of view, and seeding a thought or two along the way.

Every time we recycle something, or tilt our pension fund into an ESG option, or buy something with a smaller carbon footprint, or ask a politician to put in the systems we need, we are nudging the world toward a more sustainable path. We need every nudge we can get until the tipping point. And if we don't nudge, who will?

In this part, we explore how we as individuals can nudge toward better environmental, social, and economic outcomes in the choices we make. It covers the decisions we make:

- **Chapter 14**   As investors, through our pension or super funds
- **Chapter 15**   As consumers, every time we buy
- **Chapter 16**   As employees, every time we look for work or go to work, and
- **Chapter 17**   As citizens, every time we express our views and wants

We may not nudge the world to a better place every day, and we may be frustrated by the lack of progress and more so by the backward steps our governments may take. But we will get there in the end, and that's really the only option we have.

https://doi.org/10.1515/9783111428949-018

BOX: Sources of ESG information
At several points in this book, and especially in Part D, we will suggest you to look something up about a company's approach to sustainability or ESG. This page lists where you can go to find that information. There are now many websites providing information that is scannable by your AI partner or directly searchable. Not all websites offer the particular service you may be looking for, so it's worth looking at a few to find what suits you best.

This list was prepared in November 2024. Although it will date, most of the sources listed have been in operation for at least a decade, so are reasonably stable, and the list will make it easier for you to find other sources using your AI research tool.

These are international sources. There are also country-based sources, which are not listed here.

News services
- Responsible Investor (www.responsible-investor.com). The most comprehensive international journal.
- Corporate Register (www.corporateregister.com). CSR reports from 22,000 organizations.
- Business & Human Rights Resource Centre (business-humanrights.org). Digest of human rights issues, including legal actions.
- SRi-Connect (www.sri-connect.com). Network of experienced sustainable investors, sharing ESG investment-related insights.

Investor networks and services
- Responsible Investment Association Australasia (www.responsibleinvestment.org)
- UN Principles of Responsible Investment (www.unpri.org)
- UK Sustainable Investment and Finance Association (www.uksif.org)
- Responsible Investment Association Canada (www.riacanada.ca)
- De Vereniging van Beleggers voor Duurzame Ontwikkeling (www.vbdo.nl/en)
- The European Sustainable Investment Forum (Eurosif) (www.eurosif.org)
- The Forum for Sustainable and Responsible Investment (US SIF) (www.ussif.org)
- Japan Sustainable Investment Forum (www.jsif.jp.net/english)
- Global Sustainable Investment Alliance (www.gsi-alliance.org)
- Global Impact Investing Network (www.thegiin.org)
- Ceres Investor Network (www.ceres.org)
- Investor Group on Climate Change Australia New Zealand (IGCC) (www.igcc.org.au)
- Asia Investor Group on Climate Change (AIGCC) (www.aigcc.net)
- Institutional Investor Group on Climate Change (www.iigcc.org)
- Savvy Investor. (www.savvyinvestor.net). White papers and investment insights from top global asset managers and consultants.

ESG ratings agencies
These agencies offer the most thorough assessment of listed companies and brands. It doesn't cost anything to look up and get a score or ranking of the company, but you'll have to pay to get a report explaining why the company has earned that ranking.
- Sustainalytics (over 20,000 companies at https://www.sustainalytics.com/esg-ratings)
- Institutional Shareholder Services (ISS) (over 3400 companies at https://www.issgovernance.com/esg/ratings/)
- S&P Global (over 7300+ companies at https://www.spglobal.com/esg/solutions/data-intelligence-esg-scores)

- Refinitiv/MSCI (over 14,000 equity and fixed income issuers at https://www.msci.com/our-solutions/esg-investing/esg-ratings)
- Moody's (over 5000 companies at https://esg.moodys.io/)
- FTSE Russell (over 7200 companies at https://www.ftserussell.com/products/indices/esg)
- Bloomberg (over 11,800 companies at https://www.bloomberg.com/professional/dataset/global-environmental-social-governance-data/)

Product certification agencies
These are usually industry-specific agencies that provide a verification and branding service for companies and brands. These include the Marine Stewardship Code (MSC), Forestry Stewardship Code (FSC), the Roundtable on Sustainable Palm Oil (RSPO), the Rainforest Alliance, Fair Trade Certification, and UTZ Certification. Most products on supermarket shelves bear the certification brands to warrant their source. They are not free from controversy, as product certification has been used to assert a level of sustainability that consumers expect, but may not be being met.

Buying guides and consumer brand assessments
These websites assess the sustainability of common products and brands.
- Better World Shopper (https://betterworldshopper.org) ranks products and companies based on sustainability and social justice criteria
- Good on you (https://goodonyou.eco/) rates fashion brands
- Baptist World Aid (https://baptistworldaid.org.au/resources/ethical-consumer-report/) assesses the sustainability of global fashion brands and provides an avenue by which consumers can ask them to do better,
- SustainabilityTracker (https://www.sustainabilitytracker.com/) rates products and companies, but relies on companies registering their business

These sites offer tips on how to buy sustainable products, or offer links to the products themselves.
- Viable Earth (https://viable.earth/) scans the world for ideas, products, and companies for a sustainable future
- Ethical Consumer (https://www.ethicalconsumer.org/) discusses issues and shopping guides to assist with most consumer buying decisions
- Fashion Revolution (https://www.fashionrevolution.org) is a movement advocating for transparency and sustainability in the fashion industry, offering resources and reports for consumers
- Remake (https://remake.world) is a directory of sustainable fashion brands and ethical labor practices
- Eat This, Not That – Sustainable Food Section (https://www.eatthis.com/sustainable-food/) is an easy guide on sustainable cooking and eating etc.
- Seafood Watch (https://www.seafoodwatch.org) tracks seafood species and choices with ratings and recommendations

Award listings
These sites call for nominations and issue independent awards to companies who perform well on specific ESG areas, or generally.
- International Corporate Social Responsibility CSR Awards (www.awards-list.com)
- World Sustainability Awards (www.worldsustainabilityleaders.com)
- Investor's Business Daily Best 100 ESG Companies for Environmental, Social And Governance Values (www.investors.com)

Carbon project registries

These sites house searchable information on projects that generate carbon credits or offsets. Companies will declare the projects that they rely on for offsetting their carbon emissions, and you can verify and find out more about the projects through these registries. (If they don't declare the projects they use, that in itself is a problem.)

– Verra: https://registry.verra.org/
– Gold Standard: https://registry.goldstandard.org/credit-blocks
– UN Clean Development Mechanism: https://cdm.unfccc.int/Registry/index.html

Chapter 14
Putting your money to good work

Someone's sitting in the shade today because someone planted a tree a long time ago.
Warren Buffett, allegedly

For most people, the biggest investment choice they make is their pension fund. And far too many people don't make any choice at all. In Australia, where the much-loved super system has amassed over US$3 trillion in funds and helped make Australians the wealthiest people in the OECD, nearly two-thirds of members do not select where their money goes.[171] The superannuation (or super) they have is the one that their first employer organized for them, however many decades ago that was. Many are surprised to find out they are investing in tobacco and land mines, or in companies that resist any call to act on global warming, or that are implicated in modern slavery.

Others are more proactive. They might have chosen a super fund that suits their needs, and has performed well. Or they may have saved and invested wisely, and have money they can invest however they choose.

Either way, this chapter helps you make conscious decisions on how to invest your money or choose your pension fund, so that it makes you a good return without causing harm to others. It confirms that it's possible to help guide your money to companies that are helping to solve problems, or at least not making them worse.

Your super or pension fund is compulsory saving for your future. The professional investors who manage that money on your behalf only have it because governments have made it compulsory. These purposes should be well aligned. You will end up with money to enjoy the years after full-time work. So, it would be an enormous shame if all of that money will be needed to pay for what is now free or affordable, and perhaps taken for granted – a livable climate, security in your neighborhood, affordable transport, and affordable healthcare, among other things. There is no reason for your investments today to come at the expense of the quality of the world you and your family are going to live in.

There's no simple recipe for what might be best for you. Each person is different, with their own financial objectives, risk appetite, and personal values. But your superannuation or pension fund may well be the largest investment you have – especially as home ownership is becoming harder to reach in many countries. So you may as well put your money to good use – or at least keep an open mind and consider your options.

In this chapter, we consider:
- Investing for good returns, while protecting against harm by taking ESG factors into account

https://doi.org/10.1515/9783111428949-019

- Investing to change how companies behave, by taking a stake as an activist share-holder, and
- Investing for good, by backing companies whose primary purpose is to have a positive social or environmental impact (so-called impact investing).

Whatever your values and needs, there will be an option for you.

Part C goes into some of the content of this chapter in more depth, so you can move back to Part C if you want more detail.

Checking the fund is what it says

It's easier now to invest in these ways for good, ESG-based returns. There are more choices available from super funds, pension funds, and other fund managers. There are also more options to buy and sell funds with ESG characteristics on the world's stockmarkets, through electronically traded funds (ETFs).

Whatever the fund is, and despite the efforts of regulators, there is still an element of 'buyer beware'. Like any investment, you'll need to look at the fine print to make sure the fund does what it claims, and that it's aligned with your investment purpose and values. To assist, regulators now insist that funds disclose how they integrate ESG into their investment, and stipulate that certain words in a fund's name (e.g., sustainable) mean certain things.[172] Also, you should look for certification from a third-party organization that verifies the fund's methods and ensures that the fund is doing what it says it's doing. The Responsible Investment Association of Australasia (RIAA) has been certifying funds in this way since 2005.[173] There are more details on regulation and certification in Chapter 13.

If the fund is taking too many liberties with its naming and marketing, it could be prosecuted for 'greenwashing', that is, making unsubstantiated or misleading claims about what they do. Regulators are no longer shy about taking action against these funds. It would be unfair to single out one of the many funds that have been prosecuted, and prosecutions have been made on every continent. The fines can be significant to bring errant funds into line, with the latest one imposed by the US Securities and Exchange Commission being $4 million.[174]

Investing for good returns

Let's say you invest in companies, either directly or through a fund, and are considering having an automotive company in your portfolio. Transport has never gone out of fashion. Here are just a few of your options.

- Ignore ESG factors totally and invest in whatever car company looks like a good financial investment.

- Take ESG factors into account, and consider which well-known brands are doing the right thing with their people, with small businesses through their supply chains, on environmental issues, and have the governance needed to make the right move into electric or hybrid vehicles.
- Invest in a small, relatively unknown car company that provides affordable transport in developing countries. It is deliberately addressing a few Sustainable Development Goals, and building cars that may well end up with a large market in richer countries.
- Invest in an electric car company like Tesla that has led the auto response to climate change.
- Invest in small emerging electric car company whose brand has not been diminished by governance factors or by contrary stances on social issues.
- Avoid investing in any car company, because cars cause pollution or congestion or both.
- Avoid investing in any car company, as the next generation will use robo-taxis and mass transit instead.

You could apply the same thinking to any sector you're considering. What banks, retailers, healthcare, telecommunications, energy, or mining companies should you support with your money?

In any of these industries, you could choose to:
- Invest for financial returns only
- Invest for both ESG and financial performance
- Invest to keep clear of the 'sin' stocks, or
- Invest to favor the social or environmental issues that mean the most to you.

This section considers those four options you can take.

Ignore ESG and focus solely on historic financial returns or an Investment Index

Despite the old adage that past investment performance is no guarantee of future performance, many investors look at past performance more than any ESG considerations. We pointed to evidence in Chapter 4 that, over the long-term, the investment returns of funds that consider ESG are likely to be as good if not better than funds that do not. So, if the financial returns are equal or better, why not put your money to better use?

Still, if you want to ignore ESG, and investing in equities meets your risk/return preferences and needs,[175] selecting the right stocks or even the right fund manager is sometimes difficult. It may be easier to just choose a well-diversified index or exchange-traded fund (ETF).[176] These just track a national or global stockmarket index and tend to have the lowest fees. They will invest in every company in the index – the good, the bad, and the ugly – on both ESG and financial performance. But that's not your concern, and you save the expense of a professional stock-picker.

Investing for both ESG and financial performance

As we discussed in Part C, it makes good sense to integrate ESG into investment decisions, both in theory and practice. There is plenty of choice among fund managers, and the way they integrate ESG into their investment processes varies. To make it clearer for you, regulators are insisting that fund managers disclose if, and how, they are integrating ESG into their investment decisions. That can be quite technical, so it will be worth asking them to explain it to you. Many funds do this well. Like any investment, think twice if you don't really understand what they're talking about.

Weeding out the bad stuff – exclusion-based or 'ethical' investing

Here, your choice is to make sure your money doesn't support the things you don't like, for example, the 'sin stocks' of gambling, alcohol, tobacco, nuclear power, pornography, and weapons.

Without the sin stocks, there will be times when your financial returns will do better, but to be honest, your financial returns may also be worse over the time in which you are invested. That's a choice many people find easy to make: they're uncomfortable profiting off the harms that are deliberately or too often inflicted on others.

These days, there are funds you can choose that exclude a much wider range of potential companies. They might exclude whole sectors or specific companies that are involved in fossil fuels, genetically modified crops, unsustainable palm oil, animal testing, factory farming, pork products, and even lending. Or, they might exclude companies that are shown to have had multiple human rights violations, or environmental breaches, or breaches of an international agreement like the UN Global Compact. Your choices are almost infinite.

Whatever your choice, there are a few questions to ask, to ensure you're comfortable with that choice.

- **Does the fund exclude a 'sin' partially or entirely?** For example, it might exclude companies that produce alcohol, but not those that sell it. Or it might allow companies that 'sin' just a little. Often, there is a revenue threshold: if the 'sin' amounts to less than 5% or 10% of the company's sales, then that passes the fund's test, though it might not pass yours.

   However, there are good reasons why a fund manager may not want an absolute ban on an industry, company, or product. Investors might be using their stake to help maintain pressure for the company to transform its business in a positive way or they want to support and see the investment opportunity of a company that is making a transition for the better, for example, a power generation company transitioning to renewables. This approach is taken up in the 'Investing for Change' section below. Or the fund manager may not want to open up too much of a selection gap with mainstream funds, which might increase the investment risk beyond what the fund manager or superannuation fund wants to offer.

– **Does the fund screen its equity investments, but not its bonds?** Your money might not be buying the shares of a fossil fuel company, but it might be lent to it. Would that make a difference to you?

– **Can the fund change its mind?** A fund's marketing might say that it excludes the nuclear industry, and that may be true at the time. But the fine print may say that such exclusions are at the fund manager's discretion, which may not be what you're looking for. A potential change might be frustrating for investors, but it can also be a form of greenwashing. Either way, you need good disclosure from the fund and your own due diligence to make the choice you want.

Chasing the good stuff – positive screens or thematic investing

Here, your choice is to put your money where your mouth is – to support the industries you think are making a positive difference, or the companies you think are doing well in any industry, or both.

A positive-screen or 'best-in-sector' fund usually invests in companies that are considered 'ESG leaders' compared to their peers. They reduce risk by investing in all industries, and again by investing in the best ESG performers. You may want to check whether there are any exclusions, or you may well be investing in a tobacco company with a marginally better ESG rating than its peers. Alternatively, you can limit the screen to target companies who outperform on specific ESG issues, such as climate change, or Sustainable Development Goal alignment, or gender and diversity. The fund may rely on ESG ratings agencies to decide what companies are best-in-sector across all or some ESG factors. As we noted in Part C, those agencies will have different views on the same company, leading to one fund investing in different companies to another. This can be confusing for investors and to us.

Thematic funds invest in particular industry sectors that would either accelerate or benefit from a move to address an environmental or social issue. For example, there are funds that target sustainable agriculture, renewable energy, nature conservation, or microfinance. Or they may target affordable and accessible housing, healthcare, water and sanitation and education. There are even funds that focus on such industries, and then favor companies in it with stronger ESG ratings.

'Green bonds' are a good example of thematic investing. Our super and pension funds know that governments and companies need large amounts of money to shift the economy off carbon fuels. Governments recognize the need so clearly that their policies favor renewable energy and the switch to electricity. This makes investing in the sector less risky, and so more attractive to private investors. Unless of course the government changes.

Similarly, governments and companies issue 'social bonds' to attract investment and innovation in market-based solutions to social issues like housing and education. When we invest in a social bond, we get a fixed and, in many cases, a competitive return, and the company is bound to use our money for that declared social purpose.

There's been a sharp increase in both green bonds and social bonds over the past decade. The steady rise in green bonds (with a sharp jump in 2021, see Figure 33) reflects the need for large amounts of capital to solve the climate crisis. Social bonds burst into the market in 2020, when governments issued additional social bonds to finance the fight against the COVID-19 pandemic and try to mitigate the socioeconomic impact of the crisis.

Figure 33: Issuing of green bonds has risen steadily since 2014.

Value of green bonds issued
Global US$ billions

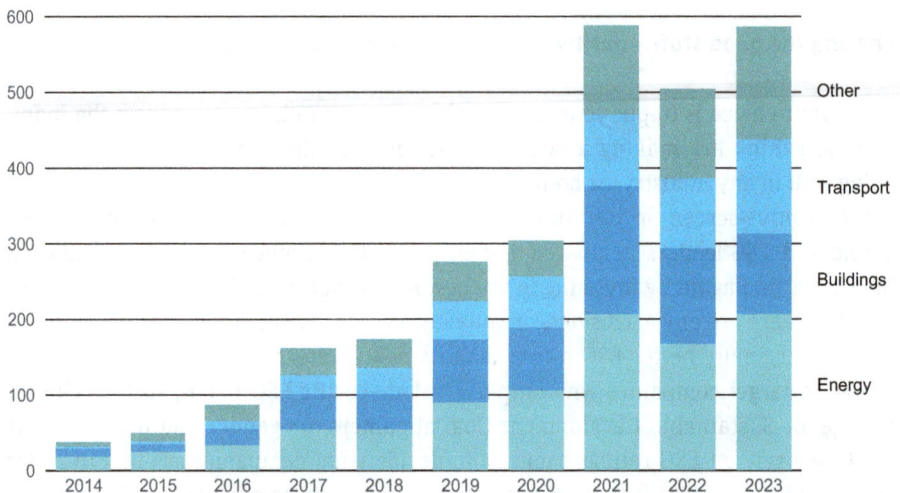

Source: Climate Bonds Initiative.

Investing for Change – Engaging with companies directly and indirectly

Engaging with companies as an individual can seem a little daunting. Like any other person, you can post on social media or write or call to express your views. As a shareholder, your voice will carry more weight because you can vote. As noted in Part C, activist shareholders will, from time to time, try to get support for a resolution to be put at a general meeting, and as a shareholder, you would see their letters seeking your support. If you agree with what is being put forward, then you can vote your shares in support of the resolution. As we explained in Part C, a resolution does not need to actually pass to bring change to a company – a solid minority vote will be enough for conversations to continue – so voting your shares is rarely in vain.

One powerful vote you have is for the appointment of directors. For example, if you believe the company's environmental or social performance is not up to scratch, you can vote against the re-election of the responsible directors. This is what many shareholders did at Rio Tinto's 2020 annual general meeting after the destruction of Juukan Gorge the previous year (see Chapter 6) when a quarter of shareholders voted against the chair of the board sustainability committee, Megan Clark. More than 60% of shareholders voted against the remuneration reports at the same AGM, with strong expressions against the then Chair, Simon Thompson, leading to departures from the Rio Tinto board and executives.

Your say becomes even more important if you're a member of a pension fund that holds shares in the company. Those funds have large holdings and are voting to represent your interests, so telling them what your interests are will certainly help them. You can make them accountable by asking them why they acted a certain way or saying why you think their action wasn't aligned with your best interest.

Increasingly, funds publish engagement reports, disclosing how they've voted and otherwise engaged with companies, and the principles that guided their actions. From this, you can tell if and how a fund has been representing your views to companies and governments. When reading these reports, try to look beyond the numbers. A fund may say how many times it has met with companies on a particular subject, but may be less clear on what the fund is actually asking the company to do on the issue.

While fund managers have influence, company responses can be slow. A fund's engagement with a company can extend over years and still not achieve change: the company board is just set in its way. In Chapter 12, we discussed what funds can do to escalate their actions if a company isn't changing. For example, investors in power companies may keep up the pressure for them to transition from fossil fuel generation to renewables, as occurred at AGL in Australia in 2022, where the board was ultimately replaced by one more likely to make that transition successfully. However, if an investor has engaged with the company, voted against its directors, or worked with other investors to put resolutions to a company vote and still there is no change – they may just have to sell the shares and work for change elsewhere.

Again, as a member of a fund, you can be part of their journey for change. Let your voice be known on what you want your fund to invest in, how you want it to influence companies for change, and what to do if there is no change coming.

Investing for Change – Impact Investing

Your next choice is to invest in a fund with the specific objective of creating a positive impact, as well as providing an investment return. These are usually managed by small, boutique fund managers who are themselves working to achieve positive outcomes. There's never a guarantee these funds will have an impact in the real world, but they are the ones most likely to. To give you a taste of what can be achieved, here are some examples of impact funds. Again, we are not implying that they will necessarily meet your investment needs but highlighting the potential for change that can come from impact investing.

The Global Impact Investing Network (GIIN) is a collaboration of fund managers who undertake impact investing. One of the managers is LeapFrog Investments, which invests in companies that provide health and financial services to consumers in Africa and Asia. Leapfrog invested in AllLife in South Africa, which offers affordable life insurance to thousands of people living with HIV/AIDS and diabetes, and improves their health experience through the company's unique adherence management program. LeapFrog's investment enabled AllLife to accelerate its growth and diversify its products and services. AllLife more than doubled its annual revenue, opened a second call center, expanded its senior team and staff, and introduced new products.[177]

The Green Climate Fund (GCF) is the world's largest dedicated multilateral climate fund, with a mandate to accelerate the shift to low emission global economy. It has invested nearly US$16 billion in 286 projects across 133 developing countries,[178] including forest conservation; deforestation-free value chains for coffee, pepper, bamboo, or fruits; and a variety of specialty products like honey, medicinal plants, mushrooms, or silk. One project in Vietnam will improve 145,000 hectares of land through agroforestry and community forest management, which will then reduce deforestation pressures on 500,000 hectares of threatened natural forests in central Vietnam, with significant environmental and socio-economic co-benefits for indigenous peoples.[179]

In October 2024, GIIN estimated that impact investing reached US$1.571 trillion globally,[180] an amount that's increasing rapidly. Different funds invest in different underlying assets. Let's say a nonprofit organization owns its own offices or warehouse. It can use that asset as security to borrow money to get its operations underway. An impact fund may lend that money – a private debt arrangement against those real assets. Alternatively, the fund can invest in the social enterprise as a venture capital or equity capital partner.

Different funds also offer a different financial return in addition to the social or environmental impact. This may be less than the promise of a fund that's focused solely on financial returns, so one must look at the investment return objectives before investing. It can be an option for investors who'd rather see their cash put to good use than have it sit in a bank. Indeed, 'doing good' doesn't necessarily mean investment returns are not meeting investment objectives. The GIIN found that over

90% of over 150 surveyed impact investors believed that their financial and impact expectations were either met or exceeded.[181]

If you are considering such a fund for your own investing, here are a few principles to consider:

- **Intentionality**. Does the fund state a clear intention of having a positive social or environmental impact – either generally or on a particular issue?
- **Additionality**. Would the positive impact have happened without the private capital from funds such as these? The danger is that if the environmental or educational benefit would have happened anyway, there is no real additionality or impact, so your money would not have had the impact you had wished.
- **Measurability**. How is the impact actually measured?
- **Disclosure**. Are these intentions, the fund's actions, and the measured impact clearly disclosed?

These four principles ensure transparency and accountability for your investment. They also build up the capacity of the impact investing sector and nongovernment organizations to collaborate on social actions that make a difference.

Chapter 14 summary
- One of the biggest investments most of us make is through our pension fund. Yet in many countries, less than half of people with a pension fund have had a say in how that money is invested.
- ESG-related funds offer a sensible range of choices that aim to ensure that you have financial capital when you retire, in a world with ample natural, social, and human capital for you to enjoy.
- There are a range of funds to look at, including those that deliver strong financial returns while having a positive ESG impact across the economy. The performance of these funds can still meet your financial objectives.
- You may also select funds that avoid 'sin' industries, or that invest to fund social enterprises with a more modest expectation of financial returns. As always, investors are wise to double-check the intention of these funds, whether they would make a difference, how they measure that, and how they disclose it and whether the fund meets your investment objectives.

Chapter 15
Buying things without harming others

Fast fashion isn't free. Someone, somewhere, is paying.
Lucy Siegle, The True Cost, 2015

As consumers, we have the right to buy whatever is on the shelves that meets our needs. That raises two questions: 'What is the right purchase for us?' and, more fundamentally, 'Do we really *need* the purchase at all?'.

For example, many of us are tempted to buy more clothing than we really need. As a result, globally, we bought 60% more garments in 2014 than in 2000, and kept the clothes for only half as long.[182] The environmental impact of the clothes we use, or don't use, keeps piling up. The fashion industry is second only to agriculture in its use of water and is responsible for 2 to 8% of global carbon emissions. Six out of every seven tons of the textiles it uses goes to landfill in the same year. Washing synthetic clothing sends microplastics to the ocean.[183]

Similarly, while an estimated 733 million people are still going hungry, about 27% of all food produced is lost as wastage through the supply chain, and another 50% of what's left is lost after it reaches retail shelves. Food waste in landfills alone contributes to 8% to 10% of agricultural carbon emissions.[184]

Obviously, we need clothes and food, but we might reconsider those needs from time to time, and how they are fulfilled. We might decide that the carbon footprint of red meat or petrol cars is just too high. Or, that a sustainably sourced and sold T-shirt is worth a little more than a T-shirt whose cotton comes at a heavy ecological cost and whose tailoring comes at a heavy human cost. Or, that we can fully use what we buy and not let it rot at the back of the fridge or cupboard.

Ignorance may be bliss, but if you're reading this book, it's unlikely to be enough. How can we find out what's going on without losing our weekends, and without losing optimism?

The main questions seem to be:

- **What everyday items might you avoid or reduce buying?** When you go into the facts, there's plenty of downside to farmed salmon, very cheap clothing, and disposable coffee cups. We'll need them from time to time, but we would argue against making them an indispensable part of your world.
- **Are your go-to retail brands part of the problem or part of the solution?** We give a large slice of our weekly budgets to grocery stores, banks, energy companies, phone companies, and the like. Similarly, we put a large slice of our income into expensive one-off purchases like a car or refrigerator. Some of these companies are making an effort to reduce their social and environmental impact, others less so. How can you check who does what?

https://doi.org/10.1515/9783111428949-020

– **What can you do to help level the playing field for companies that are seeking solutions?** At the moment, companies that responsibly bear the real cost of their business are undercut at the checkout by those who do not. We argue in Part B that the best companies will win in the end, but a lot of harm is being done by their competitors in the meantime. Letting companies know what you think may be one thing, but in the end, only regulation can set a level playing field. However, that regulation may just be the lowest bar the government believes it can set at the time, and not necessarily the standard needed to address the issues.

If you'd like to go deeper, we've listed at the start of this Part some resources that, at the time of writing, are available to guide our choices. That will help you consider the specific brands and items you're buying, and whether they're made with the values you would respect.

A shortcut may be to do an ESG 'stocktake' every year or so. Look up the ESG ratings (see beginning of Part D) of the companies you buy from, or might consider, and see which of them are leading or improving, both of which means they are taking sustainability seriously, and looking to minimize avoidable harm where possible. Make choices based on either their total ESG rating, or if you prefer the social, environmental, or governance rating, depending on which means the most to you. Stick with your choices for the year, and then take a look again next year. Alternatively, you could see whether your company is certified by B-Corp.[185] B-Corp Certification of a business indicates that it meets performance, accountability, and transparency standards on all sorts of ESG factors, from employee benefits and charitable giving to supply chain practices and input materials.

Perhaps the best thing you can do is to talk things through with your household and friends. You'll gain some perspectives for sure, not all of which would find comfort in this book. But asking questions often prompts your own thinking and your commitment to make choices.

Seeing through greenwashing

As consumers, we are the targets of advertising and messaging from companies that wish us to buy and support their products. Since marketing – and markets – first began, sellers have spruiked the benefits of their products. Over centuries, we have become accustomed to claims of being the 'world's best' this or the 'market-leading' that, and essentially ignored them. What then, should we make of claims that something is 'sustainably grown' or 'responsibly made'?

One view is that we should ignore that too. Just as we can't define 'market leading', nor can we define 'sustainable' or 'responsible'. In that view, those terms are just puffery, to use the legal term, and not a contractual promise. Nothing is meant by them except that the marketers are excited by their work and think you should be too.

These claims need to be tested, because if they can't be substantiated, they not only dupe the customer but they undermine the natural capital on which we all depend. For that reason, the terms are increasingly being subject to legal and regulatory action. They're now included in consumer protection laws, regarded as a type of 'misleading and deceptive conduct' that can be penalized and stopped. In 2008, for example, Shell boosted that extracting oil from a huge tar sands deposit in Canada was 'a sustainable energy source', a claim the UK Advertising Standards Authority found was misleading (to put it mildly).

If a company claims that its product is 'sustainable', then that claim must be substantiated by someone else whose word can be trusted. In most industries, there are frameworks for third-party certification that the product is being made or grown in a reasonably sustainable way; see the box 'Are you buying a sustainable product?' If there is no such verification, then ignore the claim, and treat the product and the company that makes it with a little more suspicion. What else might they be saying that may not be 100% certain, and what else might they not be telling you?

Then there are the advertising campaigns by whole industries who want to keep things the way they are – profits for them, and losses (of natural, social, human, or financial capital) for others. They are 'externalizing' the costs – imposing them on others, while 'internalizing' the profits. Or, as the saying goes, 'private gain and public pain'.

The examples of dishonest campaigns since consumerism really kicked in after World War II are legionary and legendary. In 1946, in response to an epidemic of lung cancer, the R.J. Reynolds Tobacco Company advertised through newspapers and medical journals that "More doctors smoke Camels than any other cigarette".[186] While asbestosis was formally identified in the 1930s, asbestos was advertised as the 'magic material' to protect farms and homes well into the 1970s.[187] In 2006, the Competitive Enterprise Institute launched a one-minute commercial on US television that concluded: "Carbon Dioxide. They call it Pollution. We call it Life."[188] In 2011, the industry peak body Clubs Australia fought back against any form of restrictions on poker machines on the basis that it was 'un-Australian'.[189] That may be true given that Australians then (as now) comfortably led the world in gambling losses per capita,[190] but we're not sure that's what the campaign meant.

Those campaigns are now being reined in, on some platforms. In 2021, Google announced that it will "prohibit ads for, and monetization of, content that contradicts well-established scientific consensus around the existence and causes of climate change".[191] The decision was market-driven. "Advertisers simply don't want their ads to appear next to this content," they said. "And publishers and creators don't want ads promoting these claims to appear on their pages or videos."

In a similar vein, many members of the advertising and public relations industry are taking a stand against helping companies that wish to deny, demean, or divert from the scientific facts of global warming. They work together through organizations like Comms Declare in Australia and Clean Creatives globally to make it harder for fossil fuel companies to hire agencies to help them. In Australia, that has extended to many journalists and cartoonists boycotting the annual national journalism awards, the Walkley's, eventually leading to the awards' having to drop its main sponsor, Ampol.[192]

Your responsibility, not ours

There's another industry sleight of hand that is worth keeping an eye on. Rather than an industry taking responsibility for the public losses it may cause, it blames you – in the nicest possible way, of course.

Consider what all the following campaigns have in common. Support from the fast-food industry for a personal fitness campaign, 'Life. Be in it.' A campaign by BP for us to all measure a new thing called our 'carbon footprint'.[193] A campaign by plastics companies to 'Do the Right Thing' when it comes to putting our garbage in the bin. A campaign by the gambling industry to 'gamble responsibly'. A campaign by the global alcohol industry to 'drink responsibly'.

What they have in common is that a complex public challenge is reduced to personal responsibility. As we have discussed, there is an element of personal responsibility in all our behavior, including our buying decisions. However, these industries seem to be saying, 'If you are worried about what climate change/obesity/plastic pollution/gambling/alcohol is doing to your society or environment, watch your carbon/sugar/plastics/gambling/drinking manners. We'll just focus on what we do best: selling carbon/sugar/plastics/odds/drinks. And, while we're doing that, we'll push back hard against any attempt to regulate our industries.'

As consumers, we can all do our best. But we are really swimming against the tide of our consumer economy, and the choices before us. Truly sustainable production is more than possible, but it is still very rare. Where a product does lead to a measurable social harm, it is possible to limit the product and its advertising, and to tax it so that harms are reduced and compensated. It would be easier for everyone if that was the way the market operated, rather than individual consumers having to ignore most of the products they need or want to buy, in the face of persistent advertising.

Which takes us back to the original question: who is most likely to force change on an industry so that natural and social capital are protected, if governments are unwilling and consumers are unable to act?

Avoiding harm

All is not lost, however. There are some simple choices that do nothing to reduce one's quality of life but help reduce social or environmental harm.

On the environmental front, we can all think twice before using single-use plastics, cheap gadgets, 'disposable' clothing, Styrofoam and other nonrecyclable plastics, single-use batteries, chemical-laden cleaning products, nonrecyclable coffee pods, and air fresheners. A quick web search will offer any number of lists.

As we noted earlier, throwaway clothing may be the most problematic item. There's no doubt that people need affordable clothing. However, the answer can't be clothing made from high-footprint materials by people in near slave-like working conditions, survive only one or two wears, lose their shape and color almost instantly, and then make up over 10% of global landfill. Some quick facts from earth.org include that 92% of our fashion ends in landfill within a year (92 million tonnes of it, 37 kg from each American), each kilogram of cotton needs 20,000 L of water, the average number of times a garment is worn is a third less than 15 years ago (7 times, down from 10), and 10% of global microplastics come from clothing.[194]

We'd also like to make mention of salmon. It may seem an environmentally friendly protein alternative to red meats, but unfortunately that is unlikely to be the case. In his ground-breaking book *Toxic*, author Richard Flanagan sets out the grim existence of retail salmon that is factory produced in marine pens. Their nitrogen-rich diet is defecated by the tonne, obliterating all sea life around them. Lacking open sea nutrition, the fish are limp grey when harvested, and dyed pink to the retailer's order. Flanagan is the only person to win both the Booker Prize for fiction and the Baillie Gifford Prize for nonfiction, and his testimony in *Toxic* has not been rebutted by the salmon industry. The downsides of eating red meat (deforestation, methane, feedlots, land clearing) are well documented, but farmed salmon may not deserve its preferred status as an alternative.

On the social front, we can think twice about disposable clothing (again), cheap gadgets (again), and the sources of our electronics, food, footwear, jewelry, toys, and furniture. All of these industries have several examples of child or slave labor being used to make the products. We might think that buying products made with cheap labor in developing countries helps to give those workers a step on the ladder out of poverty. In some cases, that can be true but it is likely their working conditions are set to keep them in poverty.

Slavery is not a thing of the past. The nonprofit organization Walk Free estimates that 50 million people were working in slavery in 2004[195] including 28 million people in forced labor and 22 million in forced marriage. About 1 in 5 were working under conditions of forced commercial sexual exploitation, and about 1 in 10 were children.[196] Alternatively, people are working in wealthier countries like the USA, the UK, and Australia under conditions of modern slavery: they may not have full working visas, and work to survive without any union or regulatory support. The Australian Federal Police made at least 206 successful prosecutions in 2022–23 alone, which would surely be only the tip of the iceberg.

If you buy a lot of something, it's worth taking a look at how it's come into your hands, and being satisfied that avoidable harms have indeed been avoided.

Checking out your brands

At the time of writing (late 2024), the brand identity of Tesla was hitting some road bumps. Tesla cars led the world in performance electric motoring, and in home batteries to store electricity generated from rooftop solar. Now, the very people who are most likely to buy those things – wealthier people who are concerned about climate change but appreciate good design – are embarrassed that their expensive and much-loved cars bear the brand of Elon Musk. Musk's political values appear far from those he had when founding the company, and far from those of his customers. Re-branding stickers are selling like hotcakes, declaring 'I bought this before Elon went crazy', or 'Anti-Elon Tesla Club', 'Elon eats my cats', or simply 'I regret this purchase'.

Tesla, it must be remembered, was at one point in 2021 valued at more than the rest of the global auto industry put together. Yet even then, there were signs all was not well with the company. Despite very high environmental ratings, its overall ESG ratings were very low – below even that of Chevron, a major fossil fuel company. This upset Musk, who decried ESG as 'the devil incarnate'. But Tesla's low performance on governance issues (too much power in the hands of the CEO) and social issues (worker disputes and conditions) were perhaps a sign of things to come.

It's rare that such a major brand has been dropped so quickly and completely by its own customers. In the same industry, Volkswagen lost customer support when it was found to have cheated on its emissions testing. In 2015, VW admitted to the US Environmental Protection Agency (EPA) that it had used 'defeat devices' in its diesel cars to disguise actual emissions data, enabling it to meet emission targets and regulatory standards. The actual emissions were up to 40 times more than that recorded by the cars' software and in testing.[197] When the EPA notified markets that it was halting certification of VW's 2016 models, VW's global share price fell 38.2%, and its earnings per share fell 382% (that is, a previous profit turned into a loss 2.82 times as great).[198]

Again, there are ways of checking whether the brands you rely on are more or less likely to one day let you down. Every year, you might:
- Do an 'ESG brand check' by seeing if the ratings of the companies you buy from are going up or down. As we saw in Part B, many is the example of an earlier ESG red flag leading to a later corporate downfall.
- See if your company has signed up for a global commitment to do better, such as the global B-Corp initiative, and had its efforts verified.
- Check if it is involved in incidents that will have legal or reputational consequences, for example, through the Business and Human Rights database; see Box 'Sources of ESG information'.

Again, these actions may not be for everyone. But they are available, and don't take much time to look up.

Nudging change

Finally, you can engage with either the companies you deal with, or the governments who set their rules. Both are keen to hear from you.

Companies do respond to their customers. It may not be immediate, or exactly what you're looking for, but your voice adds up. An NGO may be running a campaign against a government and/or industry on the issue that concerns you. Joining those campaigns in whatever works for you is another way of nudging for change.

It's not that they're doing what you say. It's that people within the company want to do what you're suggesting. Your voice adds evidence to their argument, and energy to their work. As we explored in Part B, the people most likely to want a company to be ethical and sustainable are the people who work there. Investors and consumers can easily take their money elsewhere. Employees have a much harder decision to make.

There's no formula for making your voice heard. You do not have to write an essay, or even write well. The point is that you are letting your views as a customer be known. It does help if you are a current customer. It does help if you would have bought something but for the way it is made. It does help if you know someone who works there and who will pass on the message to the people who count. But none of these things matter too much.

The one thing that may be pointless is sharing your views with the kids at the checkout, which only puts another thing on their plate to do. Best to make a phone call or send an email to the company's contact addresses, so the suggestion gets to the right place. Then, a small tip, follow it up a week later to see what's been done. That shows you care, and puts them on the spot. And get your friends to do the same.

Governments respond to people too, hard as that may be to believe at times. So, if you really want something done, you may need to get in touch, or even get involved. That's what we pick up in Chapter 17. But first, we want to check in on where you work.

Chapter 15 summary
- There is now ample information on the human, social, and environmental impacts of the goods and services we buy. Traditional and social media have been joined by all of the ESG data that companies make available to investors – and we consumers if we want it.
- Rather than agonize over every purchase, consider checking that data to do an ESG 'stocktake' on your favorite brands every year or so, and before making big purchases.
- Where companies depend on exporting harm to people and planet to make their profits, their most common tactic is to sow confusion in the community about scientific facts and corporate intent. The same tactics have been used in selling asbestos, tobacco, fossil fuels, and gambling, and we're likely to see them again when science uncovers other harms.

- A more subtle form of greenwashing is for companies to sponsor campaigns that shift responsibility onto individual consumers. This tactic has been pursued by the plastics, fast food, alcohol, and gambling industries to avoid regulations that would limit unnecessary harm more efficiently and effectively.
- Dropping a company a friendly line supports those in the company and investors know that their consumers do care about an issue. One email, phone call, or social post won't change anything by itself, but they do add up.

Chapter 16
Working for your generation's future

Don't spend time beating on a wall, hoping to transform it into a door.
- Coco Chanel

Increasingly, graduates and experienced hires expect to work for organizations whose values align with their own, whose products and services bring them pride, and whose impacts are defensible. Companies are vocal in their commitments to all of these dimensions. But do they walk the talk? How many times have we heard companies say that 'Our people are our greatest asset' or we 'need to be customer focussed'. The statement may well be true, but saying it doesn't make it happen.

In this section, we're going to suggest what you might think of doing if a company's social and environmental impact and ethical behavior matter to you. First, we'll suggest what to look at if you're considering joining a company. Then, if you're already there, we'll suggest how you could get involved in the company's social and environmental efforts. These observations, with examples from existing companies, are just thought-starters. Talking about the possibilities with your friends or colleagues will bring you to the best place.

It's worth noting here that companies may use various terms for their ESG efforts, as we discussed in Chapter 1. Most don't use the term ESG, which is really an investment term rather than a corporate aspiration. The most common term is 'sustainability', which we will use here, although you might find the company you're interested in uses 'responsibility' or 'stewardship'. As we argued in Chapter 1, they all relate to the same actions and impacts, and the slight differences some people see in their meaning rarely go beyond academic and practitioner articles and posts.

What to look for in a company

If you're not yet in a company, it is sometimes hard to get a good feel for what it really does in its sustainability efforts. The more it matters to you, the more it's worth doing a little bit of homework. In doing so, it's highly likely you'll find out other things about the company that will interest you.

Where to look

There are three places to turn to in your research. The first is the most obvious: the company's website and the documents it offers. That will lay out the company line, as it were, which you'll want to test against other sources and your own values. You

https://doi.org/10.1515/9783111428949-021

might also ask your AI research partner for first-cut answers to your queries, however, that approach (for the moment) tends to reflect the company line. For more independent views, you might try one of the ESG ratings services, using a subscriber's login for a deeper view. You can also search for one of the ESG and sustainability news services listed at the start of this Part of the book, which often reveal NGO or court action against a company, or shareholder resolutions against their climate or governance performance.

The best view, however, may come from talking with people in the company. From them, you're likely to get a more honest appraisal of how highly sustainability ranks in the corporate priorities. It's easy to get a vanilla feel from the sustainability material that companies put online: they all might sound the same. People inside the organization will know whether sustainability has been pursued consistently, whether it makes a difference to decision-making or, alternatively, whether it is a 'value' that's jettisoned when difficult decisions have to be made. If you don't know someone within the organization, many employment firms such as Seek and Glassdoor provide forums where employees can rate their company. These forums tend to focus on what it's like to work there and may not address your broader sustainability interests, but they do provide another piece to the puzzle.

Carbon offsets and other questions to ask

Whatever your sources of intel, you'll find signs that a company meets your expectations, or doesn't.

- **Action on the specific issues you are interested in.** We all have our personal priorities on what matters most to us. Many of our female colleagues, for example, will look first at whether women are well represented in senior leadership. Across our markets, strong representation of women in leadership corresponds to better governance and performance, so that's an issue for all of us. It's particularly galling where most of a company's employees or customers are women, but the executive ranks are almost all men. The athletic company Lorna Jane currently holds that distinction. Diversity in the senior ranks is just one issue. You may equally want to know what the company is doing to reduce emissions, to keep its workers safe, to take responsibility for its physical material flows, to avoid harm to the environment, to pay people fairly, and to use local suppliers. Something to consider here is whether the company has a publicly disclosed, time bound, and quantified target to improve performance on a particular issue, and publicly report back on how they're progressing. Doing so demonstrates that the company is prepared to be publicly accountable for its actions.
- **An honest appraisal of the sustainability journey**, rather than a wash of 'commitments and celebrations'. Sustainability isn't an easy path, and nobody has got to the end. It's a good sign if the company is realistic and open about the chal-

lenges it faces; most often, that's a public or internal declaration of what it needs to work on. There's no perfect company and it's not a good sign if everything is in hand (or, more likely, claimed to be in hand): either through a commitment to achieve something that is actually quite hard or a celebration of the goodwill they have generated in a community. Sometimes, this may require the company disclosing some poor performance. We need to recognize that there are no perfect companies, suspend judgment, at least initially, and acknowledge that a) recognition of a problem is the first step in addressing it and b) others in the same sector may well be facing the same issue.

– For example, Rio Tinto published the findings of a 2022 assessment of their workplace culture.[199] The report makes for some very confronting reading for anyone who reads it, and especially for the company. The front cover says it all, warning: "We wish to advise that this report contains personal stories of those who have experienced bullying, sexual harassment and racism. As a reader, you may experience a range of emotions, particularly if you have directly experienced or witnessed these types of harmful behaviours yourself. Please use your available support networks." What it says may be enough for you to decide you do not want to work in such a place, and fair enough. But Rio Tinto is far from the only mining company facing the same issues, and used the 2022 report to trigger changes. Its two-year progress report in 2024 concluded "progress is being made with promising signs of improved culture, innovation, and performance". But there were also "mixed results, with concerning behaviours persisting in some areas and requiring sustained attention to address effectively."[200] The thing is, the reports highlight a recognition by Rio Tinto that it needs to be publicly accountable for its (good and bad) culture and that is a positive step by the company.

– **Taking on something bigger than themselves.** Is the company focused on its own activities, or is it collaborating with others to take on a bigger issue? The social, economic, and environmental problems of the world are rarely the result of one company's actions. Typically, one or more industries are contributing, acting as if the world's human, social, and natural capital are theirs to use and abuse. For example, soft plastics are everywhere but rarely recycled. There is a difference between something being recyclable and whether it is ultimately recycled. Keeping them out of the environment needs the plastics, brand, manufacturing, logistics, retail, and waste industries to work together.

For reasons unknown, when an industry problem is identified, the industry often rushes to adopt a voluntary code. These don't work. The companies have to monitor their own compliance, and take it up with their competitors if there's a breach. Neither happens. The problem remains, the media becomes interested, and protests grow louder. Eventually, the government is forced to act, and starts 'consultation' on appropriate regulation to stop the problem.

– **Taking responsibility for the costs imposed on others, rather than offsetting them with community 'good works'.** It seems reasonable that, if a company's core business is shown to harm people or the environment, the company should minimize and/or pay for that harm. For example, countries including the UK, Mexico, and South Africa impose a sugar tax on drinks with added sugar, which goes some small way to pay the lost productivity and healthcare costs of diabetes. More often, however, a company can earn profits from that business, without having to pay for the costs.

The most egregious example is the gambling industry, whose tax contribution falls far short of the social cost of problem gambling. In Australia, where gambling losses are the world's highest per capita, gambling is estimated to cost gamblers $25 billion a year in direct losses, and substantially more in the social costs of crime, money laundering, distrust within families, domestic violence, bankruptcy, and suicide.[201] Gambling has been estimated to account for 22% of mental health treatment.[202] These losses are led by the poker machine industry, with 90% of machines housed in local clubs. Yet any attempt to restrain the advertising or extent of gambling, or recover its costs, is fiercely fought and has to date been lamentably unsuccessful. Restraining gambling advertising goes against the tide. In the USA, the National Football League (NFL) lobbied for decades *for* laws to keep gambling on its sport off the field and off the screen. Once the Supreme Court ruled those laws as unconstitutional in 2018, the NFL switched plays to benefit from high-volume advertising on the field and during broadcasts.[203] The small contribution to community good works cannot be held up in comparison in an attempt to net out the obvious harm.

- **An approach to sustainability that makes sense for the company.** In the early days of sustainability, many strategies or approaches seemed the same. Companies may have borrowed ideas from their peers, or from where their sustainability leads used to work, or slavishly copied the reporting frameworks. Fortunately, many companies are now linking their sustainability approaches more tightly to their broader corporate and brand strategies. You can see how they both lock together – and in some companies, there is no distinction: sustainability is part of the core strategy, just as much as the goods or services they sell, the markets they operate in, or the culture they foster.

  You'll also see connections between the company business and its sustainability priorities. A food company may stress the sustainable use of land. A social media company may make a particular effort to minimize their negative social and mental health impacts. A residential development company may focus on social connections as much as embedded carbon. If their sustainability priorities seem random or disconnected from the business, then there may not have been much thought in setting those priorities – and very little likelihood of success in pursuing them.

- **Opportunities to get involved.** This may not be for everyone, but if you're interested enough to read this passage, you may be interested in being part of your company's push toward sustainability. In reading a sustainability report, have a look at the initiatives they're celebrating. Are only the company's senior executives involved, for example, in 'sleeping out for the homeless' or other opportunities to mingle with executives from other companies? Instead, you're looking for evidence that you can bring both your capabilities and your ideas to the sustainability effort. Initiatives suggested by employees, taken up by the company, run by employees, and persisted over time offer the best proof of the company's positive intent.

– **Talking to people outside their industry.** Many companies have a systematic plan to talk with people or communities who may be affected by their products or their inputs. This could involve a regular tour of those communities by the company's own people, research by an independent agency on those impacts, an external advisory council of people made up of those communities – or all three. This will give the company a greater chance of understanding what those communities think and feel about its actions, and a greater chance of changing them when needed. There's no guarantee of course, but this community outreach improves the odds.

– **Carbon offsets that really do offset carbon emissions, and do more than that.** We've all been offered a way to offset the emissions from our purchases – most often when buying an airline ticket. Many think the airline should just offset all of its flights, and incorporate the cost into all tickets. Others feel offsets should be voluntary, as making it compulsory might offend those who feel they are to fly without paying for any environmental consequences, or that there are no environmental consequences as climate change is a myth.

Some companies do what the law requires, and leave the rest up to customers to take individual responsibility, if they wish. Others take on the responsibility themselves, and push ahead on a plan to reduce their greenhouse gas emissions not only for their operations but also through their supply chain. To get to net zero, offsets are needed, as there is no physical possibility of our economies running without emitting any greenhouse gases.

Our job as employees and consumers is to be sure that the company is first focusing on reducing its emissions. Then we can check that its offsets are real, and not a convenient (and cheap) way to avoid tackling climate change. Checking whether carbon offsets are real is not as hard as it seems. There are transparent, international registries where you can look up an offset scheme, and check how the offsets are generated. These are listed at the start of this Part of the book. If the claimed offsets can't be found on these registries, then the company is likely to be greenwashing.

When you're looking at the registries, questions to consider include:
– How are the carbon offsets being generated? This might be stopping the felling of old-growth native forests, or restoring carbon to agricultural soils, or a cleaner industrial process. All may be quite legitimate, but which would you like to be paying for?

- What are the social co-benefits? Some offset programs offer income and other social benefits to local communities. Often, those communities have found it hard
to break the poverty cycle, because the price of the commodity product they sell
isn't rising in real terms, while their land progressively loses its ability to grow it.
Offset programs that involve the community in more sustainable forms of agriculture will deliver benefits for many years to come. Often, the income from the carbon offsets has been the circuit-breaker, paying for relatively simple pipes, systems, tools, and know-how that can regenerate land that has been over-farmed or
farmed unsustainably.
- Who can I ask about the offset program? In the registries, you will find the people, communities, and companies who collaborated on the project. If you really
want to know whether the project was a success, give them a call.

Red flags for companies you really don't want to work for

The previous section suggested some of the questions you may consider before devot-
ing the next five years of your working life to a company. In this short section, we
suggest a few red flags that might exclude the company from tapping into your valuable human capital.

It's not a comprehensive list, of course, and it reveals more about our personal
preferences than yours. Nonetheless, we ask you to keep them in mind.

- **Has the company funded or published misinformation on critical social and
environmental issues, or fought against being held responsible for its harmful actions?** Why anyone would want to work for these companies, knowing
what they have done, is a mystery. The question is not just one of ethics but also
one of self-interest. How transparent would they likely be on a sensitive employee
matter? How would their win-at-all-cost attitude play out if you had an issue with
the company on the terms of your employment, or with what you were being
asked to do?

    The list of actions that companies have denied as harmful despite the evi-
    dence is long: nicotine, asbestos, thalidomide, greenhouse gas emissions, poor or
    nonexistent financial advice, the negative impact of social media on children, the
    social impact of problem gambling, the contribution of alcohol to domestic vio-
    lence or social impacts on particular social groups. It may be negligent for a com-
    pany to continue acting if they don't know of the harm. But it reveals a sickening
    disregard for humanity where a company does know and acts anyway. Often, it's
    the companies themselves who know of the harm before anyone else: their prod-
    uct research has revealed it; see Chapter 15.

    Similarly, one should question working for companies that double down on
    their right to harm others. Once called out in public, the only sensible course of
    action is to admit liability and own the mistakes. The alternative is to try to avoid

legal responsibility, as Rio Tinto did when it blew up Juukan Gorge; see Chapter 6. When companies suffer those losses, employees may bear the repercussions.

– **Do they treat ESG as little more than a marketing opportunity?** Companies that don't take environmental and social issues seriously can also harm our social and natural capital. The path of causation may not be as direct as those in the above category, but they can still do a lot of unintended damage. We are thinking of those companies that say things like 'sustainability is in our DNA', or 'we are committed to protecting our beautiful environment', but then show little evidence of either. Their sustainability reports are big on color and gloss, gorgeous locations, and smiling people, but little on facts and transparency.

Our issue with these companies is that they open all companies to the criticism that 'all ESG is just greenwashing', and cynicism against any effort. Granted, that cynicism comes from those who don't want to do anything anyway; those who stick to a very perverted notion of freedom that suggests we can do whatever we want, whatever the consequences. Yet these are powerful voices, and when singing in concert, they can prevent even the most necessary of corporate regulation.

As a potential employee, the question is how would this company treat the things that you are concerned about? How do they treat safety issues, or culture issues like bullying or racism, or diversity opportunities? If a serious issue arose on any matter, would they be more likely to deal with it honestly and responsibly, or more likely to sweep it under the carpet?

– **Is what they say publicly consistent with what they say behind closed doors or through industry associations?** Some companies are good at projecting one image but saying something very different, either directly or via their industry association, to the government. For example, a car company may advertise their EV or hybrid car models, but at the same time lobby hard against reductions in vehicle emission standards, as it might undermine their top-selling car or they know they are at a competitive disadvantage in the EV market. Companies are increasingly being asked to publicly disclose their lobbying activities. Organizations like InfluenceMap[204] track company, and industry association, lobbying on issues like climate change and plastics.

It's also worth looking at whether a company disagrees with its industry association on an issue you care about, and what it does about that misalignment. It's very rare that the company resigns from an association, though it does happen. Often, there is a genuine attempt to 'foster change from within'. Just as often, there is a desire to have a cake and eat it too: support the association's behind-the-scenes lobbying while holding an opposite view in public. Alternatively, an industry association may state that it agrees 'in principle' with the environmental or social objective of a proposed regulation, but then more forcefully argue why whatever is being proposed won't work, is too hard to be done now or there is a need to wait until someone else, or some other country, does something.

As we said in Chapter 8, investors look at a company's record on ESG matters as a proxy for their general quality of management. It indicates how they treat inconvenient issues and truths. Much of this record is in the public domain, in a way that more direct management and employee issues are not. It's often a worthwhile record to inspect.

How to help out in your company

More likely than not, you're working for a company that is serious about taking responsibility for its social and environmental impacts. Most people are good people, and good people feel uncomfortable living to one set of standards in their personal and community lives, and to another, lower, set of standards in their working lives. So, efforts are found in most companies to lessen their unintended social or environmental harm.

That being the case, there will always be a chance to join in existing efforts on sustainability, or even to initiate one. Having helped many people do so, and made a few mistakes of our own, what follows is a few of our lessons learned. It's only food for thought, and your own character and experience will be just as valuable, and likely more.

When there are already good initiatives running, think about joining in. Many people think that a good life is enjoyed when you're giving something to your family, your work, your community, and to something special of your own. There are many ways to work for your community, including its natural environment, and doing it through your workplace is just one.

As with other volunteer efforts, it may be wise to pare back your expectations. People take on these activities on top of their core work responsibilities. Although they try to apply the same work disciplines, the pressure to deliver is rarely as immediate, or as well supported across the organization. Though we always advise companies to 'manage your sustainability initiatives just like you would any other', they rarely do. So, people tend to muddle their way through to what is possible, rather than drive to a stretch target. To prosper in these circumstances, which can be a little uncertain and frustrating, you need to bring your best self to the party: friendly, positive, patient, curious, helpful, and thoughtful. Realize that the learning and relationships that you gather are just as important as the end goal. (And conversely, if you're not gaining either, invest your time in something else.)

Deciding to kick off an initiative of your own is another matter entirely. You'll need all of the above, of course. And you'll need to be able to see it through. The history of corporate sustainability is littered with half-hearted attempts to support a good cause, before petering out in disappointment. The problem is that these efforts can eat up your personal goodwill or social capital and, if they involve people outside the company, the company's social capital. We shouldn't fear failure, but should be ready to give the initiative a very strong shot, over a significant period of time. Choose your battles carefully.

Ideally, you'll gather a few colleagues willing to work with you, and think through the best approaches. As we saw back in Chapter 6, you'll need to be able to connect your idea to a company priority – it's hard for people to back things that are totally removed from their purpose at work, and they won't back it to the end unless that connection is clear. And you'll need to articulate that connection to those who don't immediately see it, even if they don't understand it immediately. And if you can't connect the dots between your initiative and their priorities, think twice before asking for their help. Most people are time-poor at work, as much as they'd like it differently, and the pressure to meet corporate targets can be intense.

It will help if you have already established a value that people respect you for, and that value can be expressed through your initiative. People will be more likely to support your push to ditch disposable coffee cups and food containers, if they know you've been doing that yourself for some time. While people don't always agree on values held by others, they do respect people who act on them consistently, assuming that's not to the cost of others. They won't actively resist you if that's what you want to do, and with luck and good humor, the values may catch on.

Finally, be open to someone else taking over 'your initiative', at anyone's request. That can be hard, but it's actually a sign of your success. Your initiative will now be bigger than you alone can make it. The social or environmental benefit is now one step closer. If that's your primary concern, then you can continue to make it happen as part of a bigger team. Or, if your primary concern is to lead something positive of your own, no matter how small, then there will be other issues you can act on – and people will be more likely to support you, given your earlier success.

If your job is directly related to a company's sustainability effort, don't be surprised or take it personally if you get pushback. It may be because they don't understand the reasons well enough, or they may genuinely disagree with what you are proposing. It may be that people are very good at the very thing you want to change, or have been doing it for a long time. All of us have faced a change at some point in our lives, which we have found threatening. That's where real cultural and personal values are needed, respect for others and a commitment to work together.

Chapter 16 summary
- If you are considering working for a company (or giving it your human capital), have a look at its ESG record in the same way an investor would. It can be very revealing.
- Issues to consider are what they are doing on issues that are important to you, whether they take or shift responsibility for harm to others, and whether their sustainability approach actually matches their business or seems disconnected.
- Companies that are willing to treat their communities and consumers poorly are more likely to treat their employees poorly as well.
- Getting involved in a sustainability effort may not be easy, but it is likely to be worthwhile in lessons learned, relationships, and fulfillment.

Chapter 17
Being a citizen

We here highly resolve that these dead shall not have died in vain – that this nation, under God, shall have a new birth of freedom – and that government of the people, by the people, for the people, shall not perish from the earth.

Abraham Lincoln, dedicating the dead at Gettysburg, 1863

In an ideal democracy, it is 'we the people' who rule as citizens. We elect our representatives in government, and they set policy and get things done. If we're happy, we elect them again; if not, we elect someone else. If we're not allowed a fair vote, we're not in a democracy. If we choose not to vote, we can hardly complain of the outcome.

We would argue that governments are essential, and that their purpose is to nurture the social, human, natural, and financial capital of the people they serve. Ultimately, we judge their performance on how they advance and balance these assets.

We have included this section in the book to help make the point that ESG is not the answer to social and environmental issues. It can certainly help, and help we capitalists prosper for the long term, but it is a weak instrument on its own. It helps influence our markets, but it is governments that set the purpose, tone, and direction of those markets. As we say in Part A, the markets of capitalism are enormously powerful engines for getting things done. Governments set their direction, their limits, and the way they operate. Governments have the final say.

Our observations are informed not only by our experience as citizens, but by being involved in both the political process and with the machinery of government. We have worked with economically conservative, socially progressive politicians who act as centrist independents in Australia's parliamentary system. We have also worked with government departments seeking to get things done on economic, social, and environmental issues. We seek to raise questions, rather than answer them.

We need a government

If a government's purpose is to nurture the four capitals, the extent to which it leaves outcomes to 'the market' helps define its economic philosophy, while its 'values' define its social philosophy. There is always a tension between the two.

Markets aren't perfect. In theory, they work fine when everyone has all the information, and equal power to act on it. This never happens, so markets fail us. The employment market is a classic example. Consider an individual trying to get a job in a large company. Unless the individual has a particular skill or experience which gives them leverage, it can be a pretty one-sided affair: 'Here's the job; take it or leave it'. Or consider hiring a tradesperson to do something you desperately need done, but

https://doi.org/10.1515/9783111428949-022

couldn't work out how to do in a month of Sundays. In both cases, there is unequal knowledge and unequal power. The end result will come down to trust.

Markets aren't self-directed to provide what people need. People might need affordable housing close to their jobs, but the housing market is set to build only costly housing near job centers, or affordable housing far away. So, unless a government steps in, people will have ever-longer commutes to their work.

Markets create losses for others. People want affordable furniture. As long as the piece does the job and looks good in the store, people will buy it. Firms then compete on looks and price. So they look for the cheapest (copied) designs, the cheapest materials, and the cheapest labor. If that means the supply chain logs native forests for chip, bonds materials with carcinogens, and uses slave labor, then human, natural, and social capital are eroded. Companies and investors may fight against this through their ESG policies, but that gives the companies that take shortcuts an even greater financial advantage. People are protected from these harms only when governments set and enforce laws.

In times past, one might think that a conservative government would prefer a relatively free market: let business roll and seek financial stability before spending on social goods. A more progressive government would take the opposite approach: define the social goods it wants, and then set market rules both to deliver those goods and to raise the funds to pay for it.

If that used to be the case, recent political outcomes suggest the lines are no longer so clear-cut. 'Conservative' governments are just as prone to direct and constrain markets for political ends as are progressive ones. Increasingly, indeed, progressive ones stand for a rules-based order to maintain national and international markets, though they do want to set clear rules.

In the end, the choice of government comes down to a simple question: how much money and power does a government need to deliver the society we want?

Every day, you have the power to help determine its answer. It may not feel that way, but it's true. And it's also essential that you do. The results of citizen inaction can be alarming. If citizens aren't active, then louder, paid industry voices will have too great a say, and outcomes will favor those industries rather than the broader population. Then, all the individual efforts made in our financial, corporate, community, and political spheres may come to naught.

In this brief chapter, we offer some thoughts on how you can take up your rights as a citizen with more power and purpose. We will talk about engaging with your government:

- on the basis of what they deliver (that is, from a four capitals perspective), and
- on the basis of how they are doing it (that is, from a good governance perspective).

Your governments and organizations are not so different after all. It's just that the government's job is so much harder. It serves all of us, not just the customers and employees it chooses. It takes on the jobs that markets leave alone. It must do everything according to the rules it sets. It is subject to deep and painful public review every step of the way. And those who take on this impossible task on our behalf are typically rewarded a fraction of what they would earn in the private sector.

Still, we should sack them all if they don't do a good job.

Voting and engaging from the four capitals perspective

Increasingly, it seems that politics are becoming tribal. You belong to either blue or red or another tribe, and take their side no matter what. This is a deliberate view of democracy, advanced in rather disturbing ways by Perry Jotter in his book *Modern Tribal Politics,* and more subtly by think tanks like The Heritage Foundation. The rebuttal by the Irish journalist Fintan O'Toole is compelling,[205] but it seems tribalism is here to stay, at least for a while.

Unless you're locked into the red or blue no matter what, if you have an open mind on who might do a better job for the next term, it's worth weighing up the political candidates from the four capitals perspective. This means considering the natural, human, social, and financial capitals together, and making decisions around them.

It's the job of our governments to trade off short-term losses of one form of capital for greater and more lasting gains in others, so that at the end of their term in office, all four of the nation's capitals are enhanced. Too often, however, one or more capitals are pursued to the detriment of the others, or governments don't think beyond the election cycle, and we all suffer in the long term.

Having a vote

So, how can you assess what a political candidate might do to the four capitals? You have to assess their track record, their declared principles, their declared policies, and your belief on whether they will actually deliver on those principles and policies (that is, do you trust them to do what they say?). We still find it astonishing that in seeking re-election, governments do such a poor job in laying out their track record and what they have achieved. The media may not run with it, but at least it's there for the curious.

From the capitals perspective, you could first consider each independently:
– **Would they leave their patch in a stronger financial position than before?**
  That doesn't mean having more or less of a surplus. It could be that they have spent public moneys on things, like infrastructure, that will generate more money in the future. If they underspend on these things, then they'll break down, and be more costly for future generations to fix. Yet if they overspend, then the interest bills will crowd out more worthwhile things.

- **Would they leave their patch with a stronger well of human capital to draw on?** This may mean increasing any combination of the number of people, or the education of people, or the energy of people, or the basic security of people to do productive things (that is, the peace, safety, shelter, and nutrition people need to apply themselves). Which are they intending to do? Given human capital can be spread unevenly across a population, will the government focus on the human capital of everyone, on providing education and basic security to those without, or some other subsection of the population? Would it even measure those things, or recognize and act if the stock of human capital or its foundations were dangerously low?
- **Would the political candidate add to social capital, or diminish it?** Remember that social capital is simply the capacity of one group of people to do things with another group of people. Would a nation be in a better or worse position to do things with other nations? Would it be harder or easier for people within the nation to work together and agree on things? Would there be more or less trust in a community? Would there be more or less understanding of what people need to work together and agree on things? Would it even measure those things, or recognize and act if the stock of social capital or its foundations were dangerously low?
- **Would the candidate leave their patch with more or less natural capital than before?** This would take in both the extent of natural resources (flora and fauna, atmosphere, minerals, water, visual landscapes) and the quality of that resource. Would it even measure those things, or recognize and act if the stock of natural capital or its foundations were dangerously low?

It also requires the government to think about how they manage the future risks to these capitals.

Thinking in this way is a useful first step. But pretty quickly, you appreciate that the four capitals are interdependent. If there is too much imbalance in the community's sharing of financial and human capital, then social capital will be at risk. Financial capital is needed to reinvest in the other three capitals, but if the focus on financial capital is too great, then each of the others may be at risk. Natural capital is needed to provide for people's needs and inspire their human existence, but if the focus on natural capital is too great, then financial and social capital may be at risk.

This is the constant judgment and juggle that good governments attempt. A candidate that doesn't consider each of the four capitals and their interdependencies may not be your best choice.

Having a say

Your vote is not your final say, though.

While in office, governments can and do respond to people who have a say. That may seem to be through the clutter of media generated by opinion polls and advocacy groups. More powerfully, it is through your direct interaction: responding to their official and personal social media, writing, phoning; either individually or as part of a movement.

In doing so, it helps to say why you are voicing your concerns. It may be because you or someone close to you are directly affected by bad policy or gaps in the law. It will also help to voice your complaint by pointing out the false trade-offs. Fight the advertising and access that leads to problem gambling not just because of the people you may know to be its victims (and the probability of that is extremely high). Remind your representatives that the deep personal harm far outweighs the slightly constrained 'fun' (human capital); that the shame, loneliness, suicide, theft, and family violence far outweigh the fun from the odd occasion of hanging out with friends (social capital); and that the losses in physical and mental health, social services and productivity far outweigh the gambling market profits, across the population (financial capital).

It also helps to be part of the political life of your community. This is one form of the volunteerism on which our societies depend. You'll have to go a long way to find a person who has volunteered for a community organization and regretted the time they spent there (despite the obvious and many frustrations!). Spending time with your local charity, or sporting or musical club, adds to our human and social capital and can be a lot of fun. So too can engaging with the more serious side of life. Non-profit service or advocacy groups, policy think tanks, and even a local politician are all opportunities to have a say in the society you want, adding your voice and effort to those of similar views. The more people like you get involved, the more likely society will get past the destructive tribalism that weakens our political culture and our human, social, natural, and financial capital.

Voting and engaging from a governance perspective

In a democracy, it also matters how government decisions are made and implemented. The ends do not justify the means. That's because democracy depends on trust. If decisions and deals are not transparent and do not abide by the rules, people may have cause to believe they're not made for the right reasons. The public benefits when governments take an efficient, effective, and equitable path toward something we desire, appreciate, or accept.

The rules by which a government takes action matter. Most of us would agree that everyone is equal before the law and must comply with the law. The alternative is anarchy, which history suggests works out well in the short term for the most powerful at the expense of everyone else, and ends in catastrophe not long after. The laws extend to how a government must act: through a transparent process in which voices are heard and rights are respected. As laid out by Ian Dunt in his 2020 masterpiece *How to be a Liberal*,[206] these laws have been forged and tested through the fires of revolution, government action, law courts, and civil protest since the mid-1600s. They work.

No good comes from a government choosing to shortcut these rules. You might like one or two of their actions, but you won't like the end result of hundreds of actions taken together. If policies are made without open debate, they're likely to favor only those in the room. If contracts are awarded without an open process, they're likely to favor only those with connections. If decisions are made without all sides being considered, they'll be unlikely to lead to the best outcomes.

Over time, these shortcuts erode trust in government. Any government decision will lead to some people losing a little of what they have, so that most can have more. We accept that situation if we have faith that decisions are being properly made, and that we won't be on the losing end too often. Shortcuts in governance erode that faith, and will likely lead to some of us being on the losing end too often. Then people become disillusioned and disengaged, then angry. It becomes harder for governments to do anything at all for the public good. In Australia, one measure of trust in governments fell from 53% in 2020 to 34% in 2024, and the fall in trust in large businesses almost as great from 33% to 26%, while trust in local community information held up at 45%.[207]

For these reasons, in considering a political candidate, ask whether they are likely or not to follow the rules of good governance that apply as much to a government as your own organization. All of these questions would be part of an ESG scan of an organization's board and management,[208] and could equally apply to our governments.

- Do they represent the values, culture, and integrity you would expect?
- On issues that they are a party to, would they accept independent and objective oversight, evidence, or court rulings?
- Would they be transparent in their decision-making, consider a range of diverse opinions, and resist industry lobbying?
- How would they perform in a crisis?
- Have they been subject to any misconduct or disciplinary measures?
- Have they been disclosed their funding sources and financial holdings?
- Do they keep a public record of their meetings?
- Have they supported legislation to combat core ESG concerns such as tax avoidance, anticompetitive conduct, modern slavery, and environmental pollution?

No politician would have a perfect record on these matters – none of us would either. In the same way, we're not likely to agree with every decision even our most favored politician will make. Yet we're looking for the ones we'd agree with the most, and would most likely act toward the outcomes we want. A candidate with a better governance record would be more likely to take those actions, than one who did not.

* * *

Investors have found that ESG improves their outcomes or reduces their risk, or both. Companies have found that keeping an eye on their natural, human, and social capital tends to lead to greater financial capital. As individuals and as a community, we benefit if they do. So it makes sense to ask whether the companies we spend our capital on – those that we work for, buy from, or invest in – apply those principles or not. We can also ask whether the candidates who seek our vote are more or less likely to benefit our communities. Or, if they claim they're on your side, we can test that claim using the four capitals and governance lenses. That's a big ask, so it's lucky we don't vote every day.

Chapter 17 summary
- Markets are powerful and essential, but they aren't perfect. People have unequal information and bargaining power. Markets aren't self-directed to provide what people need. Markets create losses for others.
- Governments are also essential, with a purpose to nurture the social, human, natural, and financial capital of the people they serve. They should correct the market where if fails through regulation or policy or nudge it in the right direction when it is not sending the right signals. They trade off short-term losses of one form of capital for greater and more lasting gains in others, so that at the end of their term in office, all four of our capitals are enhanced.
- In considering a candidate, ask: Would they leave their patch in a stronger financial position than before? Would they leave it with a stronger well of human capital to draw on? Would they leave it with more or less natural capital than before? Would they add to social capital, or diminish it?
- Governance also matters, things a company is assessed on, like integrity, respect for our laws, transparency, and responses to a crisis or misconduct. No one has a perfect record on these matters. Yet a candidate with a better governance record would be more likely to act for the benefit of the community than one who did not.
- If we do not vote or otherwise participate in the election of candidates, then we can hardly complain about the results.

ESG Unlocked

This book was written to capture the joint experience of our 52 years working in capital markets and for capitalist firms. We were motivated by the mounting evidence that our markets are not safeguarding our long-term natural, human, social, and financial capital. All of us – companies, investors, individuals, and governments – can help halt and reverse this self-defeating trend.

To help appreciate ESG's potential, we've traced some historical threads, not least of which is the democratization of capital and the power of individuals to make a difference through their work, communities, and investments. We have shown how companies that take a responsible stance on governance, social, and environmental matters will have more access to capital, and to more diverse sources of capital.

Those who hold a slice of the four capitals are as different as the companies that seek them. So there's no one way to 'do' ESG. What matters is that the company has a clear, coherent, and connected approach to ESG and the value it can create and can articulate that to those who count.

This set of beliefs has been openly challenged every day we were writing the book. Indeed, the last months of its writing coincided with direct attempts to malign ESG. If ESG is being questioned at this time, it is because it is not well understood. It is one of many convenient scapegoats for problems whose causes lie far deeper in our economies and nations.

We have therefore sought to unlock the mysteries of ESG, and to show how – far from being a constraint on capitalism – it is essential for its survival. ESG helps to future-proof capitalism by protecting and growing the natural, human, and social capital on which it depends.

Investors and companies will continue to consider ESG factors because they recognize that capitalism and its markets are never zero-sum games. They know that others don't have to lose for them to win, and that the deal currently on the table is not the only one that matters. They understand that their wealth is dependent on our shared natural, human, and social capital, and that actions that take or erode those capitals will only work in the short term.

To put it bluntly, capitalism will not survive if our markets lead to a sudden shift to an uninhabitable climate, the loss of our biodiversity, a loss of hope and dignity in our human capital, and the shredding of trust in our social capital. The market economy that we capitalists have learned to enjoy will be replaced by something less forgiving and less able to offer opportunities to future generations. And that will be accompanied by political systems that are also less forgiving and less able to offer opportunities to future generations.

Recent global events suggest that these concerns are not far-fetched. But those events need not be the direction of our future. We have choices. And we hope that this book will contribute to a capitalism in which the right choices are made for this and future generations.

https://doi.org/10.1515/9783111428949-023

Acknowledgments

We first acknowledge the generation of corporate sustainability and ESG leaders we have been fortunate to witness firsthand in the lead up to 2006 – when the UN Principles of Responsible Investing was launched – and the vastly larger generation that has brought ESG into mainstream investing since that date.

In particular, we thank the work and inspiration of Thomas Clarke, Stirling Habbitts, Steve Drummond, Steve Hatfield-Dodds, Stephen Burt, Siobhan Toohill, Siobhan Leach, Sasha Courville, Sarah Colenbrander, Rory Sullivan, Rob McLean, Rob Lake, Rob Koczkar, Rachel Alembakis, Pru Bennett, Pieter Winsemius, Paul Gilding, Nick Robins, Nichole Hertogs, Mike Tyrell, Mike Murray, Mick Lovely, Michael Anderson, Matthew Kiernan, Martijn Wilder, Mark Lyster, Mark Diesendorf, Mark Campanale, Mark Bytheway, Maria Atkinson, Mara Bun, Louise Davidson, Kingsley Slipper, Kelvin Templeton, John Elkington, Jed Sturman, James Connelly, James Coleman, Grant Hunt, Gerard Castles, Gavin Gilchrist, Fiona Reynolds, Duncan Patterson, Dexter Dunphy, Ben Spruzen, Andrew Peterson, Amory Lovins, Alison Ewings, and the AMP Capital ESG Research team.

Thank you to those friends and family who have continued to believe in this venture and give guidance on either how to execute it or recover from it. Nick Fowler, Sara Dowse, Merren McArthur, Fiona Reynolds, and Rory Sullivan have been kind enough to read and comment on the whole manuscript. Neil Young did an amazing job bringing all the charts to life from various sketches and sources.

Our agents, Nick Wallwork and Christopher Newson, found the right publisher in the patient and thorough Stefan Giesen at DeGruyter, where Maximillian Gessl guided the book through production.

Any errors that remain are those of the authors, despite our best efforts.

https://doi.org/10.1515/9783111428949-024

Endnote references

1 Kerber R and Jessop S (2024), 'How 2021 became the year of ESG investing', *Reuters News*, 24 December.

2 UN Secretary-General (1987), Report of the World Commission on Environment and Development: Our common future.

3 Porter ME and Kramer MR (2011), 'Creating Shared Value', *Harvard Business Review*, January 2011.

4 Gleeson-White J (2014), *The Six Capitals: The revolution capitalism has to has*, Allen & Unwin.

5 Fink L (2022), 'Letter to CEOs: The Power of Capitalism', https://www.blackrock.com/corporate/investor-relations/larry-fink-ceo-letter accessed 26 October 2022.

6 Harari YN (2011), *Sapiens*, Vintage.

7 Carson R (1962) *Silent Spring*, Houghton Mifflin. First published as a serial in *The New Yorker*.

8 Freshfields (2005), 'A legal framework for the integration of environmental, social and governance issues into institutional investment', UN Environmental Program Finance Initiative.

9 Porter ME and Kramer MR (2006), 'Strategy and Society: The Link between Competitive Advantage and Corporate Social Responsibility', *Harvard Business Review*, December 2006.

10 Fink L (2022) Letter to CEOs: The Power of Capitalism, https://www.blackrock.com/corporate/investor-relations/larry-fink-ceo-letter accessed 26 October 2022.

11 Principles of Responsible Investment (2023), *Signatory Update*, December 2023.

12 The Economist (2022), 'ESG should be boiled down to one simple measure: emissions (Three letters that won't save the planet)', Leader, 21 July.

13 Quoted in Gleeson-White (2014), *The Six Capitals: The revolution capitalism has to has*, Allen & Unwin. Again there is natural capital, then social capital, then human as well as intellectual capital (or IP), then manufactured as well as financial capital. There are real distinctions within the two sets of capital that have been merged. Human capital stays with the person, while intellectual capital can be transferred. Material capital includes physical assets, while financial capital is cash. Nonetheless the four capitals correspond to the original six quite directly but are easier to talk about. There is also a convenient correlation between human capital and an organisation's people, and social capital and its external stakeholders.

14 Ocean Tomo (2020), 'Intangible Asset Market Value Study', https://oceantomo.com/intangible-asset-market-value-study/ accessed on 15 March 2021.

15 Druckman P (2013), 'Internal Audit is the Glue', speech to the Institute of Internal Auditors International Conference https://integratedreporting.ifrs.org/news/paul-druckman-internal-audit-is-the-glue/ accessed 14 December 2024.

16 The model applies to any public or private organisation, for profit and non-profit, however this discussion focuses on a private or listed company, for whom action on the ESG cycle is most urgent.

17 Blume ME, Crockett J and Friend I (1974), 'Stockownership in the United States: Characteristics and Trends', *Survey of Current Business*, Federal Reserve Bank of St Louis.

18 ASX (2023), 'Australian Investor Study 2023,' https://www.asx.com.au/content/dam/asx/blog/asx-australian-investor-study-2023.pdf accessed 15 December 2024.

19 The Economist (1999), 'Fuel cells meet big business', July 24.

20 Friede G, Busch T and Bassen A (2015), 'ESG and financial performance: aggregated evidence from more than 2000 empirical studies', *Journal of Sustainable Finance & Investment*, 5(4).

21 Giese G, Kumar N, Nagy Z and Kouzmenko R (2021), 'The Drivers of ESG Returns - A Fundamental Return Decomposition Approach', MSCI, https://www.msci.com/documents/10199/f31964d0-c79b-02af-45cc-fada2887d085# accessed 16 December 2024.

22 Morgan Stanley (2015), 'Sustainable Reality: Understanding the Performance of Sustainable Investment Strategies', Institute for Sustainable Research https://www.riacanada.ca/research/sustainable-reality-understanding-the-performance-of-sustainable-investment-strategies/ accessed 16 December 2024.

https://doi.org/10.1515/9783111428949-025

23 Du J, Thomas B, Zvingelis J (2014), 'Exploration of the Cross-Sectional Return Distributions of Socially Responsible Investment Funds', *SRI Journal,* Elsevier, 31 July.

24 Morgan Stanley (2021) 'Sustainable Funds Outperform peers in 2020 Coronavirus', Institute for Sustainable Investing, https://www.morganstanley.com/ideas/esg-funds-outperform-peers-coronavirus accessed 16 December 2024.

25 McKinsey & Co (2023) 'How do ESG goals impact a company's growth performance?, https://www.mckinsey.com/capabilities/growth-marketing-and-sales/our-insights/next-in-growth/how-do-esg-goals-impact-a-companys-growth-performance accessed 17 July 2023..

26 SenateSHJ (2022), *Crisis Value Erosion Index: A report on the financial impacts of crises on 70 listed companies from around the world,* www.senateshj.com.au accessed 15 December 2022.

27 SenateSHJ (2022), *Crisis Value Erosion Index: A report on the financial impacts of crises on 70 listed companies from around the world,* www.senateshj.com.au accessed 15 December 2022.

28 Norton Rose Fulbright (2021), 'ESG: What boards of directors should do now', https://www.nortonrosefulbright.com/en/knowledge/publications/bed17bb0/esg-what-boards-of-directors-should-do-now accessed 15 December 2022.

29 Lumsden A and Fridman S (2007), 'Corporate Social Responsibility: The Case for a Self-Regulatory Model' 25 *Company and Securities Law Journal* 147 at 167, quoting from Porter M and Kramer M (2002), 'The Competitive Advantage of Corporate Philanthropy', *Harvard Business Review.*

30 Freshfields (2009), 'Fiduciary responsibility: Legal and practical aspects of integrating environmental, social and governance issues into institutional investment', UN Environmental Program Finance Initiative.

31 Freshfields (2005), 'A legal framework for the integration of environmental, social and governance issues into institutional investment', UN Environmental Program Finance Initiative.

32 US Securities and Exchange Commission (2022), 'SEC Announces Enforcement Results for FY22', Media Release, 15 November.

33 Grantham J (2018), 'The race of our lives reconsidered', GMO white paper, https://www.gmo.com/australia/research-library/the-race-of-our-lives-revisited accessed 24 November 2024.

34 US House of Representatives Judiciary Committee (2024), 'Climate control: exposing the decarbonization collusion in environmental, social, and governance (ESG) investing', interim staff report, 11 June.

35 US House of Representative Judiciary Committee (2024), 'Jordan and Massie Demand Information From Over 130 Companies Surrounding Their Involvement with Woke ESG Cartel Climate Action 100 +', press release, 30 June.

36 Note that investors typically look at 'risk' more positively: they may be happy to take an informed, calculated and acceptable risk in the expectation of a return that reflects that risk.

37 Lee J, Koh K and Shim ED (2024), 'Managerial incentives for ESG in the financial services industry: direct and indirect association between ESG and executive compensation', *Managerial Finance,* 50(1), 10–27.

38 Elkins H, Entwistle G and Schmidt RN (2024), 'Expectations for sustainability reporting from users, preparers, and the accounting profession', *International Journal of Disclosure and Governance,* 21(1), 143–164.

39 Jebe R (2019), 'The Convergence of Financial and ESG Materiality', *American Business Law Journal,* 56(3).

40 Hand G (2001) *Naked among cannibals: what really happens inside Australian banks,* Allen & Unwin.

41 Giese G, Nagy Z, Lee LE (2021), 'Deconstructing ESG Ratings Performance: Risk and Return for E, S, and G by Time Horizon, Sector, and Weighting', *Journal of portfolio management,* 47(3).

42 Liu S, Jin J and Nainar K (2023), 'Does ESG performance reduce banks' nonperforming loans?' *Finance research letters,* 55(7).

43 Basu S, Vitanza J, Wang W and Zhu X (2022), 'Walking the walk? Bank ESG disclosures and home mortgage lending', *Review of accounting studies,* 27(3).

44 *The Australian* (2019), 'CBA chief first to face public flogging,' 9 October. *Global Banking News* (2018), 'Banking royal commission says National Australia Bank charged fees to dead customers', 8 August.

45 Crofts P (2020), 'Strategies of denial and the Australian Royal Commission into Misconduct in the Banking, Superannuation and Financial Services Industry', *Griffith Law Review* 29(1). Both the Chair and CEO of the National Australia Bank were forced to resign.

46 The question asked both at McKinsey & Company and Macquarie Group, where the author worked.

47 Australian Prudential Regulation Authority (2018), *Prudential Inquiry into the Commonwealth Bank of Australia.*

48 Dai Nippon Printing (2024), *Integrated Report,* p 19.

49 Dai Nippon Printing (2024), *Integrated Report,* p 101.

50 Dai Nippon Printing (2024), *Integrated Report,* p 102.

51 Dai Nippon Printing (2024), *Integrated Report,* p 109.

52 Dai Nippon Printing (2024), *Integrated Report,* p 56.

53 Australians for Negotiated Treaties and Restitutions (ANTAR 2024), 'The Destruction of Juukan Gorge', https://antar.org.au/issues/cultural-heritage/the-destruction-of-juukan-gorge/ accessed 4 March 2024

54 Winning D (2020), 'Rio Tinto Chief Exits Over Site Destruction', *The Wall Street Journal,* 11 September.

55 Ker P (2021), 'Rio chairman flags 2022 exit after Juukan Gorge "failings"', *Australian Financial Review,* 2 March.

56 G Cochrane (2020), 'Social science could have saved sacred site', *The Australian Financial Review,* 15 July (since retitled in the online edition as "Rio Tinto's Aboriginal desecration shows folly of rote ESG".

57 Rio Tinto (2024), website history https://www.riotinto.com/en/about/history#rt-rio150-1980 accessed 15 September 2024.

58 Altman J (2009), 'Indigenous Communities, Miners and the State in Australia' in Altman J and Martin D (eds.), *Power, Culture, Economy: Indigenous Australians and Mining,* ANU Press.

59 Ker P (2020), 'Rio slashed communities team prior to Juukan debacle', *Australian Financial Review,* 4 September.

60 Kemp D, Kochan K and Burton J (2023), 'Critical reflections on the Juukan Gorge parliamentary inquiry and prospects for industry change', *Journal of Energy & Natural Resources Law* (41)4.

61 Reinhardt FL (1999), *Down to Earth: Applying Business Principles to Environmental Management,* Harvard Business Review Press, pp 61-65.

62 O'Rouke D and Strand R (2017), *Patagonia: driving sustainable innovation by embracing tensions,* Sage.

63 Interface (2019), *Lessons for the Future: The Interface guide to changing your business to change the world,* https://interfaceinc.scene7.com/is/content/InterfaceInc/Interface/Americas/WebsiteContentAssets/Documents/Sustainability%2025yr%20Report/25yr%20Report%20Booklet%20Interface_MissionZeroCel.pdf accessed 24 November 2024.

64 Crain Communications (2015), 'Top 15 Ad Campaigns of the 21st Century', *Advertising Age.*

65 Busch T, Barnett ML, Burritt RL, Cashore BW, Freeman RE, Henriques I, Husted BW, Panwar R, Pinkse J, Schaltegger S and York J (2024), 'Moving beyond the business case: How to make corporate sustainability work', *Business Strategy and the Environment,* 33(2).

66 Packham C and Macdonald-Smith A (2023), 'Batteries and hydro to drive AGL transition, *Australian Financial Review,* 10 February.

67 Potter B and Whyte J (2024), 'CEO hails progress as AGL ups guidance again', *Australian Financial Review*, 7 May.

68 Allianz (2023), *Group Sustainability Report*, p 5.

69 Allianz (2023), *Group Sustainability Report*, p 8.

70 Allianz (2023), *Group Sustainability Report*, p 13.

71 This example is an amalgam of insights from H&M's global recycling initiative, and the Salvation Army (UK)'s commercial arm SATCoL. See Harrell A (2023), 'H&M Rewards Fashionistas for Recycling Clothes on Roblox', *Sourcing Journal*, 9 January; Safaya S (2024), 'SATCoL to create UK's 'first' fibre farm, trials 'worn out' clothes recycling', *just-style.com*, 29 February; Singhai S, Agarwal S and Singhal N (2023), 'Chemical recycling of waste clothes: a smarter approach to sustainable development', *Environmental Science and Pollution Research* 30:54448–54469.

72 Gillan C (2023), 'Top US chemical firms to pay $1.2 billion to settle water contamination lawsuits', *The Guardian*, 3 June.

73 Yamada H (2023), 'Johnson & Johnson to pay $8.9 billion to settle claims baby powder, other talc products caused cancer', *abcnews.com*.

74 Monsanto (1992) Annual Report, quoted in Reinhardt FL (2000), *Down to Earth*, Harvard University Press p 23.

75 Farrell M (2023), 'Years After Monsanto Deal, Bayer's Roundup Bills Keep Piling Up', *The New York Times*, 6 December.

76 Dowse J (2013), 'Valuing intangibles and ESG performance, *Keeping Good Companies*, July.

77 Michel M (2024), 'Increasing influence: 66% of new Chief Sustainability Officers report to CEO', *CSO Futures*, 9 January.

78 Dai Nippon (2024), *Integrated Report*, p 24.

79 BT (2007), *Sustainability Report*, p 5.

80 Macintosh A (2008) LaFarge Advisory Council notes, http://www.alastairmcintosh.com/general/quarry/lafarge-panel.htm accessed on 4 January 2008.

81 Chevron (2023), *Climate Change Resilience Report*, p 51.

82 Henkel (2024), *Sustainability Report*, p 43.

83 Henkel (2024), *Sustainability Report*, p 52.

84 Henkel (2024), *Sustainability Report*, p 52.

85 Henkel (2024), *Sustainability Report*, p 12.

86 Henkel (2024), *Sustainability Report*, p 113.

87 IFRS Foundation (2024), 'Progress on Corporate Climate-related Disclosures', October, p 4.

88 Malone L, Holland E and Houston C (2023), 'ESG Battlegrounds: How the States Are Shaping the Regulatory Landscape in the U.S.', *Harvard Law School Forum on Corporate Governance*, 11 March. The States with laws or policies that restrict ESG considerations in public investment or procurement were at the end of 2023: Idaho, Indiana, North Dakota, Arizona, Florida, Kentucky, Mississippi, Oklahoma, Tennessee, Texas, West Virginia, Wyoming. All are Republican. The states that have encouraged ESG considerations were Illinois, Maryland, New Mexico and Oregon. Other states have limited pension funds support for fossil fuels (Maine, Massachusetts, New York) or guns (Connecticut, Nevada, Rhode Island).

89 Charlin V, Cifuentes A and Alfaro J (2022), 'ESG ratings: an industry in need of a major overhaul', *Journal of Sustainable Finance and Investment*, 1–19.

90 Europe's Directive on Green Claims was passed in March 2024 to insist that there is some independently verifiable evidence to support making a green claim: see Segal M (2024), 'EU Parliament Agrees to Ban Unverified Green Product Claims', *ESG Today*, 12 March.

91 Stapledon A (2022), 'Mind the splashback: greenwashing and greywashing in sustainability-linked financing', *Mondaq Business Briefing*, 20 September.

92 They also invest in what is collectively called 'alternative assets' such as infrastructure, or private equity funds. These generally account for a relatively small amount of the total investment. Investors also invest in risk instruments such as derivatives – options based on price movements on the underlying assets – which help to manage potential investment risk or liquidity issues.

93 Ozili P (2020), '100 Quotes from the Global Financial Crisis: Lessons for the future', *SSRN Electronic Journal*, 10.2139/ssrn.3500921.

94 United States Government Accountability Office (2013), *Financial Regulatory Reform: Financial Crisis Losses and Potential Impacts of the Dodd-Frank Act*.

95 Bakkar Y (2023), 'Why did Lehman Brothers fail?', *Economics Observatory* https://www.economi csobservatory.com/why-did-lehman-brothers-fail accessed 24 November 2024.

96 United States Government Accountability Office (2013), *Financial Regulatory Reform: Financial Crisis Losses and Potential Impacts of the Dodd-Frank Act*.

97 Meacham J (2007), 'A Candid Conversation with Greenspan', *Newsweek* 23 September, updated 2010.

98 Commonwealth of Australia (2019), *The Royal Commission into Misconduct in the Banking, Superannuation and Financial Services Industry*.

99 US Department of Interior (2015), 'U.S. and Five Gulf States Reach Historic Settlement with BP to Resolve Civil Lawsuit Over Deepwater Horizon Oil Spill', media release 5 October, updated 2021.

100 Court C, Hodges A, Coffey K, Ainsworth C and Yoskowitz D (2020), 'Effects of the Deepwater Horizon Oil Spill on Human Communities: Catch and Economic Impacts', *Deep Oil Spills*, Springer.

101 Bousso J (2018) 'BP Deepwater Horizon costs balloon to $65 billion', *Reuters*, 17 January.

102 US National Oceanic and Atmospheric Administration (n.d.) 'Deepwater Horizon oil spill settlements: Where the money went' https://www.noaa.gov/explainers/deepwater-horizon-oil-spill-settle ments-where-money-went accessed 19 November 2024.

103 BP (2010) 'Deepwater Horizon Accident Investigation Report - Executive Summary', https://www. bp.com/content/dam/bp/business-sites/en/global/corporate/pdfs/sustainability/issue-briefings/deepwa ter-horizon-accident-investigation-report.pdf accessed 19 November 2024.

104 National Commission on the BP Deepwater Horizon Oil Spill and Offshore Drilling (2011), *Deep Water - The Gulf Oil Disaster and the Future of Offshore Drilling*.

105 United States Coast Guard (n.d.) 'Report of Investigation into the Circumstances Surrounding the Explosion, Fire, Sinking and Loss of Eleven Crew Members Aboard the Mobile Offshore Drilling Unit Deepwater Horizon', https://www.dco.uscg.mil/Portals/9/OCSNCOE/Casualty-Information/DWH-Ma condo/USCG-ROI-Deepwater-Horizon-Vol-I-Redacted.pdf accessed 19 November 2024.The Bureau of Ocean Energy Management, Regulation and Enforcement (2011) 'Report Regarding the Causes of the April 20, 2010 Macondo Well Blowout', https://www.dco.uscg.mil/Portals/9/OCSNCOE/Casualty-Informa tion/DWH-Macondo/BOEMRE-Macondo-Well-Blowout-Report-Vol-II.pdf accessed 19 November 2024.

106 Kanter RM (2010), 'BP's Tony Hayward and the Failure of Leadership Accountability', *Harvard Business Review*, 7 June.

107 Coase RH (2013), 'The problem of social cost', *The Journal of Law and Economics*, 56(4).

108 e.g., Baumol WJ and Oates WE (1971), 'The Use of Standards and Prices for Protection of the Environment' *Swedish Journal of Economics*, 71(1); Montgomery WD (1972), 'Markets in Licenses and Efficient Pollution Control Programs' *Journal of Economic Theory*, 5.

109 Title IV of the Clean Air Act Amendments 1990 (US) to control sulphur and nitrous oxide emissions that were creating acid rain.

110 For example, fishing rights in New Zealand, see Richardson B (1988), 'Economic Instruments and sustainable management in New Zealand', *Journal of Environmental Law* 10(1).

111 The Hunter River Salinity Trading Scheme, established under *Protection of the Environment Operations Act* 1997 (NSW) s 293 to limit salt discharges.

112 Ellerman AD (2003), 'Ex post evaluation of tradable permits: the U.S. SO2 cap-and-trade program', *Center for Energy and Environmental Policy Research, MIT*, February.

113 ICAP (2024), *Emissions Trading Worldwide: Status Report 2024*, International Carbon Action Partnership.

114 Principles for Responsible Investment (2024), 'Understanding the data needs of responsible investors'.

115 As of 19 January 2024.

116 Personal knowledge of author from working in Papua New Guinea in 2007. The funds were administered by the Papua New Guinea Sustainable Development Program, with an international board independent from the government.

117 Cash D (2024), 'Chapter 5: Systemic signalling' in *ESG Rating Agencies and Financial Regulation*, Edward Elgar.

118 For example, ESG ratings providers in the European Union will have to be authorised and supervised by the European Securities and Markets Authority.

119 For example, Japan has developed six principles as part of a Code of Conduct for ESG data providers. The code is designed for voluntary adoption on a 'comply or explain' basis. Firms may choose not to comply with the code if they can explain why.

120 S&P Global, https://www.spglobal.com/en accessed 19 November 2024.

121 The S&P 500 is widely regarded as the best single gauge of U.S. large-cap equities. The index includes 500 leading companies spanning all sectors of the U.S. stock market. It covers approximately 80% of the U.S. equity market capitalization and over 50% of the global equity market.

122 For example, see ASCOR Project, https://www.ascorproject.org/.

123 Friede G, Busch T and Bassen A (2015) 'ESG and financial performance: aggregated evidence from more than 2000 empirical studies', *Journal of Sustainable Finance & Investment* (5)4.

124 Atz U, Van Holt T, Liu Z and Bruno C (2022), 'Does Sustainability Generate Better Financial Performance? Review, Meta-analysis, and Propositions', *Journal of Sustainable Finance and Investment*, 22 July.

125 American Business History Centre (2024), 'Most Valuable American Companies 1995-2024', https://americanbusinesshistory.org/most-valuable-companies-the-last-25-years/ accessed 19 November 2024.

126 BBC News (2015), 'Petrobras corruption costs hit $2bn', 23 April.

127 El-Hage J (2019), 'Shaking the Latin American Equilibrium: The Petrobras and Odebrecht Corruption Scandals', *Fordham Journal of Corporate Financial Law*, 4 November.

128 Klobucista C and Labrador RC (2018) 'Brazil's Corruption Fallout', US Council on Foreign Relations, https://www.cfr.org/backgrounder/brazils-corruption-fallout accessed 19 November 2024.

129 Office of the High Commissioner on Human Rights (2011), *Guiding Principles on Business and Human Rights*.

130 CCLA (n.d.), 'Mental Health', https://www.ccla.co.uk/mental-health accessed 19 November 2024. CCLA is a re-branding of the former Churches, Charities and Local Authorities Investment Fund.

131 Vanguard (n.d.), 'Stewardship in action - A voice for investors', https://www.vanguard.com.au/personal/about-us/investment-stewardship accessed 19 November 2024.

132 State Street Global Advisers (2024), *Asset Stewardship Report*, https://www.ssga.com/au/en_gb/intermediary/insights/asset-stewardship-report accessed 19 November 2024.

133 Blackrock (2024), *Investment Stewardship Engagement Priorities Summary*, https://www.blackrock.com/corporate/literature/publication/blk-stewardship-priorities-final.pdf, Blackrock website accessed 19 November 2024.

134 Climate Action 100+ (2024), https://www.climateaction100.org/.

135 Australian Council of Superannuation Investors limited (n.d.), https://acsi.org.au/.

136 Federated Hermes Limited (2024) 'EOS Stewardship', https://www.hermes-investment.com/uk/en/institutions/eos-stewardship/ accessed 19 November 2024.

137 FAIRR Initiative (2024), https://www.fairr.org/about accessed 19 November 2024.

138 Mining 2030 (2024), https://mining2030.org/about/ accessed 19 November 2024.

139 Principles for Responsible Investment (2024), 'Advance: A Stewardship Initiative on Human Rights and Social Issues', https://www.unpri.org/investment-tools/stewardship/advance accessed 19 November 2024.

140 CCLA (n.d.), 'Mental Health', https://www.ccla.co.uk/mental-health accessed 19 November 2024.

141 Global Tailings Portal (n.d.), https://tailing.grida.no/about accessed 19 November 2024.

142 As of January 2024.

143 Principles for Responsible Investment (2024), 'Collaborative engagements' https://www.unpri.org/investment-tools/stewardship/collaborative-engagements accessed 19 November 2024.

144 Starbucks (2023), '2023 Notice of Annual Meeting of Shareholders and Proxy Statement', https://www.sec.gov/Archives/edgar/data/829224/000082922423000007/a2023proxystatementfinal.htm accessed 19 November 2024.

145 National Labor Relations Board (NLRB) (n.d.), 'About NLRB', https://www.nlrb.gov/about-nlrb/what-we-do accessed 19 November 2024.

146 Starbucks (2023) 'Message from Sara: Our Outreach to Resume Contract Bargaining with Workers United', https://stories.starbucks.com/press/2023/message-from-sara-our-outreach-to-resume-contract-bargaining-with-workers-united/ accessed 19 November 2024.

147 A list of some of the successful shareholder resolutions is given at Principles for Responsible Invesment (2024), 'Are corporate boards responding to successful shareholder ESG proposals?', https://www.unpri.org/active-ownership-20/are-corporate-boards-responding-to-successful-shareholder-esg-proposals/11160.article accessed 19 November 2024.

148 Glencore (2023), 'Results of 2023 AGM', https://www.glencore.com/media-and-insights/news/results-of-2023-agm accessed 20 November 2024.

149 Sasol (2024) 'Results of The Annual General Meeting of Sasol Limited Held on Friday, 19 January 2024', https://www.sasol.com/node/6325 accessed 20 November 2024.

150 Woodside Petroleum Limited (2022), 'Woodside Shareholders Approve Merger', https://www.woodside.com/docs/default-source/asx-announcements/2022/woodside-shareholders-approve-merger.pdf accessed 20 November 2024.

151 Woodside Energy (2023), '2023 Annual General Meeting Voting Results', https://www.woodside.com/docs/default-source/asx-announcements/2024/2024-annual-general-meeting-voting-results.pdf accessed 20 November 2024.

152 International Energy Agency (2021), *Net Zero by 2050: A Roadmap for the Global Energy Sector*.

153 Welsh H (2023), *Assessing Anti-ESG Efforts in the 2023 Proxy Season*, Si2 Institute, https://siinstitute.org/reports.html accessed 25 November 2024.

154 Tobacco Free Portfolios (n.d.), https://tobaccofreeportfolios.org/ accessed 25 November 2024.

155 350.org (n.d.), '350 Campaign Update: Divestment', https://350.org/350-campaign-update-divestment/ accessed 20 November 2024.

156 Norges Bank Investment Management (2024), 'Ethical exclusions', https://www.nbim.no/en/responsible-investment/ethical-exclusions/ accessed 20 November 2024.

157 PwC (2022) 'ESG-focused institutional investment seen soaring', https://www.pwc.com/id/en/media-centre/press-release/2022/english/esg-focused-institutional-investment-seen-soaring-84-to-usd-33-9-trillion-in-2026-making-up-21-5-percent-of-assets-under-management-pwc-report.html accessed 20 November 2024.

158 RepRisk (2024), 'A turning tide in greenwashing? Exploring the first decline in six years', https://www.reprisk.com/research-insights/reports/a-turning-tide-in-greenwashing-exploring-the-first-decline-in-six-years#ix-banking-and-financial-services-sector-sees-a-20-global-drop-in-climate-related-greenwashing accessed 25 November 2024.

159 Australian Securities and Investment Commission (2024), 'ASIC's first greenwashing case results in landmark $11.3 million penalty for Mercer', https://asic.gov.au/about-asic/news-centre/find-a-media-release/2024-releases/24-173mr-asic-s-first-greenwashing-case-results-in-landmark-11-3-million-penalty-for-mercer/ accessed 20 November 2024.

160 RepRisk (2024), 'A turning tide in greenwashing? Exploring the first decline in six years', https://www.reprisk.com/research-insights/reports/a-turning-tide-in-greenwashing-exploring-the-first-decline-in-six-years#ix-banking-and-financial-services-sector-sees-a-20-global-drop-in-climate-related-greenwashing accessed 25 November 2024.

161 Principles of Responsible Investment (2022), 'Review of the trends in ESG Reporting Requirements for Investors', https://www.unpri.org/driving-meaningful-data/review-of-trends-in-esg-reporting-requirements-for-investors/10296.article accessed 20 November 2024.

162 European Commission (n.d.), 'EU taxonomy for sustainable activities, https://finance.ec.europa.eu/sustainable-finance/tools-and-standards/eu-taxonomy-sustainable-activities accessed 20 November 2024.

163 United Nations Environment Programme Finance Initiative (n.d.), 'Join the Alliance', https://www.unepfi.org/net-zero-alliance/join-the-alliance/ accessed 20 November 2024.

164 Net Zero Asset Managers Initiative (2024), website https://www.netzeroassetmanagers.org/.

165 Pleiades Strategy (2024), '2023 Statehouse Report: Right-Wing Attacks on the Freedom to Invest Responsibly Falter in Legislatures', https://www.pleiadesstrategy.com/state-house-report-bill-tracker-republican-anti-esg-attacks-on-freedom-to-invest-responsibly-earns-business-labor-and-environmental-opposition accessed 25 November 2024.

166 Azizuddin K (2024), 'CA100+ slams Republican attempts to deter US investors from climate initiative', *Responsible Investor*, 5 August.

167 Stempel J and Mandl C, (2024), 'BlackRock, Vanguard, State Street sued by Republican states over climate push', *Reuters News*, 30 November.

168 New Civil Liberties Alliance (2024), 'NCLA Asks Appeals Court to Stop SEC's Unconstitutional New Climate Disclosure Rules', media release 29 April, https://nclalegal.org/press_release/ncla-asks-appeals-court-to-stop-secs-unconstitutional-new-climate-disclosure-rules/ accessed 25 November 2024.

169 National Association of Manufacturers (2023), 'Manufacturers Challenge SEC's Authority to Politicize Corporate Governance', media release 24 May, https://nam.org/manufacturers-challenge-secs-authority-to-politicize-corporate-governance-23172/ accessed 10 December 2024.

170 Gambetta G, (2024), 'US asset management giant joins Climate Action 100+ exodus', *Responsible Investor* 6 December.

171 Australian Productivity Commission (2020), *Superannuation: Assessing Efficiency and Competitiveness, Inquiry Report*. Rainmaker Information (2020), *Superannuation*.

172 For example, European Securities and Markets Authority (2024), *Final Report: Guidelines on fund names using ESG or sustainability-related terms*; and UK Financial Conduct Authority (2023), *Policy Statement PS23/16, Sustainability Disclosure Requirements (SDR) and investment labels*.

173 See Responsible Investment Institute of Australasia website at https://responsibleinvestment.org/ri-certification/.

174 U.S. Securities Exchange Commission (2024), 'SEC Charges Advisory Firm with Failing to Adhere to Its Own Investment Criteria For ESG-Marketed Funds', 21 October, https://www.sec.gov/newsroom/press-releases/2024-173 accessed 5 December 2024.

175 You may need financial advice to assist you to understand to understand your investment risk and return preference and overall financial needs.

176 Index funds typically try to mirror an investment index, such as the US S&P 500, the MSCI All World Index or the Australian ASX200 to give a broad exposure to different sectors in the economy. Equity based indices are typically constructed such that the amount invested in a company is proportional to their size in market capitalisation.

177 Global Impact Investing Network (2017), 'Case Studies: AllLife, LeapFrog Investments', https://the giin.org/publication/case-study/alllife/ accessed 12 December 2024.

178 Green Climate Fund (2024), 'About Us', www.greenclimate.fund accessed 12 December 2024.

179 Green Climate Fund (2024), 'Projects and programmes', https://www.greenclimate.fund/project/ fp250 accessed 12 December 2024.

180 Hand D, Ulanow M, Pan P and Xiao K (2024) 'Sizing the Impact Investing Market', GIIN, https:// thegiin.org/publication/research/sizing-the-impact-investing-market-2024 accessed 12 December 2024.

181 Hand D, Sunderji S, Nova N and De I (2021), 'Impact Investing Decision-Making: Insights on Financial Performance', GIIN, https://thegiin.org/publication/research/impact-investing-decision-making-insights-on-financial-performance/ accessed 12 December 2024.

182 Remy N, Speelman E and Swartz S (2016), 'Style that's sustainable: A new fast-fashion formula', McKinsey&Company, https://www.mckinsey.com/~/media/mckinsey/business%20functions/sustainability/our%20insights/style%20thats%20sustainable%20a%20new%20fast%20fashion%20formula/style-thats-sustainable-a-new-fast-fashion-formula-vf.pdf, accessed 14 December 2024.

183 Geneva Environment Network (2024), 'Environmental Sustainability in the Fashion Industry', https://www.genevaenvironmentnetwork.org/resources/updates/sustainable-fashion/ accessed 12 December 2024.

184 UN Food and Agriculture Organisation (2024), 'Get Involved: International Day of Awareness of Food Loss and Waste', https://openknowledge.fao.org/handle/20.500.14283/cd1406en accessed 12 December 2024.

185 See the B-Corp website at www.bcorporation.net.

186 Little B (2018), 'When Cigarette Companies Used Doctors to Push Smoking", *History Channel*, 13 September, https://www.history.com/news/cigarette-ads-doctors-smoking-endorsement accessed 8 December 2024.

187 See the Mesothelioma Help website at https://www.mesotheliomahelp.org/asbestos/history/.

188 Competitive Enterprise Institute (2006), "We Call it Life", advertisement, https://www.youtube.com/watch?v=7sGKvDNdJNA accessed 4 December 2024.

189 Blight D (2011), 'Clubs Australia under fire over ad campaign', *AdNews*, 13 April.

190 By 2017, Australians lost US$958 per adult, followed by Hong Kong $768, Singapore $725 and Finland $515. No other countries reach half of Australian per capita losses. See https://www.statista.com/statistics/552821/gambling-losses-per-adult-by-country-worldwide/ accessed 4 December 2024.

191 Hiar C (2021), 'Google Bans Ads That Spread Climate Misinformation', *Scientific America* 8 October.

192 Comms Declare (2024), 'The Walkley's drop Ampol Sponsorship', 16 May, https://commsdeclare.org/2024/05/16/the-walkleys-drop-ampol-sponsorship accessed 30 November 2024.

193 Amy Westervelt (2023), 'How Big Oil helped push the idea of a 'carbon footprint', NPR Radio 18 December, https://www.nprillinois.org/2023-12-18/how-big-oil-helped-push-the-idea-of-a-carbon-footprint accessed 30 November 2024.

194 Earth.Org (2024), '10 Statistics About Fast Fashion Waste', https://earth.org/statistics-about-fast-fashion-waste/ accessed 29 November 2024

195 Walkfree (2024), *Global Slavery Index*, https://www.walkfree.org/global-slavery-index/ accessed 29 November 2024.

196 Australian Institute of Health and Welfare (2024) 'Family, domestic and sexual violence' webpage, https://www.aihw.gov.au/family-domestic-and-sexual-violence/types-of-violence/modern-slavery accessed 29 November 2024.

197 Lynch LJ, Coleman AR and Cutro C (2016), 'The Volkswagen Emissions Scandal', Emerald Publishing, 21 July, https://doi.org/10.1108/case.darden.2021.000009.

198 SenateSHJ (2022), *Crisis Value Erosion Index: A report on the financial impacts of crises on 70 listed companies from around the world*, www.senateshj.com.au accessed 15 December 2022.

199 Elizabeth Broderick & Co (2022), *Report into Workplace Culture at Rio Tinto,* https://www.riotinto.com/-/media/Content/Documents/Sustainability/People/RT-Everyday-respect-report.pdf accessed 15 December 2024.

200 Rio Tinto (2024), *Everyday Respect Progress Review,* CEO speech 20 November, https://www.riotinto.com/en/invest/presentations/2024/everyday-respect-progress-review accessed 15 December 2024

201 Australian Productivity Commission (2010), *Gambling Inquiry Report.*

202 Breen M (2021), 'How policy reform can solve Australia's gambling problem', *In the Black,* CPA Australia.

203 Drape J and Hsu T (2021), 'The N.F.L.'s New Play: Embrace Betting Ads, Watch the Money Pour In', *The New York Times,* 15 September.

204 See https://influencemap.org/index.html.

205 ABC Radio National (2024), 'Fintan O'Toole on why politics is becoming more tribal' Late Night Live, https://www.abc.net.au/listen/programs/latenightlive/fintan-o-toole-tribalism/104396624 accessed 25 September 2024.

206 Ian Dunt (2020), *How to be a Liberal,* Canbury Press.

207 SenateSHJ (2024), *The Togetherness Index Report,* https://senateshj.com.au/project/togetherness-index/ accessed 20 August 2024.

208 World Economic Forum (2022), *Defining the 'G' in ESG Governance Factors at the Heart of Sustainable Business.*

Index

https://doi.org/10.1515/9783111428949-026

www.ingramcontent.com/pod-product-compliance
Lightning Source LLC
Chambersburg PA
CBHW061813210326
41599CB00034B/6982